PENGUIN BOOKS
MORAL MATERIALISM

Joseph S. Alter is an anthropologist who earned his doctoral degree from the University of California, Berkeley. He teaches at the University of Pittsburgh, where he is professor and department chair. He was born in Landour, Uttarakhand and divides his time between Pittsburgh and the Allegheny mountains of western Pennsylvania and Mussoorie in the Himalayas.

For thirty years he has been conducting research on various aspects of society and culture in South Asia with a particular focus on physical fitness, sport, and the culture and history of medicine. He has written five books, including *The Wrestler's Body* (University of California Press, 1992), *Knowing Dil Das* (Penguin India 2010), *Gandhi's Body* (University of Pennsylvania Press, 2000), *Asian Medicine and Globalization* (University of Pennsylvania Press, 2005) and *Yoga in Modern India* (Princeton University Press, 2004). He has also published extensively on a range of sports, including *kabaddi* and *jori/mugdal*, on the cultural history and philosophy of Ayurveda and Unani medicine, and on the impact of colonial and postcolonial development on the political economy of Mussoorie.

Moral Materialism
Sex and Masculinity in Modern India

JOSEPH S. ALTER

PENGUIN BOOKS

An imprint of Penguin Random House

PENGUIN BOOKS

USA | Canada | UK | Ireland | Australia
New Zealand | India | South Africa | China | Singapore

Penguin Books is part of the Penguin Random House group of companies
whose addresses can be found at global.penguinrandomhouse.com

Published by Penguin Random House India Pvt. Ltd
4th Floor, Capital Tower 1, MG Road,
Gurugram 122 002, Haryana, India

First published by Penguin Books India 2011

ISBN 9780143417415

Typeset in Sabon MT by Eleven Arts, Delhi
Printed at Repro India Limited

www.penguin.co.in

MIX
Paper from
responsible sources
FSC® C047271

This is a legitimate digitally printed version of the book and therefore might not
have certain extra finishing on the cover.

Contents

Acknowledgements

This book reflects approximately twenty years of study in India, from 1988 until 2008. Funding for research projects upon which most of the chapters are based came from the National Science Foundation, the American Institute of Indian Studies, the Fulbright Foundation and the University of Pittsburgh. I am most grateful to all of these institutions for their financial and professional support.

Three of the chapters in this book have been previously published in academic journals. Chapter two was published as 'Celibacy, Sexuality and the Transformation of Gender into Nationalism in North India' in the *Journal of Asian Studies* (1994: 53.1: 45–66). A version of the chapter was presented at the 1992 annual South Asia Conference, University of Wisconsin–Madison, and at a symposium on *Dimensions of Ethnic and Cultural Nationalism in Asia* organized by David Buck under the auspices of the Association for Asian Studies, at the University of Wisconsin–Milwaukee, February 1993. Chapter three was published as 'Seminal Truth: A Modern Science of Male Celibacy in North India' in *Medical Anthropology Quarterly* (1997, 11.3: 275–298). A number of anonymous reviewers provided valuable comments and criticisms on early drafts. I am grateful to them as well as to Don Brennies, David Gilmore, Lawrence Cohen, Michael Herzfeld, and Gay Becker. Chapter four was published as 'The Celibate Wrestler: Sexual Chaos, Embodied Balance and Competitive Politics in North India' in *Contributions to Indian Sociology* (n.s.), (1995. 29.1&2: 109–131). A version of this chapter was presented at a conference on *Social Reform, Sexuality and the State* held at the Institute for Economic Growth at Delhi University in 1993. I am grateful to Patricia Uberoi for organizing the conference and for providing valuable comments and suggestions.

Four of the chapters have not previously been published, but have been presented in various forms to a number of different groups. Chapter five was written as a contribution for a panel organized by Martha Ann Selby for the annual South Asia Conference at the University of Wisconsin–Madison, 2005. Versions of the chapter were also presented at the University of Indiana, Bloomington and at the University of Pittsburgh. A version of chapter six was presented at the Indiana University of Pennsylvania and at the Honors College at the University of Pittsburgh. A version of chapter one was presented at the University of California–Santa Cruz.

My thanks to Sumit Ganguly, Edward McCord, Loki Pandey and Tamar Reich for extending kind invitations and for their hospitality.

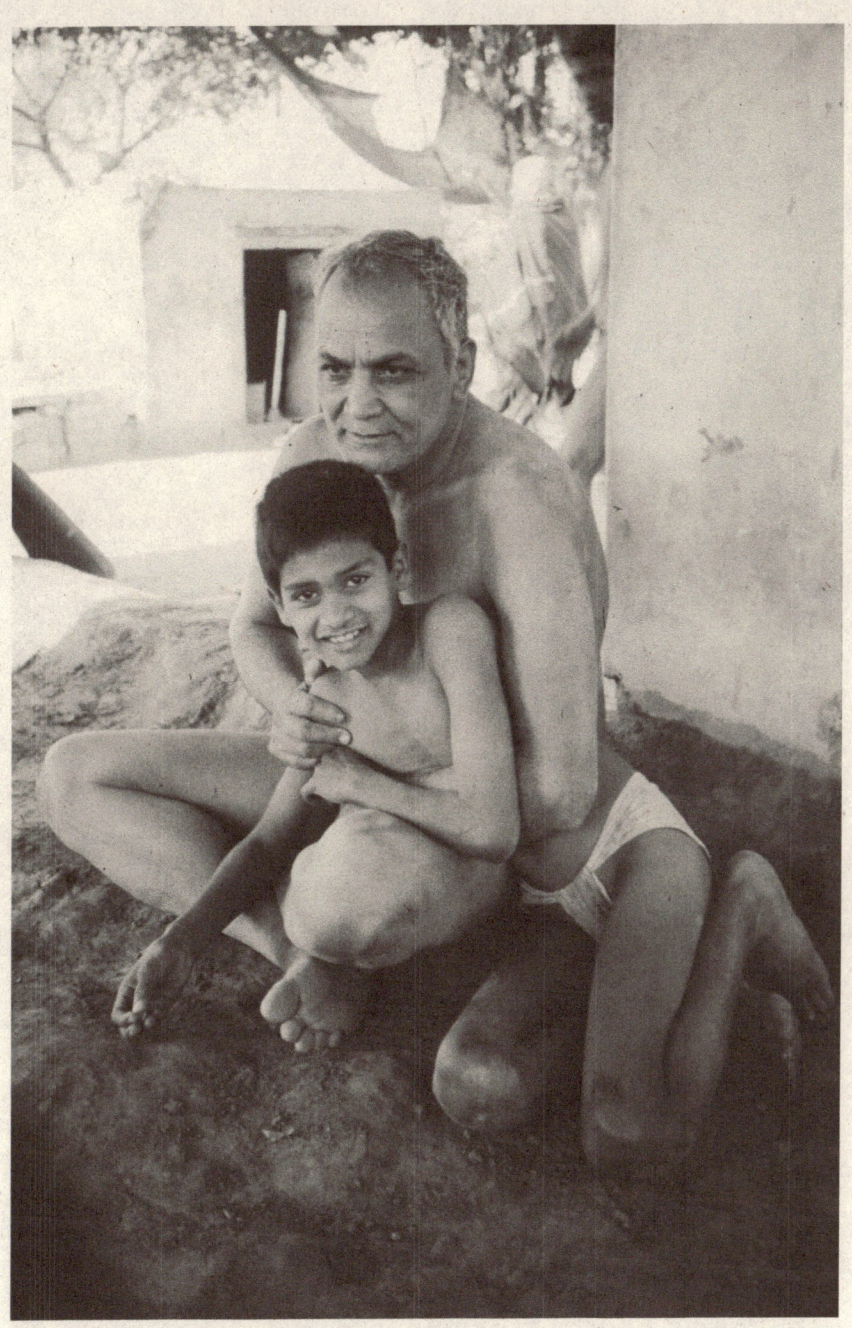

Guru and Chela, Akhara Ram Singh. Varanasi, 1988

Introduction
Sex, Substance and Embodied Identity

In spite of the fact that the words 'sex' and 'masculinity' invoke very general, common-sense meanings, this book is about a very specific articulation of sex and masculinity in modern India: an articulation that complicates a history of sexuality in which pleasure, morality and power are unquestioningly keyed to the social act of sexual intercourse. It is about the way in which sexual meanings are encoded in substances rather than acts, ideas and conceptions, and it is about the regulation, containment and embodied expression of substances. One might say that it is about the worlds of meaning that are created in relation to things that are implicated in sex, but that are not exclusively or directly involved in the act of sex, the acts that lead up to sex, or what follows as a direct consequence of the act as such.

Apart from whatever intrinsic interest this may hold as a topic, and despite problems to be addressed shortly, it is important to highlight the particularity of this perspective on contained embodiment simply because sex is almost always understood in terms of a range of meanings, feelings and emotions that emerge from, or devolve into, desire, erotics and pleasure on the one hand, and fertility and reproduction on the other. Beyond the domain of sexual meanings that spring from pleasure, sex as a social act with consequences—involving two or more individuals (and not necessarily of the same gender or species)—entails obligations and expectations, even if one of the expectations is that there are no consequences. With reference to this, the kinetic physicality of sex manifests a very specific, and, I will argue, limited articulation of meanings, even though when thinking of sex one is most often left with the impression that 'intercourse' engages the body in obvious—if endlessly creative, experimental and novel—ways that involve, but are ultimately limited by, gross anatomy. When the Bard has Iago respond to Brabantio by saying, 'I am one, sir, that comes to tell you your daughter and the Moor are now making the beast with two backs,' one knows, by way of suggestive analogical imagery, everything: but also really nothing at all beyond the obvious. In terms of sex and masculinity, functional anatomy—as a hegemonic signifier—would appear to sharply circumscribe meaning. Apart from the red herring of incidental Moorish involvement—*sala betichod!*—is there, in fact, a way of talking about sex without suffering under the burden of the beast with two backs?

One might well ask, rhetorically, if the fact of an erection at stage two arousal, which appears to be the emergence of instinctual nature into the domain of culture, does not prefigure a whole world into which it fits as the point of ultimate and definitive contact between masculinity, meaning and feeling. Is not sex—in its endless permutations, involving any combination of human genders and species and sexes of species—held in place by the instinctual physiology, neurology and biochemistry of the sexual response cycle?

To question this seemingly rhetorical question, to raise a finger in protest, involves taking a very different and subversive—if not by any means disconnected—perspective on the whole fucking category: the physiology of sex and the recursive logic of the five-stage sexual response cycle. Forcing the question involves taking a critical analytical attitude towards a trajectory of meaning, identification and categorization that does not follow the path of desire, excitement, plateau and orgasmic ejaculation: the pleasurable fulfilment of desire in 'final resolution', from where the cycle starts all over again, and again, having produced a whole spectrum of other things—babies, crimes, poetry, guilt, social bonds, shame, infection, affection, love, hate, murderous resentments, violence, valentines or what have you.

There is a different way in which the physiology of sex can be understood to be linked to the body, and in this conceptualization an erection is important, as a sign, but does not define the ways and means by which the body is implicated in sex. To be sure this alternative conceptualization of sex is a cultural construction, but this can also be said about the 'natural' sexual response cycle. As such it defines the base point of a trajectory of meanings that are very different from those that spill forth from the entelechy of endless orgasms. This book is, simply, about the trajectory of these other meanings in modern India: the outward expressions of masculinity—personal, political and medical—of an inward orientation concerning the essence of sex and sexual fluid. My goal is to explore the structural disjuncture of moral materialism: bodies that are animated by sexual fluids, but oriented away from the physiology of desire.

Over the course of the past ten or fifteen years there has been a spate of research and publishing on questions of sex and sexuality in southern Asia. Although this can in part be accounted for by the intensity and pervasiveness of academic interest in the topic of sex and sexuality on a larger, global scale (see Altmann 2001; Bhattacharya 2002; Bose and Bhattacharya 2007), and the obvious correlation between academic interest and changing social, political and medical investments—consider how the function and cultural meaning of condoms has changed since 1984—it is important to place the development of the South Asian academic literature in the context of a more local intellectual history.

Realizing, of course, that there is no single, linear history of intellectual development, it is nevertheless fair to say that the general developmental trend in South Asian sexuality studies has been from an engagement with the 'exotic extreme'—mythopoetic bestiality, androgynous onanism, sexually insatiable goddesses, erotic asceticism, tantric ritual, debilitating semen anxiety, and more-or-less sober examinations of Khajuraho temple art and interpretations of the *Kama Sutra* (see "A Member of the Royal Asiatic Society" 1952)—to studied examinations of sex in all of its various normative, modern permutations.

What I mean by 'normative'—as such, or in the extreme—should not be confused with hetero-normative as a designation for identity and choice within the framework of sexual orientation. In the chapters that follow, 'normative' is a point of contrast that includes all expressions of sex and sexuality that take cultural advantage, so to speak, of the pleasure principle and desire. In understanding the point I am trying to make in this book, the term 'normative' must be applied much more broadly to encompass the reductive logic whereby local expressions of sexual meaning make sense in terms of unexamined derivative categories, and acts of categorization, that have been normalized through the homogenizing ebb and flow of globalized understandings. Sex that resolves into erotic gratification is all of a type, regardless of degrees of subtlety or whether it includes or involves other men, women, children or animals; that is, regardless of how much *difference* is factored into the equation of who has, or wants to have, what kind of sex with whom.

Added to this is the critical problem of perspective and interpretation when dealing with sex, which is a deceptively straightforward articulation of culture; deceptively straightforward since drives, instincts and repressed desires define behaviour, and the components of individual experience that are linked to said behaviour define perspective and interpretation. In other words, it is extremely difficult to think beyond the beast with two backs, since stage one ineluctably moves the body into position for stage five, so to speak.

Directly implicated in this is the critical problem of what counts as sex, and at what point something that is not sex becomes, in some sense, sexual. There is, for example, nothing intrinsically sexual about nakedness. Here there can be manifold misunderstandings, miscommunications and blunders, as well as fractured, violent encounters based on a spectrum of different individual feelings and the intensity of feelings. While blunders and violence point to serious and important ethical questions concerning the relationship between embodiment, meaning and power (Brittan 1989), as well as other things, a focus on the material essence of the body provides a different perspective on how morality corresponds to meaning.

The position I wish to take is not, by any means, completely new and original, although my point of entry and engagement is somewhat unique, and my argument rather explicit.

As I understand it, Lawrence Cohen's refusal to let sex define the parameters of identity—especially, or in particular, when it appears to be the singular point of cultural reference—is congruent with the way in which my analysis seeks to destabilize the nature of sex in relation to society at large (1995). Similarly my argument concerning the hegemonic structure of sex, and the limitations this places on how individuals and groups come to understand their identity in relation to the sexed body, resonates very well with Gayatri Reddy's analysis of *hijra* identity and experience in Hyderabad (2005). This may seem counterintuitive and ironic, since in the popular imagination to be a hijra is defined with reference to the essence of sexual difference and expectations of behaviour. But in many respects, the fact that sex as such means so much in terms of defining the articulations of hijra identity means that it can be made to mean many different things. As Reddy points out, being hijra extends beyond the narrow limits of sexual identity, even though genitalia remain a critical point of reference.

Beyond the pale of masculinity—where it has been virtually impossible to imagine the fate of sexual fluids in anything other than the functional kinetics of sex—it is important to point out that, especially with the development of new in-vitro technologies, there are significant structural parallels to the argument presented here in terms of the disaggregation of sex, the physiology of fertility and reproduction in the female body. As cogently argued by Emily Martin (1987), it is only by way of the contrived logic of essentialized sex and sexual intercourse, and the presumed entelechy of fertility, that menstruation and menopause are conceptualized in terms of failed reproduction and metaphors of wastage and missed opportunity. Another way of putting this is that although there is an almost universal conflation of sex and reproduction with respect to processes that intersect in the body, the two are completely different with reference to biology as such. The fact that reproduction is no longer dependent on either male anatomy or a large percentage of the fluid stuff that is ejaculated makes it that much easier to conceive of sex as something independent from semen.

Whereas Cohen and Reddy unpack the significance of sex with reference to problematically essentialized difference, my goal is to question the way in which sex is defined as the normative articulation of sexuality, as this articulation encompasses essentialized differences. In pursuing this goal I have most likely overcompensated and will plead guilty to a degree of counter-essentialism in the following discussion of such things as semen, celibacy, physical fitness and health in middle age. This would be a critical flaw if it were not for the fact that, as with respect to all things cultural, the analytical focus is ultimately on the social structure of meaning, not on the contingent vagaries of meaning as such. What is important about questions concerning the limits of essentialized categories is the way in which these questions suggest alternative social realities and provide critiques of those established realities that constrain imagination and experience.

Discussions of sex take shape with reference to normative conceptualizations of cultural meaning based on the recognition of cross-cultural patterns. Consequently there is much to be admired in works that have problematized our understanding of pornography, desire, erotics, and the seductive, all-consuming pleasure of cinema, as well as sex work and 'sexuality in the time of AIDS', to borrow the encompassing title of a book that provides fabulous insight on the nitty-gritty of behaviour on the ground, both in and out of the home, in relation to the full spectrum of experiences that anticipate and stem from the sexual response cycle (Verma, Pelto, Schensul and Joshi 2004). In a very different vein, William Mazzarella's work on advertising, consumption and commodification is an excellent example of scholarship that is on the cutting edge of the sex/desire nexus in the context of Indian modernity. His analysis of the marketing of KamaSutra condoms in Bombay (2001), as well as advertising more generally (2003), provides fascinating insight into the dynamics of fetishization— both commodity and sexual—and the tensions and fault lines that surface as bodies, markets, and representations of each take shape in the public sphere.

As distinct from the different articulations of 'sexuality' that are deftly and insightfully brought into analytical focus by Mazzarella (2001, 2003) and others (Adams and Pigg 2005; Dwyer 2000; John and Nair 1998; Srivastava 2004, 2007; Vanita 2002, 2007), the nature of sex itself is left unexamined in much of the recent literature. This is by no means a criticism, only a conceptual bracketing of things into discrete categories. It is simply to point out that even when trying to understand such things as aphrodisiacs, celibacy and virility my concern is not with the rich discourses of sexuality that otherwise structure meaning in this arena of experience. With respect to how far to push the issue, my interest is in difference, all the way down to that point at which the body would seem to prohibit cultural intervention; that point at which an articulation of answers forces one to ask, with inquisitive insight rather than self-doubt: what was the question? With regard to sex, 'what'—as different from how, why, when, where and with whom—is a critical question, especially when embodiment is an issue.

In many respects, unsurprisingly, the trajectory of scholarship on sexuality over the course of the past half century in southern Asia is parallel to the structure of Indian modernity. With reference to points of interface between the body, sexuality and culture, Sanjay Srivastava has aptly characterized this in terms of a generalized movement from the self-sufficient production orientation of a planned, socialist economy in the years immediately following independence, to the consumption orientation of contemporary free-market globalization (2007: 1–38). Although obviously this is a schematic generalization, changes in the political economy of the state reflect changing perspectives on sexuality as concerns over the dynamics of producing and conserving semen shift towards a preoccupation with the conditions under which it might be spent.

While a number of other factors are involved—such as the disciplinary formalization of anthropology and sociology—it is almost as though late nineteenth century Orientalism's engagement with the 'exotic erotic' in the mythological and ritualized world of southern Asia complicated the problematic question, both analytic and open-ended, of making sense of sex in real life. Independence and freedom suggest a whole spectrum of questions that are liberated from the limitations of libidinous libertinism and the constraints of being, at once, the object of desire, an imperial subject, and engaged in struggle. Along these lines Caroline and Fillipo Osella's *Men and Masculinities in South India* (2007) is both an explicit critique of the 'exotic erotic' in South Asian studies of masculine sexuality, as well as a nuanced ethnographic intervention on analytical questions about the relationship between sex and a spectrum of masculinities. On one level their rich ethnography serves to disaggregate sexuality and masculinity—and then see how individuals draw specific correlations between articulations of the two—in the context of contemporary South India. As such, *Men and Masculinities in South India* examines new trajectories of desire, and brings to light the many points of intersection between desire, the social entailments of sexuality and various articulations of modernity. It is an outstanding study of sex and masculinity conceived of in terms of the way in which these categories are normally conceptualized.

But the albatross of normative structure and mythology hangs heavy on the neck of history, and the history of relative differences.

As a number of scholars have recently pointed out, it is noteworthy that despite what obviously seems to have been the case—increased rates of fertility and HIV infection being conveniently 'normative' measures of a certain kind of sex on the ground—literature that ventured to address the question of sex and masculinity in the decades following independence became obsessed with the issue of semen anxiety. One might say that the post-colonial stage of 'final resolution'—the morning after the imperial sun finally set—gave rise to a set of concerns that made good sense within the framework of five-year plans for growth that were based on the dissemination of centralized wealth and self-contained development. But, innuendo aside, G. Morris Carstairs's book *The Twice Born* (1957), based on research conducted near Udaipur in 1951 as well as nine years of childhood experience in Rajasthan, had a profound effect on the field by bringing together psychological and sociological insights to locate the nexus of 'Hindu' masculinity in semen, and highlight the logic of semen retention in terms of a Freudian reality principle .

There can be no question that Carstairs was on to something. Many others have subsequently made note of the fact that men from various communities and social backgrounds express concern about their health, broadly defined in terms of 'anxiety' over the volume, quality and fluid integrity of their semen. However, what is more important, and interesting, than the problem of either ethnographic accuracy or reductive over-generalization is the issue of how 'semen anxiety' has been analytically framed by a psychological reading of culture and masculinity, as this reading of 'sex in real life' resonates with the mythopoesis of erotic asceticism on the one hand and post-colonial political economies of desire on the other: Nehru, Shiva and the 'Hindu' everyman as a kind of postmodern trinity of secular creation, holy destruction and mundane, embodied self-preservation.

There are a number of reasons why a psychological interpretation of semen anxiety has popular validity as an argument for explaining the cultural construction of masculinity at large in South Asia. In essence, psychological interpretations are based on the logic of displacement, and semen, as a substance that is metonymically linked to sex, can very easily absorb a spectrum of metaphorical entailments. Put another way, it is possible to very convincingly read a panoply of subtle issues concerning the development of sexuality into gross anxiety about the causes and consequences of semen loss. Beyond purely psychological analyses focused on child rearing, sexual intimacy and the relationships that boys and young men have with their mothers and fathers, semen anxiety is a very seductive and powerful trope for the interpretation of culture at large. It can reflect a whole spectrum of value-laden scenarios involving self-control, restraint, modesty and non-violence on the one hand and volatility, frustration and aggression on the other. Given this, it is not at all surprising that recent scholarship has taken issue with the trope of semen anxiety, pointing out that it is reductive, two-dimensional and ignores a whole world of experience where inhibition is expressed if not unleashed (see Derné 2000; John and Nair 1998; Osella and Osella 2007; Srivastava 2004).

The problem, however, is that the critique is directed at a trope that reflects a highly problematic misunderstanding of the cultural logic at play. In essence—and to slightly overstate the issue—semen 'anxiety' has very little to do with sex and sexuality, as these terms are commonly understood. The logic of displacement is completely misplaced in terms of providing a theoretical answer to the question of what semen anxiety means. Consequently, those who have rightly criticized the pervasive trope of semen anxiety in the literature on masculinity tend to over-compensate by shifting the focus onto the manifold expressions of 'uninhibited' sexuality. To do so provides insight on issues of importance with respect to masculinity, but only within the rather restricted and dislocated parameters of a standard history of sexuality as such.

One way to better understand the trajectory of this misunderstanding is in terms of physiological categories and their cultural entailments. Needless to say, semen finds expression, and is expressed, in the enactment of kinetic sex, but it factors into the logic and experience of health in ways that render it much more potent as a cultural signifier of fitness and strength. To reiterate, if one simply takes fitness and strength to reflect a Freudian reality principle based on the displacement of desire one has succumbed to the fate of Oedipus—the blinded parent, not the iconic, patricidal child. Health, and a concern for physical health built upon the production and retention of semen, is every bit as meaningful and coherent as a conceptualization of sexuality in terms of desire and the physiological entailments of desire that end-to-begin-again in orgasm. The pleasure of sex as an embodied experience must not blind one to the fact that culture can make of semen much more than the body and culture-bound instinctual drives make of it.

And, although the point of reference here is modern India, it is comparatively instructive to point out that a history of sexuality intent on questioning assumptions—rather than discovering origins—shows that what worried the ancient Greeks was similarly not sex as such but the relationship between sex, health and civic life. Aretaeus, a first-century physician, connects the dots of masculinity and semen as follows: 'If any man is in possession of semen, he is fierce, courageous and physically mighty like beasts. Evidence of this is those athletes who are abstinent' (quoted in Scanlon 2002: 29). In fact, pleasure in the fifth century BCE was not so much a guiding principle as an independent variable in the functional calculus of a highly fluid, ecologically grounded body defined by the risk of excess.

Perhaps not surprisingly, the body's relationship to semen was recognized as a particular kind of problem in the context of the gymnasium—rather than the bedroom—and not only, or even primarily, because young naked athletic boys drove Plato, Aristotle and other philosophers to distraction. The problem was not sex, or even too much sex, but rather, the problem of too much of anything, including exercise, food, sleep and the like. As Thomas Scanlon puts it in his comprehensive work *Eros and Greek Athletics*, 'It would seem, then, that moderate fitness and moderate sexual activity were in keeping with the life of the healthy Greek, and that athletics is part of a recommended regimen for those concerned with counteracting the potentially debilitating effects of intercourse' (2002: 229). While sex was as important, and problematic, as anything else, it did not stand out as especially significant; the guiding principle was the equipoise of *aidos* reflected in *arete* as the antithesis of uncivilized, violent, animalistic *hybris*.

While early Greek conceptions of the body are ultimately neither here nor there with regard to modern India, it is useful to keep the classical gymnasium in mind precisely because it shows how the materialism of the body can structure meaning. In a word, despite being central to the development of classical philosophy, the gymnasium suggests a radically alternative history of sex and masculinity: Plato, the iconic philosopher of the polis, takes his name from the Greek word *platon* meaning broad and robust. Although there is some question as to whether it was his back or his forehead that was broad, the point is that the problem of too much sex, among other things, was framed with reference to the fitness of the fluid body and in terms of a whole spectrum of ideas that are now the bedrock of modern philosophy. Given what wrestling has come to mean in the public sphere of popular imagination, as a somewhat plebeian, anti-intellectual masculine activity, it is very easy to lose sight of this—the framing of masculinity in terms of embodied principles that relate to ideas and high ideals: to philosophy, citizenship, physical fitness, *and* a certain understanding of sex.

This is my point, albeit with reference to a different philosophical tradition and geo-historical context: to interpret a concern with the dynamics of retaining semen as 'anxiety' is to indiscriminately read a linear history of normative sexualities into the formulation of cultural meanings that have different trajectories. There is no need, or space, to go into the logic that produces this misreading, but a significant role is played, quite obviously, by morality, notions of sin and religious values in general, as well as individual and public health factors of risk. What is most important to keep in mind, however, is not the disciplinary forms of punishment, either formal or informal, or even the secular manifestations of morality and inhibition in the articulations of psychology, psychotherapy and legislation. What is of central importance is the way in which an organic discourse of sexuality—with global scope and numerous, deep, local roots—is almost exclusively concerned with questions of what is good or bad, pleasurable or distasteful, safe and unsafe, erotic or perverted, normal or abnormal, in relation to uncritical assumptions about the nature of sex as a physiological act that involves bodies. These issues are important—perhaps critically so, with respect to public health, basic human rights and justice—but they do not at all exhaust or encompass what is meant by the term 'sex' or its entailments.

Each of the following chapters in this book engages with specific points of intersection between masculinity and physiology as these points of intersection provide critical insight on questions of public health, politics, nationalism, colonialism and medicine, among other things.

Chapter Two explores the articulation of nationalism in relation to a discourse about celibacy wherein the male body, weakened by maladies of modernity, is subject to an elaborate, scientific rhetoric of virtue and is disciplined with reference to ideals of embodied citizenship.

Chapter Three develops and extends this point to a general critique of psychological approaches to 'sexuality'. Many scholars have noted that *brahmacharya* (celibacy) is an important concept in South Asia (cf. Kakar 1981, 1982, 1990; Obeyesekere 1976, 1981; for comparison, see Gilmore 1990). Although the psychological basis of this concept has been studied, there is very little in the literature on the 'medical mechanics' of being and becoming a *brahmachari*. Nor is there a comprehensive account of the precise relationship between sex and the meaning of physical health in modern urban India. Through an examination of the popular Hindi literature on brahmacharya, interpreted within the context of therapeutic celibacy as put in practice by a modern yoga society, this chapter shows how a discourse about sex, semen and health is conceived of in terms of embodied truth.

Chapter Four focuses on the tension between celibacy and potent sexuality in the cultural practices associated with wrestling (*pahalwani, kushti*), and in the development and expressions of embodied masculinity manifest in different aspects of the sport. The argument here is that wrestlers articulate a critique of institutionalized politics—which is cognate with sex as such—on the basis of their concern with balance and power.

Chapter Five is concerned with the specific problem of how to make sense of various expressions of modern yoga, given that postural yoga is intimately linked to very old theories of embodied sexual potency and to mediaeval experiments with the internalization of alchemy and magical power. The focus of analysis is on the seductive 'post-modern' conflation of *asana* postures and sexual positions with an intent to articulate a politics of knowledge in relation to questions of power and truth in the representation of culture and history.

Chapter Six elaborates on this theme with reference to a very controversial form of practice—competitive postural yoga. Purists, concerned with transcendence, decry the way in which yoga has become a gymnastic sport. Using literature on the 'problem' of sex, desire and self-control in the gymnasiums of classical Greece—where sport and philosophy were conceived—and the kinaesthetics of sex and embodied perfection in mediaeval South Asian yoga, the argument here is that while *asana* competitions may be anathema in relation to many other articulations of modern practice, competitive 'sexy' yoga has a rather pure pedigree in relation to various other hybrid bastardizations of this alchemical tradition.

Chapter Seven focuses on a unique brand of practice that has taken shape at a point of intersection between various articulations of modernity, gender and medicine: *gupt rog chikitsa*. Gupt rog—'secret disease'—is a euphemism for problems of sex and sexuality that can be medically treated. Medical practitioners who draw on a wide range of medical knowledge—Ayurvedic, herbal, Unani, biomedical—have developed clinical expertise in the treatment of sexual problems, in particular impotence, infertility and deficiencies of energy, strength and desire. Taking 'secrecy' as a point of ambiguous and uncertain orientation, this concluding chapter is a meditation on the somatic semiotics of sexual meaning in modern India.

It is necessary to directly address what may well be a post-colonial criticism of the argument put forward in this book: that the concept of celibacy, encoded in cultural categories such as brahmacharya and theories of internalized *shakti* in the form of *vajikarana, rasayana, masti, kundalini* and *samadhi*, reflect nothing more than a fetishistic concern with the 'oriental exotic'—the sleeping hydra of imperial intellectualism—and have no place in Indian modernity. Why, one might ask, focus on Gandhi's 'curious personal habits' concerning diet, celibacy and nature cure (see Alter 2000b) when his politics of nonviolence may be regarded as an iconic articulation of modernity at large? Why is it necessary to take 'sexy yoga' seriously when it is patently ridiculous? Why worry about a discourse of sexuality that revolves around the hydraulics of 'night fall' when the vectors of infection and risk behaviours associated with HIV/AIDS are of paramount and unequivocal importance in the field of public health? Why frame the high ideals of philosophical enlightenment achieved by twentieth-century sages and savants in terms of 'mediaeval' concerns with embodied alchemy and the correlation between semen, breath and consciousness? Why not focus instead on ideas and practices that are 'really important' and that unambiguously reflect a contemporary state of affairs?

My view is that a consideration of these things—exotic as some may be in the post-colonial imagination—provide insight into alternative modernities wherein sex means something significantly different from what it means in the banal context of a global Google search. It is, I think, a preoccupation with Bollywood erotica and the manifold ways in which sex is consumed in contemporary India that reflects a fetishization of one particular articulation of modernity and its sexual exploits. Clearly there are many ways in which modern sexuality has consumed India, but it is necessary to keep in sharp focus the ways in which these articulations are derivative of globalization as a process that extends beyond the scope of both European colonialism and post-colonial nationalism. The coupling of globalization with the behavioural entelechy of the sexual response cycle simply reproduces—with local colouring—the standardized bathwater in which baby after baby is repeatedly washed.

What do I mean by masculinity as a sexed construct that is derivative of globalization? One clear example is found in both the militant rhetoric of nationalist organizations and extremist groups, as well as in secular critiques of this rhetoric and the ways in which sexed masculinity is played out in public. Hindu nationalism has produced a form of militant masculinity wherein violence and virility have become virtually synonymous. Herein the displacement of meaning from *lund* to *lathi* is fractional, both for those who wield the latter as well as those who are seduced, in their articulation of the critique, by that which is suggested by alliteration and rhyme.

The point is that there are two trajectories of logic that intersect to produce a singular, powerful, and seemingly all-consuming image of masculinity–sex–violence. One trajectory is reflected in the subject matter of Sudhir Kakar's book *The Colours of Violence* (1996) and Anand Patwardhan's documentary film *Pita, Putra, aur Dharmayuddha* (1995). Kakar, with wit, empathy and a palpable sense of ethnographic nuance, provides an intimate account of how two *goonda*s from different communities—Majid

Khan and Mangal Singh—embody and express their respective communal antipathy. Far from being two-dimensional caricatures of masculinity, Majid Khan and Mangal Singh radiate visceral power. 'A middle-aged, barrel-chested man of medium height, with a short thick neck that took its function of joining the head and the trunk more seriously than of separating the two, Majid Khan, even in his undervest and the rumpled green-and-black checked *lungi*, dominated the room with a miasma of raw power' (1996: 53).

Sexuality and violence permeate and animate the bodies of Mangal Singh and Majid Khan, and, in an extended sense, Kakar concludes that both men, although purposefully involved in orchestrated communal violence—and 'unusually dominant and of a marked authoritarian bent' (1996: 81)—otherwise manifest a relatively normal psychological profile.

Kakar's analysis is extremely perceptive and nuanced insofar as he succeeds in putting his analytical finger on the latent impress of extremity that characterizes these particular manifestations of masculinity. Following the seductive logic of a psychoanalytic interpretation however, Kakar disaggregates the embodied experience of visceral masculinity and essentializes sex as *different* from power in articulations of nationalism:

> Although egalitarianism between men may be missing from some modern Western conservative ideologies, it can very well be a part of Hindu conservative traditions and is, of course, available in the ideology of Islam. Egalitarianism, for instance, is a point of emphasis for the deeply conservative ideologies of the RSS, the organizational vanguard in the current revival of militant Hinduism. *The litmus test of revivalism and fundamentalism remains the attitude toward, sex rather than power* (1996: 84–85, emphasis added).

Rather dramatically, Mangal Singh and Majid Khan are stripped of their textured masculinity when it is an 'attitude towards sex'—sex as such rather than the relative size and essential composition of their bodies, and saturated body parts—that tests, and stands as a testament to, the nature of their fundamentalism. Once sex and power are disconnected, the risk of semiotic slippage, between masculinity and muscles as well as violence and virility, is significantly increased, both for those directly implicated, as well as for those of us looking on.

But there are different formulations.

The image on the front of this book is taken from the front cover of an inexpensive medical manual entitled *Sambhog Samrat Bananewalen Oshdiyan* that provides instructions and recipes for the decoction of formulas designed to 'produce sexual potency like that of an emperor'. One could say 'imperial sexual potency', but the sun has long since set on that tryst!

The key term used in the title of the book is *sambhog*, which has come to mean sex as such. The picture on the front, depicting 'loins and lions', is of the same order of displacement as 'lunds and lathis' in the rhetoric of militant Hinduism. In any case, the meaning of sexual potency would seem to be self-evident and irrefutable, as would the dynamics of masculinity invoked by a powerful, muscular man wrestling with a lion. Consequently, I was reduced to tears of laughter, which gave way, eventually, to critical reflection and a willingness to accept that sex and masculinity are never just what they seem to be, when my son, then just eleven years old, asked me when I showed him the picture: 'Dad, why is the lion sucking on the strong man's teat?' Some *bhog*, you might say!

But, all joking aside, there is an important and often misunderstood connection between the fluid meaning of the masculine body and the body's sexual fluids; and this connection—as often oriented towards a production of self, as it is to re-production, violence, pleasure and the mass consumption of erotica—does not just occupy a place in the cultural history of contemporary India. It provides a critical perspective on the orientation of modern sexuality at large by allowing for a history of semen and other vital fluids to raise a number of questions that are otherwise lost in the endless illusion of the sexual response cycle.

ब्रह्मचर्य की प्रचण्ड शक्ति

The Awesome Power of Celibacy. Cover image of an anonymously authored book: *Brahmacharya Ki Prachand Shakti*. Barelli: Sanskriti Sansthan, n.d.

Celibacy and Sexuality
Transformations of Gender into Nationalism

Introduction

It is well known that Mahatma Gandhi felt that sexuality and desire were intimately connected to social life and politics and that self-control translated directly into power of various kinds, both public and private. Gandhi's enigmatic genius and his popular appeal among India's masses may be attributed, at least in part, to the degree to which he was able to embody a powerful ideal of sexual self-control that linked his socio-political projects to pervasive Hindu notions of renunciation. Affecting the persona of a world-renouncer, Gandhi was able to mix political, religious and moral power, thus translating personal self-control into radical social criticism and nationalist goals. Gandhi's mass appeal was partly effected on a visceral level at which many Hindu men were able to fully appreciate the logic of celibacy as a means to psychological security, self-improvement, and national reform. Although my concern in this chapter is not directly with Gandhi's notion of self-control, it is against the larger backdrop of his political legacy that I situate this discussion of sexuality, gender, and nationalism in contemporary India.

My specific purpose is to analyse the concept of *brahmacharya* (celibacy) as it relates to questions of gender and politics. I will show that a male concern with celibacy is couched in terms of a discourse about truth, and that truth translates directly into the moral politics of nationalism.[1] At the outset, I must point out that the nationalism that emerges out of this discourse is of an oblique and somewhat utopian sort. In other words, it is not formalized or institutionalized in any sense, but takes shape culturally, I would argue, on two primary levels: that of rhetoric on the one hand, and the body on the other. Rhetoric and the body come together in terms of health, for the celibate body is regarded as supremely fit, and as such evokes a divine and heroic mystique of epic proportions. What emerges is a kind of medical poetics in which the male body is sexually analysed, systematically diagnosed and, finally, as rhetoric and theory are put into practice, disciplined according to a rigorous regimen. This regimen is thought to produce a citizen who embodies the essence of national integrity and strength.

There is not a great deal in the standard literature on nationalism to help make sense of this process. For the most part, contemporary writers such as Dumont (1986), Hobsbawm (1990), Smith (1971) and Gellner (1983) focus on the overtly political, institutionalized forms of nationalism wherein the primary issues are ethnic, religious, or linguistic ideologies. Benedict Anderson, whose analysis of nationalistic 'imagined communities' is less formal and more open to the dynamics of power/knowledge and cultural transformation, is still primarily concerned with questions of language and the history of ideas, even when those

---

[1] Various interpretations of celibacy have, of course, been incorporated into the rhetoric and institutionalized, militant politics of the Rashtriya Swayamsevak Sangh and its various affiliate organizations (cf. Andersen and Damle 1987; Ashby 1974; Chandra 1984; Embree 1990; Fox 1989). As I have argued elsewhere (Alter 1994), the RSS interpretation of physical fitness is one among many interpretations of how the body can be construed as a political object in nationalist projects. My purpose in this chapter is to argue that brahmacharya's political salience is not limited to the interpretation given it by a single political ideology. It is part of a larger, more ambiguous discourse in which sex, health and politics blur together.

ideas concern the political implications of such somatic signs as the colour of a person's skin (1983: 129–47).

A small but significant body of literature is being developed on the relationship between explicitly somatic problems and nationalist sentiments (cf. Martin 1990; Mosse 1985). Much of this work emerges from the intersection of feminist scholarship and critical studies of colonialism (cf. Alloula 1987; Ballhatchet 1980; Callaway 1987; Etienne and Leacock 1980; Hyam 1990; Stoler 1989; Cooper and Stoler 1989; Strobel 1987).[2] British imperialism in India seems to have provided particularly fertile ground for the study of sexual politics, and some innovative recent work has been done on the place of female bodies in the nationalist projects of the late nineteenth and early twentieth centuries (cf. Chakravarti 1990;Chatterjee 1986, 1989, 1990; Sangari and Vaid 1990; Tharu 1990; Mani 1987). Discussions of male bodies in this context are, unfortunately, more difficult to find (cf. Alter 1992, 1994; Rosselli 1980). However, my own research in north India clearly shows that physical fitness and nationalism are dramatically embodied in the heroically masculine physique of the Indian wrestler (*pahalwan*),and that this masculine physique took shape as a form of colonial and postcolonial critique (Alter 1993a).

Along these lines, Partha Chatterjee's general formulations about gendered nationalism are of particular relevance. He argues that Indian nationalists in the mid to late nineteenth century made a distinction between a material sphere of power, regarded as

[2] Much of this literature focuses on the colonizers' perceptions of their sexual encounters with people of other races. Ballhatchet (1980) and Hyam for example, analyse colonial discourse on prostitution, sexual health, and interracial marriage, but do not concern themselves with the way the colonized people reflected on these same issues. Nandy (1980), and Mani (1987) have pointed out that there were sexual aspects to the indigenous discourse on *sati* (widow burning), and others (Alloula 1987; Marglin 1985; Oldenberg 1991) have shown how erotic entertainment was implicated in the construction of gender relations. But the focus of these authors, and almost all others who write on sexuality and the sexual politics of imperialism, is on the embodiment of gender and not on the physiological aspects of sex.

exterior to the individual, where the British were superior, and a spiritual sphere of moral value where 'traditional' Hindu beliefs, located within the individual, were regarded as superior to, and somewhat immune from, the Western culture of imperialism (1989: 624). He concludes that the notion of an inner purity of tradition—imputed by colonized men onto the bodies of colonized women—was the product of an alien discourse of power that classified certain aspects of Hindu culture as inherently private and apolitical (p. 631), thus producing what he calls 'the new patriarchy' of modern liberalism (p. 627).

While I agree in general with the distinctions Chatterjee makes, I think his use of the term 'spiritual' is somewhat misleading since it evokes notions of mystical devotion and secret knowledge about mysterious truths. Clearly, 'Hindu' notions of somaticity—both in terms of ritual, health, and social hierarchy—fall within the domain of what Chatterjee refers to as the spiritual discourse of nationalism, and yet bodies are concrete material objects. While certain aspects of 'Hindu' physicality may, indeed, be construed as 'inner' and therefore outside the purview of imperial power, in other ways the material body is a naked object upon which the forces of imperial power directly impinge. As distinct from ideologies about the body, physiological issues of gender, health, and hygiene tend to blur the important distinctions that Chatterjee argues the early nationalists were trying to make. The literature on brahmacharya clearly illustrates the extent to which, in the late twentieth century at least, the 'spiritual' male body became a focal site for a discourse of nationalism.

Celibacy, Semen, and the Science of Sex

Many scholars have noted that brahmacharya is a concept with social, psychological, medical and religious significance in Hindu society (Carstairs 1958; Kakar 1981, 1982, 1990; Obeyesekere 1981; O'Flaherty 1973; Spratt 1966), and there can be no doubt that semen retention is a theme with powerful resonance in the psyche of many men who feel that sex is enervating. While the basic theory of celibacy has been analysed and explained in various ways by many authors, my concern is primarily with the technical aspect of the brahmachari's regimen, and with what the logic of those techniques implies. Aside from Gandhi's own writings, there is very little on the mechanics—the science—of being and becoming celibate.

The modern concept of brahmacharya clearly derives from the classical life-cycle prescriptions of dharma articulated in the *Manusmriti* (see Olivelle 2005). The four-fold *ashrama* cycle of life stages, of which brahmacharya (initiated studentship) is the first, when understood in conjunction with the 'four ends of man'—*dharma*, *artha*, *kama*, and *moksha*—clearly articulates an encompassing code of moral, civic, ritual, political, and economic conduct. The status of the initiated student defines one specific phase in the larger structure of society, and the 'structured' integration of the individual into that society. Specifically, it marks the 'second birth' of Brahmin, Kshatriya, and Vaishya boys and sets them on a path of disciplined Vedic learning. In this regard, brahmacharya may be seen as a crucial phase in the articulation of difference within society insofar as the ritual of initiation defines the particular trajectory of the various *varna* categories and who has what rights and duties within those categories.

Most of the rules of conduct for the brahmachari concern his religious status vis-à-vis his guru and the ritual protocol of his community. It is clearly within the ritualized contexts defined by *The Sacred Laws of the Aryas* (Muller 1897 [1965]), *Bhagavad Gita* (1945), and the *Ashvalayana Grhya-Sutra* (1923) that the vow of chastity must be understood. For the initiated twice-born student, chastity in particular and self-control in general were requisite for learning the Vedas, since sex was regarded as both defiling and distracting. In this regard, chastity was a practical pedagogical principle and not a general rule of moral conduct prescribed for all Hindus. Nor was the ritual vow of chastity—as distinct from the modern concept of nationalistic celibacy—medicalized in any sense; the initiated student did not, it seems, practise celibacy as a form of personalized public health. It was simply part of his religious training.

Despite the very narrow, ritualized meaning of celibacy within the classical life-scheme of the twice-born (cf. Stevenson 1920 [1971]), one is able to discern a nascent political agenda in Vedic and post-Vedic discourse on sexuality. Within the life-cycle of the twice-born male, there was most certainly a time and place for sex. However, the Vedas and other classic texts sought to regulate the nature of who, what, where, and how one might engage in sex (cf. *Kama Sutra*), but not sex itself as a monolithic construct that defined the moral conduct of some equally monolithic 'Hindu' citizen. Social, political, aesthetic, and economic distinctions were all important when reckoning the moral propriety or appropriateness of sex, whereas universal standards were virtually meaningless: what was good for one was by no means good for all, particularly when it came to abstinence. In this regard, the classical authors seemed to see sex as one behavioural facet among many others to be regulated in the interest of maintaining the social hierarchy. As Romila Thapar has noted, however, the world-renouncer who abstained from sex completely was able to act as a social critic precisely by virtue of his position outside of this hierarchy (Thapar 1976). Similarly, for the Naga sect of the Ramanandi order (see Pinch 2006) the discipline of brahmacharya was central to the practice of various martial arts put to use in sixteenth- and seventeenth-century political campaigns. Thus, asexuality functioned as a form of socio-political power while deriving authority from the renouncer's mystical, 'other-worldly' spirituality. It was this connection between sex, spirituality, and social criticism that Gandhi was able to translate so effectively into his programme of militant nonviolence. Although I think the Vedic and post-Vedic perspective on sex is radically different from the modern discourse on sex and nationalism that emerged in the twentieth century—since the classical renouncer, unlike Gandhi and his modern heirs, did not advocate that everyone become like him in order to reform society—it is important to keep in mind that the 'laws of dharma' were incipiently political. It is easy, therefore, for modern advocates of Hindu reform to recast the narrow rules of 'ancient sex' in terms of social criticism and a more encompassing, nationalistic vision of moral propriety.

Like his classical forebear, the modern brahmachari is, first and foremost, celibate, but to maintain absolute control over his sexual desire his discipline mandates that he must control all of his senses by means of a rigid and carefully regimented programme of diet, exercise and rest. Moreover, control of the senses entails careful management of a wide array of daily activities, including what and how to read, where and how to sleep, and what to wear, among many other things. In other words, brahmacharya is a way of life that is focused on sexuality but includes a much broader spectrum of activities and concerns.

In contemporary north India, a genre of popular/technical literature on brahmacharya is published by large, mainstream establishments as well as by smaller, regional presses. Booklets, pamphlets and 'medical manuals' advocate celibacy, explain its merits and provide precise instructions on how to control desire and stay healthy. These publications also, and perhaps primarily, offer home-remedy treatments to cure specific ailments that threaten to undermine self-control. In virtually all of this literature, the concept of brahmacharya is systematically opposed to Indian modernity. Although it is only logical that this literature should have proliferated in the decades of rapid change and increasing literacy after independence, my argument is that brahmacharya developed as a strategically modern Indian concept opposed to Westernization. More specifically, it was developed as the moral/physical alternative to various forms of postcolonial desire—both gross and subtle—which were thought to directly afflict the body and undermine its strength and integrity. The forces of postcolonial desire are manifold, and mostly defined by way of contrast to the pristine, natural, and non-erotic environment of 'traditional' India. As one critic writes:

Because the youth of today are destroying their semen they are courting the worst disaster and daily being condemned to hell ... Mother nature stands, stick in hand, watching their abominable behaviour, and for every drop of semen spilled she lashes out and strikes their vital organs. ...

These days it is common to see the deep wounds of her stick on young people's backs. How many of these unfortunate people lie shaking on their cots like the grievously ill? Some are suffering from the heat. And others, carrying the same deep wounds, pretentiously puff out their chests and walk about piously exchanging garlands while nervously checking their pulse for any sign of illness. There is no trust of God in their hearts, only lust. Now tell me, what future do such people have? ... They only glow with the light of fireflies, and neither humility nor glory are found in their flickering hypocrisy. (Sivananda 1984:41)

Many authors are very specific about what forms of erotic and sensual stimulation cause young people to destroy their semen. Popular cinema, which is saturated with romantic themes and suggestively lurid images, is unanimously regarded as the most debauched aspect of modern life.

As a form of entertainment, cinema is a great enemy of modern society. It is full of obscene, erotic and indecent images which enter the sub-conscious, lie dormant, and then result in night-emission. (Shastri n.d.:29)

Similarly, so-called 'pornographic' novels and magazines are said to stimulate desire through fantasy. However, it is the whole ethos and institutional structure of modernity that is considered sensually decadent, including everything from effete toiletries and coeducation to hair-styles and family-planning policies. While sex is certainly not said to be categorically bad, its public manifestation and subtle permeation of the culture is thought to be fundamentally disruptive.

The literature on brahmacharya is directed specifically, but not exclusively, at teenage boys and young men in college who would be the primary consumers of films, 'pornography', and the other effete products of modernity. Books on celibacy are often sold at school bookstores along with classroom texts and other educational literature. Although their precise circulation is unknown, the literature is widely available. Among wrestlers, who comprise a broad class and caste spectrum of society, the practice of brahmacharya is highly developed and provides a clear example of how the discourse on celibacy finds popular, public expression. In many north Indian villages and cities, wrestling is a popular sport that attracts tens of thousands of spectators who are exposed to a dramatic display of how semen retention can enhance the character, strength and skill of otherwise ordinary men. The wrestling *akhara* (public gymnasium) provides a social environment in which the ideas expressed in the popular literature on celibacy are both confirmed by practice and disseminated among village and neighbourhood men. The public gymnasium thus provides a context within which the critique of postcolonial desire finds popular expression. Thereby a 'moral' form of popular culture is pitted against the popular hedonism of modernity.

Numerous scholars have noted that sexual lust and desire are regarded as volatile, dangerous, and chaotic by many in South Asia (Edwards 1983; Kakar 1987, 1990; O'Flaherty 1973, 1980; Obeyesekere 1976, 1981; Spratt 1966). Even so, it is not primarily on moral grounds that public sexuality is decried. While one may discern a tone of approbation and indignation in the tracts on brahmacharya, where many authors use words such as 'filthy', 'dirty', 'evil' and 'sinful' to describe so-called reprobate sexuality, their concern, ultimately, is with substance and not with the behavioural components of virtue and vice. Celibacy is more of a hydraulic and biochemical problem—an issue of fluid balance and flow that has a powerful moral effect on the individual's overall health—but it is not moral in a puritanical or prudish sense simply by virtue of being intrinsically opposed to sex and sexuality. Thus, a person is good or bad not only because of what he does, but because what he does, sexually speaking, fundamentally changes the biochemical nature of his being. In these terms, moral reform is not so much an issue of 'building character' as it is an exercise in building the body in terms of a theory about moral substance. Consequently, there seems to be an inverse correlation between the extent to which brahmacharya is subjected to a microscopic and comprehensive analysis, and the magnitude of those forces that threaten to undermine celibacy. Confronted with the overpowering chaos of transcultural sensuality—satellite TV and MTV, to name but two of the most recent forces—those who advocate brahmacharya as a strategic form of defensive health do so by way of a scientific discourse designed, at least in part, to combat the nonsense of sexual stimulation with the logical sense of medical knowledge about sex and desire.

In a similar vein, the literature on brahmacharya pays a great deal of attention to the plethora of so-called 'doctors' and 'sex specialists' who treat sexual problems in various ways. Those who advocate celibacy are unanimous in their criticism of these specialists, who, they claim, undermine self-control by either prescribing tonics that enhance virility and sexual potency, or else administering purely symptomatic rather than holistic cures for semen loss (see chapter 7). In essence, the writings regard these specialists as quacks and charlatans who profit at the expense of debauched and deluded youth. One aspect of the criticism of these specialists is that they perpetuate a discourse of seductive secrecy about sexuality. Their whole mode of operation is said to be framed by an erotic mystique that magnifies the allure of passion's forbidden fruit. It seems to be in direct opposition to the secretive nature of this kind of modern sexuality that the tracts on brahmacharya are written. In this literature, a detailed, systematic and holistic analysis of male sex is designed to break down the mystique and power of secrecy by advocating a form of public, sexualized truth.

What is most striking about the literature on brahmacharya is the degree of detail provided about all facets of male sex, sexuality, and health. Rather than focusing on the moral psychology of erotic desire—as might similar books published by, say, church groups in America, or the Boy Scouts—books on brahmacharya strive to analyse the mechanics, hydraulics and chemistry of sex with particular emphasis on the various properties of semen, since semen is regarded as the most essential fluid of life. The whole purpose of brahmacharya is to build up a resilient store of semen so that the body—in a holistic, psychosomatic sense—radiates an aura of vitality and strength.

The production and protection of semen is based on what might best be described, somewhat awkwardly, given the incompatibility of English with the language of 'Hindu' sexuality, as a regimen of the plain and simple truth. One writer explains that the term brahmacharya is a conjunction of two words which mean truth and conduct (Saraswati1982:89). More specifically, conduct is of three types—diet, exercise and work. To be a brahmachari is to eat simple food, live simply, and engage in the simple exercise of walking. The term 'simple', as Saraswati uses it, is synonymous with truth, and may be contrasted to the imbalanced chaos of modern life—the deceit of modernity.

The process by which the body makes semen is fundamental to the brahmachari's regimen. Diet is perhaps the single most important variable. According to a clearly defined and predictable ratio, food is transformed into blood, blood into flesh, flesh into fat, fat into bone, bone into marrow, and marrow into semen. Thus, semen is a highly condensed distillate of pure and wholesome food. As Shastri notes, the brahmachari's food should be of the purest quality, since 'pure food produces pure truth, and pure truth produces pure wisdom. With great and absolute wisdom one will always be successful' (n.d.:50). He then provides a long list of specific items which, on account of being either *tamasi* or *rajasi*, ought to be avoided.[3]

[3] *Tamas* and *rajas*, along with *sattva*, comprise a triadic scheme of food classification. Tamasi foods make one dull and lethargic, while rajasi foods make one feel hot, agitated, and restless. Rajasi foods are generally thought to excite passion, whereas tamasi foods inhibit the production of semen and prevent the

Another example of the importance of dietary health to the regimen of self-control may be drawn from Yogananda Saraswati's *Brahmacharya Raksha Hi Jiwan Hai* (*Celibacy is Life Itself*, 1982). Saraswati explains that good digestion is crucial to the production and retention of semen, which, in turn, is essential to good health. He thus begins his book on celibacy by explaining the anatomy of digestion with carefully drawn diagrams of the stomach and intestines, and a two-page discussion of how food is broken down into various properties. Indigestion in general, and constipation in particular, are regarded as factors that disrupt the production and balanced flow of semen within the body. Saraswati explains the causes of constipation and then provides a list of exercises one may perform while defecating to relieve the symptoms. These exercises are diagrammed, analysed and evaluated in terms of their particular effectiveness (1982: 9–25). Indigestion is, in fact, a common symptom of a much larger and more pervasive problem: overeating. From the following critique of gluttony and unbridled consumption, the reader gets a sense of how important a proper, balanced diet is for the brahmachari.

> The poor die from not having enough to eat, and the rich gluttons from eating too much. Only one who eats moderately can live the long life of a true celibate. Plague and cholera are caused by gluttons because rich people are dirty. They earn, consume, and eliminate; these are their 'three worldly tasks', and in the end they die eating. A glutton is sad, lazy, sickly, and has a short life span. Whenever there is an epidemic in the country, it is the gluttons who are the first to be infected. (Sivananda 1984: 91)

---

body from being able to exercise self-control. *Sattvik* foods, on the other hand, stabilize semen and calm passion. Without indicating which foods contain which property, Shastri provides the following list of foods that ought to be avoided: red pepper, oil, molasses, sour things, tamarind, fried or baked breads made from finely ground wheat, spiced greens, spicy condiments and sauces, savouries made from lentil flour, peanuts, onions, garlic and cloves (n.d.a:51).

As the most primary of fluid substances, semen is thought to permeate and flow within the body much the way blood does. However, as a vital fluid, its properties are not only life-giving, but energizing in a heroic, epiphanal, and almost supernatural way.

> The more a person conserves his semen, the greater will be his stature and vitality. His energy, ardour, intellect, competence, capacity for work, wisdom, success and godliness will begin to manifest themselves, and he will be able to profit from a long life. . . . To tell the truth, semen is elixir. (Sivananda 1984: 10–11)

Although semen has phenomenal properties, it is regarded as a tangible, natural substance. This point must be emphasized because the reader is likely to forget that semen is an elemental fluid with basic physical properties when its power to transform is taken into consideration. No distinction should be made here between the gross nature of seminal fluid and the subtle properties of *ojas*, which animate the body with vital energy.[4] The regimen of brahmacharya, and the analysis and rationalization of that regimen in popular medical literature, fundamentally conflates concrete substance—the stuff of wet dreams, masturbation and intercourse—with abstract social, political and spiritual power. Celibacy is not a theory based on analogy and metaphor, but

[4] Those who have studied yoga theory and the practices associated with world renunciation are aware that ojas is the term used to describe the aura of enlightenment. As O'Flaherty (1980: 179–90) has pointed out, the yogic theory of *kundalini* meditation is based on a literal model of what might be called internal ejaculation, in which semen is shot upwards along the spine through the various *chakra* centres of the 'subtle' body until it reaches the brain and becomes the *shakti* of enlightened consciousness. Interpretations of this process emphasize the metaphorical transformation of substance into mystical insight, where semen is regarded as a symbol of the ultimate truth. A tacit distinction is made between the ideational construct of subtle ojas and the substantial nature of gross semen. My argument is that such a distinction ought not to be made, particularly in the case of a politicized discourse on celibacy where it is essential that the somatic, and therefore generic, nature of truth not be compromised.

a practical scheme based on the metonymical correspondence of somatic health, psychological and intellectual maturity, and the socio-political power to change the nature of society. It is, therefore, not the action of self-control that builds character and resolve through a discipline of the disembodied self in a game of mind over matter. It is the matter itself from which the essentials of character and virtue emanate.

Although the positive effects of semen are envisioned in terms of stupendous glory, and chronicled in florid and sublime prose, the negative effect of semen loss is a far more common condition. It is important to note, however, that while semen loss is a serious problem, it is not simply the consequence of libertinism. To be sure, sexual intercourse and masturbation are two of the most common ways to lose semen, but night emission, spermatorrhea, and various other 'illnesses' in which semen is lost 'involuntarily' are also regarded as problems whose moral effect is essentially the same, even though volition and personal responsibility are less clearly defined.[5]

Most books on brahmacharya contain a list of between fifteen and thirty 'symptoms' which afflict a person who suffers from semen loss. What is most interesting about these lists is their comprehensive nature. A person who suffers from semen loss, for example, walks with his head bowed and eyes averted, perspires constantly, has no sense of humour, is irritable and aggressive; his eyes are sunken and lacklustre; his jaw bone protrudes and his cheeks are colourless and sunken; he never finishes the work he

[5] I was first surprised and perplexed by the inordinate attention given in the literature on brahmacharya to the problem of night emission. My reasoning was that the involuntary emission of semen could not be considered a moral problem since it was purely accidental and related to forces over which the individual could not be expected to exercise control. However, my logic was backward. I was operating under the false assumption that celibacy was the product of self-discipline, and morality a measure of the strength of one's resolve. Instead, the strength of one's resolve is directly related to the power inherent in semen, which means that it makes virtually no difference how you lose it; the moral effect is the same.

starts and prefers to be alone; he is restless; he has gum disease, halitosis and tooth decay; he drinks, smokes, and takes drugs; perhaps most enigmatic (and to my mind inexplicable), he chews on pencils, chalk, dirt and the coloured pages from his copy book; he suffers from memory loss, is depressed and dull-witted; his unconscious mind is unstable, and he is plagued by conflicting thoughts, mental anguish and dementia (Shastri n.d.:36–40).

The picture of one afflicted by semen loss is certainly not a pretty one—ultimately a toothless, skinny, prematurely old half-wit who blindly sweats, grumbles and hobbles his way to a suicidal end. However, those who paint such pictures are, for the most part, being neither accusatory nor judgemental. Their primary concern is medical, with an intent to understand and cure rather than zealously condemn. If one looks carefully at the epidemiological arguments presented in the texts on celibacy, it becomes clear that 'weak moral character' and 'perversion' are not, in and of themselves, definitive traits that explain behaviour. They are, rather, the socio-psychological manifestations of a more primary array of psychosomatic imbalances. When the authors of books on brahmacharya are specific about what can be done to prevent semen loss, they do advocate abstract notions of conviction, resolve, and self-control, but only within the context of treatments for constipation, nasal congestion, high blood pressure, tooth decay, acne, and other 'somatic' problems that destabilize semen. In any case celibacy, in general, is regarded as a cure for semen loss, and the larger intent of effecting a cure is to turn the chronically ill into heroically healthy citizens.

Gender and Postcolonial Desire

A discourse on the power of semen produces an unambiguously male ideology. In spite of the fact that some authors, in keeping with Ayurvedic theory, say that women's bodies also contain semen, albeit of a different kind and nature than that of men, there can be little doubt that the entire construct of brahmacharya is conceived of in male terms. Although it is intriguing to consider the implications of genderless semen for a discourse on sexuality and nationalism, typical discussions of the subject consist of one or two disappointingly vague and insignificant lines.

One might argue that the distinctly male features of celibacy render the whole question of gender moot and uninteresting by virtue of the relatively two-dimensional relationship between social, political, and physical power that is implied. However, in most instances of male dominance, power is largely an ideological construct that is only nominally, and therefore tenuously— although often forcefully and vigorously—based on images of strength (cf. Brown 1988; Elshtain 1981). It is relatively rare, and therefore of some theoretical interest, to find a case in which a logic of male dominance is inverted, so to speak, where what becomes problematic is not the politics of status and authority, or the production of a heroic identity but that which might seem most essentially and ineluctably male: the nature of semen.

In *The Woman in the Body: A Cultural Analysis of Reproduction* (1987), Emily Martin clearly shows how women's bodies have been fragmented by science, technology, and labour (cf. also Martin 1989, 1991). Most significantly, she shows how an opposition to fragmentation and alienation is often effected through the medium of the body in general, and specific parts of the body or body processes in particular—menopause and birthing, for example. Martin's argument is that disempowered women are not only able to see the process of fragmentation for what it is, but are able to imagine 'alternative visions' to that process. Significantly, these reconfigurations of the self are not only imagined, they are embodied, and the logic of embodiment is worked out in exact detail.

Distinct from the medical discourse by men about women's bodies, which Martin critically deconstructs, the discourse on semen within the literature on brahmacharya is both by and about men. However, it is 'unreflexively' male, which is to say that the men writing about semen write, for the most part, as though the world were exclusively, if unremarkably, male. Clearly this discourse emerges from a comfortable position of unself-conscious power: a world in which women simply do not figure except in their sharply circumscribed roles as mother, sister and wife on the one hand, and seductive whore on the other. The whole discourse on brahmacharya is so fantastically skewed that gender—what it means to be a man in modern India—becomes a purely self-referential question rather than a problem of distinguishing between masculine and feminine attributes, between male and female roles, or, indeed, between male and female aspects of sexual intercourse. A preoccupation with the nature of semen—rather than, say, machismo or masculine values—tends to structure the discourse on male identity in a way that unintentionally deconstructs a mythology of dominance by penetrating deep into the body and soul of every man. However, the deconstruction is only nominal, for the male discourse on semen ends up constructing an alternative and perhaps more covert mythology of gendered truth.

Although the men who write about celibacy do so—in terms of gender, at least—from a position of almost total power, their motivation to write comes from a feeling of impending powerlessness in the face of radical socio-moral change. In other words, they feel compelled to reconfigure the nature of their identity in order to prevent nothing less than the debauchery of every man and the total disintegration of society. It is this feeling of impending powerlessness and disintegration that puts those who write about celibacy in a frame of mind to reflect critically—if not always self-consciously—on the nature of the 'man in the body'. The impending fragmentation of the male body in terms of modernity and the various forces of postcolonial desire entail a radical reconfiguration of 'self and body image', to again adapt Martin's phrase. These reconfigurations are, needless to say, quite different from those of 'the woman in the body' where powerlessness is real and encompassing rather than putative and contextual, and where there is a gendered world of difference between those who structure the discourse about bodies and those who 'live' in those bodies. Under certain circumstances, Emily Martin argues, women are able to see through the thick walls of patriarchal ideology and see it for what it is. My argument is that men in a position of power, confronted by what they perceive to be an almost apocalyptic transformation of society, are forced to see the extreme contingency of their gendered position—the fictional basis of their ideology if you will. As a result, what they do is critically deconstruct the elements of that ideology in search of a more primary, natural truth about themselves—which is, in essence, what some of the women Emily Martin writes about are trying to do. Although there are phenomenal differences between these women and the Indian men who advocate celibacy, lessons may be drawn from the former about how the latter seek to embody their gender.

To understand the problematic nature of male identity in contemporary India, it is necessary to consider briefly a few historical points. Edward Said, among others, has argued that there is a close connection between the culture of imperialism and the power and imagery of male-oriented aggressive sex (1978; cf. also Ballhatchet 1980; Stoler 1989; Alloula 1987). While the connection is perhaps most apparent in the common metaphor and experience of rape, there were more subtle, if no less insidious, ways in which the Orient, as female, was eroticized and then passionately consumed by those in positions of power. This power depended not only on the construction of an erotic feminine mystique, but also on the deconstruction of an indigenous male identity.

From a British perspective—and I use 'a' rather than the more general and totalizing 'the' advisedly (cf. Cooper and Stoler 1989)—it was relatively easy to conclude that Indian men in general, and upper-caste Hindu men in particular, were effete. They had, after all, been defeated and turned into subject citizens by a dominant power. Accusations of political, military, and sexual impotence were powerful metaphors in this kind of argument. Although there were loud and sustained protests by Indian politicians, reformers and educators alike, John Rosselli has indicated, through historical research in Bengal, that for a significant period of time this image of effeteness was accepted and perhaps even affectedly popularized by a certain class of Indian men, primarily, although not exclusively, the educated *babu*s and clerks who worked in the vast imperial bureaucracies (1980). The trend was certainly strong enough to elicit a powerful nationalist response by those who felt compelled to 'remasculate' their impotent brethren through the medium of physical education (Nandy 1980:60). A striking example is provided by Abdus Salam's short treatise, *Physical Education in India* (1895). After applauding the vitality and vigour of India's early Muslim heritage, Salam makes the following observation, which, although directed at the Bengali Muslim intelligentsia, may be taken as a more general statement on the condition of all 'Westernized' Indians.

> In contrast with this brilliant past as regards physical vigour and manliness, the lack of physical energy which now more or less characterizes the Mahomedans [sic] in India stands out in bold. Our one-sided Western education, so far . . . has acted with us like a bad liver: it is making us assimilate what has to be rejected of the Western import, and reject what has to be assimilated. We are rapidly parting with our own national ways and manners. . . . In the case of a few here and there might be visible some surface Western polish, but it is no more than skin deep; the result being that whilst the sweet guilelessness and gentle suavity of the East is absent, the genuine sturdiness and masculine straightforwardness of the West is also wanting. (1895: 17–18)

At issue amidst all this acrimony, from a British perspective at least, was the largely metaphoric connection between heroism, strength and courage on the one hand, and virility on the other. Their disparagement of Indian men was, in effect, based on an analogic theory of how personal strength translated into public virtue. Virility was a metaphor for political power and socio-moral strength: a metaphor that mixed together elements of masculine psychology and colonial ideology. Virility, in British terms, was of course associated with a particular form of sexuality wherein strength and power were a function of potency, stamina, size and appetite. In other words, power was measured in terms of one's ability to spend semen—either literally or figuratively—which was, in turn, dependent on one's ability to control conditions under which it was spent. An echo of this reverberates in Salam's anglicized, English prose.

> [I]n these piping-days of peace and high intellectual pressure and especially in this enervating Indian climate, when more than ever a race is apt to get emasculated, it is absolutely necessary that we should have recourse to physical exercise . . . (1895:22).

It is important to point out that the effete, Westernized babu was only one of a number of sexually-based stereotypes of Indian men. As many scholars have pointed out, the British in India were intent on various schemes of racial/caste classification. One of the categories developed in these schemes was that of the so-called martial castes, who, in direct contrast to the effete Bengali babu and mercantile Vaishya, were aggressive, virile and courageous. These martial castes, which included Marathas, Pathans, and Rajputs, were constructed in terms of a classical masculine image that probably had as much to do with imputed British ideals as with indigenous values (Nandy 1980:72). One can, for example, clearly locate the moral empathy in the opening sentence of Sir George MacMunn's *The Martial Races of India*.

> Who and what are the martial races of India, how do they come, and in what crucible, on what anvil's [sic] hot with pain spring the soldiers of India, whom surely Baba Ghandi [sic] never fathered? (1933:1)

Although bombastic almost to the point of parody, MacMunn's rhetoric serves to illustrate the extent to which a scheme of sexual classification functioned to make sense of Indian masculinity. Whereas Salam blamed Western education for sapping the strength of India's young and noble, MacMunn places the blame on religion and 'early marriage, premature brides, and juvenile eroticism' (1933:2). Applauding the chivalry of Rajput soldiers and other 'virile races' who would rather immolate their wives than have them captured in war, MacMunn again castigates Gandhi and 'the mass of [Indian] people [who] have neither martial aptitude nor physical courage.' (ibid.)

The gentle yet merciless race of hereditary moneylenders, from which Lala Ghandi [sic] springs, only kept within bounds by an occasional flaying and roasting, have never been able or even tried to protect their own hoards. (ibid.:3)

Despite their radical differences, the effete babu, the gentle yet merciless Vaishya and the heroic Rajput were conceived of in terms of a single theory of sexual power: aggressive virility or a lack thereof.

The logic of this analogy between semen and power is, I believe, crucial to understanding the nature of what I am calling postcolonial desire and the logic of various indigenous responses to it. In most general terms, the colonial conception of sexuality in particular, but sensuality in general, with its emphasis on male potency and personal gratification, helped change what might be referred to as the structure of erotic passion in late nineteenth- and twentieth-century India. Needless to say, eroticism was not a British invention, and it could be argued that Victorian prudishness mitigated against the public—as distinct from private and elite— proliferation of erotica in colonial India. However, it was, in part, this same prudishness that contributed to the 'pornographication' of erotica in Indian culture on the one hand, and on the other, the construction of a moralistic, Christian discourse on sex in general. As Ballhatchet (1980) and Hyam (1990) show, there was a great deal of disagreement about, and ambivalence towards, sexuality, prostitution, concubinage, and interracial marriage among the British in India. Attitudes and practices did not always conform to policy. Regardless, what is most significant about colonial sexuality was the tremendous politico-moral discourse it generated by linking sex and identity with questions of power and authority. The modern advocates of celibacy who criticize the youth of modern India for being 'sex addicts' often trace the history of their addiction back to the virtual invention of 'sexuality'—in the modern Foucauldian sense of the term—during the colonial period. Prior to that time there was sex, passion, and sensuality, to be sure, and there was an elaborate discourse on the art of sex—replete with categories and modes of classification (cf. Chakravarti 1963; Meyer 1930)—but there was no sense in which an apparatus of sexuality provided a definitive moral yardstick against which to measure the appropriateness of various acts or the status of the actors. Sex was a thing unto itself, but certainly not an encompassing socio-moral force whose seductive influence permeated the entire cultural fabric.

Those who advocate brahmacharya however, argue that sex began to permeate society at about the turn of the century and since that time men have become progressively more enslaved to the idea that sex is the most important aspect of life. One might say that a more encompassing, libertine concept emerged out of the self-image of effeteness, and the ascribed identity of race-specific martial virility—at least in the critical, conservative judgement of those who favoured celibacy. The colonial discourse on sex seduced those who were colonized and distorted their self-concept by structuring the very nature of sexuality.

Rather than celebrate Independence and the achievements of modern India, those who write about celibacy often point out that postcolonial India is enslaved by its 'freedom' to develop and Westernize: enslaved not so much to sex itself—although certainly that—as to the idea that power is a function of potency, and virility the coefficient of modernization. In other words, the authors are adamantly opposed to the institutionalized sex of prostitution and concupiscence, but they are more strongly opposed to a Victorian theory of sexuality that underwrote the vast industry of prostitution and attitude of covert concupiscence in colonial India: a theory whose legacy they regard as a form of neocolonial domination. They would most likely agree with Lawrence Birken's general analysis of modern Western sexuality as a 'consuming desire', and with the notion that sexualization and the idiosyncratic nature of desire is a function of radical 'neoclassical' individualism (1988:35; cf. Dumont 1986 for the basis of this kind of individualism).

Those who champion the cause of brahmacharya target for particular criticism the gross manifestations of sex. However, the larger issue they address is the nature of modern sexuality in India and the impact of colonial domination on male identity. As they see it, the basic problem is hydraulic. Modern life in general, and a discourse preoccupied with intercourse and erotic stimulation, both figuratively and literally cause semen to flow and then structure identity in terms of that flow. In the context of postcolonialism, where sex is measured in terms of the gratification it gives, power is defined in relation to the flow and expenditure of semen. You are who you are in terms of the sex you have. For example one might look, to adapt the rhetoric of the brahmachari, at the way popular film heroes and villains are portrayed; at the accusations levelled against corrupt, licentious policemen; at the proliferation of sex manuals; and, perhaps most alarmingly, at the rate of population growth and all it signifies of the ways men are trying to define themselves and assert their position in society. In other words, everywhere one looks there are more or less horrific signs of men trying to build themselves up by the very means that will ultimately bring them down, quite literally, by drying up their liquid assets.

The celibate, on the other hand, is defined by the sex he does not have, and by the semen that he does not allow to flow. However, there is a more fundamental distinction between the brahmachari's conception of sex and that of the postcolonial 'libertines' whom he criticizes. For the brahmachari, it is not sex as an act that defines identity nor is power conceived of in terms of one's sexual prowess—quite the opposite: identity and power are inherent in semen and not in those situations in which semen is made to flow. What this means is that gender gets defined in two radically different ways by the brahmachari and his 'libertine' counterpart: for the postcolonial 'libertine', masculinity is an ideology of domination, self-gratification and the control of others, an ideology almost pathologically individualistic in the priority it places on the egocentric self in relation to others. For the brahmachari on the other hand, gender identity derives from a regimen of self-control, balance, and integration of the self with natural truth. It is, in part, the sheer abomination of contemporary masculinity, the utter waste of vital fluids, which has made celibacy a persuasive form of embodied opposition to the legacy of colonial sexuality.

Nationalism and Truth

In his treatise on night emission and celibacy, Kaviraj Jagannath Shastri writes:

> Today the disease of night emission is widespread. It not only afflicts the young and unmarried, but also those who are married and old. Wherever you look you will see that about 85 per cent of the population suffers from this disease. But the greatest sorrow is in fact that it is these same people who man the rudder of this dear country of ours; who must shoulder the heavy burden of protecting India; who must steer the nation into the future; who provide the standard upon which all else rests; and who are the heart and soul of our society. These students, children, and youth are worn down and left virtually defeated by the battle this evil power wages against them. (n.d.a:17)

Shastri and many others feel that India's vital potential is being wasted on a scale that only those who believe in the phenomenal power of a single drop of semen can truly appreciate. As Shastri concludes, the loss of semen means the total demise of 'the nation, the present era, prevailing circumstances, the environment, the natural order of things, and the social order of caste and religion' (ibid). Although the magnitude of the problem here imagined is noteworthy, it is the nature of the problem that has particular relevance. Shastri and others believe fundamentally that the body is the site of national reform: that nationalism must be embodied to have any real effect. On the other hand, the nationalism of 'pure ideology' is 'like the roar of a paper tiger, and the loud rhetoric of false prophets'. As Sivananda writes:

> Without reforming the body one will never achieve a state of freedom and satisfaction; nor will one ever be successful. There is nothing—no substance or person—who can give satisfaction and peace to one whose body is unhealthy. You alone can make yourself free and blissfully happy. In other words, physical reform must be our primary goal, for it is the basis for all of man's other four aims, and essential for our salvation and independence. (1984:29)

As a tangible, corporeal whole, the body is regarded as more fundamental and natural than are ideas and concepts; it is incontrovertible, and therefore moral in a biological rather than an ideological way. As the body is made the site of nationalism, and brahmacharya its agency of reform, the individual is held responsible for embodying such things as freedom, glory, peace, and happiness, as well as more typically physical attributes such as strength and good health. The regimen of celibacy is clearly meant to turn sick men into progressive citizens who could, single-handedly, reform the nation. Sivananda writes:

> Open your eyes and set your resolve in order to regain the glory of the past through the regimen of celibacy. One who is able to control a single drop is able to control the seven seas. There is nothing in the world—no object or condition—which a celibate man cannot overcome. (1984:34–35)

As we have noted, celibacy is an inwardly focused regimen. The logic of self-control is also purely reflexive in a microscopic mode, insofar as the ultimate goal of celibacy is to magnify the power of that which is most elemental, essential, and basic—the smallest common denominator of everyman. But as the regimen of brahmacharya turns inward and becomes concerned with the minute intricacies of how to breathe, bathe, defecate, and eat, it becomes less and less individuated and progressively more integrated into the 'natural environment' of Mother India.

The place of nature in the regimen of brahmacharya is important, for there is a logical correspondence between each drop of semen on a microscopic level and the natural order of things on a universal level. Harmony and balance—which translate easily into the freedom, happiness and peace of national revival—are achieved when the body and its reservoir of semen are enveloped by, or in tune with, the natural world. 'Brothers!', writes Sivananda, and the reader should not forget the implications of his gender-specific appeal:

> Return to the arms of Mother Nature. She is truly compassionate! She will help you reform. Have faith. You cannot live for even one hour without the kindness of Mother Nature. Through the nose, ears, mouth, anus, skin, and hair she takes the poison out of our bodies and keeps us fit. We should daily avail ourselves of the 'five natural substances'—light, water, earth, air and space. Abandon those things which aggravate in favour of things which impart happiness and bring redemption. Salvation is in our own hands. (1984:43)

Although the nationalism invoked through this kind of rhetoric is embodied on an individual level where citizenship is constructed as a kind of psychosomatic attribute, there are some important ways the body has an impact on social institutions. As noted above, those who advocate celibacy are critical of postcolonial sexuality in general, but they are adamantly opposed to 'legitimate' sexuality as it is practised within the family. In their view, the family is not a place where one may freely indulge in sex. In fact, it is precisely the notion that one may freely have sex with one's wife as often as one likes—'every hour of every night', as Sivananda sarcastically quips (1984:51–52)—which makes the family a dangerous and potentially destructive institution, a kind of sanctioned den of iniquity where the veneer of public morality—to say nothing of social status and prestige—hides the truth of a more insidious demise. One's legal rights as a spouse in no way change the biomorality of semen flow.[6] On the other hand, one can certainly be married and remain 'celibate' as long as one engages in sex only for procreation. The argument presented for this case is drawn from animals and the natural environment, where relationships are balanced, rather than from the world of modern society, which is corrupt. Men are admonished to draw their genitals up like horses and bulls, thus limiting sex to the act of intercourse while remaining otherwise passively unsexed. Unlike the late nineteenth-century discourse on 'spiritual' nationalism (cf. Chatterjee 1989) wherein the family was constructed as pure, impervious and outside the purview of politics, the discourse on brahmacharya not only makes the family a focal site of national reform, but directly criticizes the basic sexual premise upon which the family itself is founded.

Although institutionalized sex within the family is generally regarded as dangerous precisely because it appears to be 'legitimate', brahmacharis reserve their harshest criticism for the practice of child marriage. The logic of this position is not hard to grasp. Youth in general are thought to be easily seduced by the pleasure of sex and particularly apt to take advantage of the

---

[6] As Carstairs (1957) and more recently Daniel (1984) point out, there are many in South Asia who would disagree with the rigid and rather dogmatic nature of this particular argument. A more common, and less trenchant, interpretation given to the biomoral effect of sexual intercourse takes into consideration the social status, age and health of the individuals involved, a general feeling that sex with one's wife does not have the same effect as does sex with a young, low-caste prostitute or an older, twice-born widow, for example. Daniel, in particular, provides a detailed case of how the biomorality of sexual intercourse is interpreted in Tamil Nadu (1984: 163–81).

sexual licence that early marriage provides. To put children in a situation where they can easily satisfy their erotic appetites clearly undermines every principle of self-control and all potential for self-development. Sivananda writes:

> In this country we even undermine the potential of our children. Before teaching them how to swim, parents tie the lead weight of a young wife around their sons' necks and then push them out mercilessly into the ocean of life. How can a country in which this kind of thing goes on advance!? (1984: 56)

The nation of which the reformist celibate speaks is both a figment of his utopian imagination—a world where every man is strong, hard-working, and happy—as well as a world where the natural order of things—clean air, pure food, cool water, and fresh air—prefigures, and to some extent supersedes, the social order. In general, modern social life, which from most perspectives would be the central constituent category of a reformist ideology, is in this case both preempted and subverted. In part, this is because postcolonial modernity is regarded as irredeemably debauched; but, in an important sense, 'Hindu' epistemology also makes it difficult to separate out social facts from biological or natural ones (cf. Marriott 1991). This point brings us back to the question of truth and its relationship to the nation and to the body.

Mahatma Gandhi's autobiography appears in translation as *The Story of My Experiments with Truth* (1929). Although it is an account of his early political and social life, the autobiography is intensely personal and, as Sudhir Kakar has noted, characterized by extreme 'candor and honesty' (1990: 85). Gandhi was preoccupied with issues of social and political justice and felt that truth was the only means by which justice could be achieved. For Gandhi, however, truth was far from self-evident; one had to experiment in various ways to both realize its nature and subscribe to its tenets. Although he was concerned to some extent with abstract metaphysics, what is most striking about Gandhi's experiments is their utterly banal character, and Gandhi's own virtual obsession with seemingly mundane, utilitarian issues of diet, health, and above all else, the control of sexual passion (see Alter 2000). Although Gandhi's own theory of celibacy was derived in more or less equal parts from Christian and Hindu doctrines, the regimens he developed were extreme and highly idiosyncratic. However, it is clear that Gandhi, in keeping with classical prescriptive teaching, believed in the power of semen, that there was an intimate connection between the elusive nature of truth and the seductive power of sexuality: to conquer the latter was to realize the former.

Although Gandhi believed in the power of celibacy and was keenly aware of what Kakar refers to as the 'metaphysical physiology' of semen (1990: 115), it would seem that for him truth was a somewhat mystical function of the regimen he devised rather than the actual, biomoral substance itself: a problem of overcoming the body in order to realize truth through enlightenment rather than embodying truth as semen itself. At times Gandhi seems to write as though it is the semen itself that matters, but more often it is what the spillage or waste of semen represents in terms of his personal failure to put mind over matter. For Gandhi, celibacy was a physical and personal means to a socio-political, and ultimately spiritual, end.

Unlike Gandhi, whose enigmatic genius was in part the function of his vital suspension between the world of Christian and Hindu ethics, contemporary advocates of brahmacharya provide a much more tangible and one-dimensional version of what constitutes truth, and the connection between that truth and national reform. For them celibacy is not the means to an end; it is an end in and of itself, a way to engender nationalism by cultivating the seeds of truth.

Conclusion: Gender into Nationalism

The ideology of nationalism is arguably one of the most masculine expressions of patriarchal politics. Certainly, the rhetoric of brahmacharya is aggressively male. And yet, male sexuality—the metaphors of conquest, penetration and violent domination—are strikingly absent from the whole scenario of celibate power. In a similar vein, Gandhi's nationalist politics of nonviolence seems to go against the grain of overt masculinity (cf. Nandy 1980: 73, 74). Despite his preoccupation with sex and semen—and perhaps on account of it—Gandhi felt that women could be celibate, and through their celibacy work towards a realization of the truth. As Kakar has argued and others have noted, Gandhi's personal treatment of women was not particularly enlightened, but at least on the level of theory he did not discriminate and may, in fact, be regarded as a champion of gender equality, remembering, of course, with a caveat drawn from Chatterjee (1989), that Gandhi's discourse on women was part of the larger 'new patriarchy' of liberal nationalism. A number of scholars have pointed out the ways in which Gandhi's ambivalence towards women and femininity and men and masculinity led to the construction of what might be called an androgynous politics (cf. Erikson 1969; Kakar 1990; Nandy 1983; Rudolph and Rudolph 1967). The notion that one could become powerful by dominating others—sexually or physically—was anathema to Gandhi, whose most cherished ideal was that of selfless service. Gandhi's regimen of satyagraha, with its emphasis on celibacy and dietetics, was designed to translate selfless service into national reform. To this end, Gandhi made it clear that both men and women were equally qualified to experiment with truth, equally qualified to turn themselves into citizens who would work to reform India, equally qualified to turn willpower into social service—but only if they stopped being sexual objects to one another. In the Gandhian utopia—to paraphrase an often-quoted model—male and female citizens would be as brother and sister, mother and son, father and daughter, with all that these relationships imply in the context of the new patriarchy of modern India.

I do not want to get into the particulars of either Gandhi's ideology or his programme of reform. However, Gandhi's concern with celibacy and his policy towards women provide an important point of contrast to the engendered nationalism of contemporary brahmacharis. One might say, to somewhat oversimplify, that Gandhi undermined the old ideology of patriarchal politics by turning the aggression of virility into the energy of androgynous nonviolence. Although Gandhi's nonviolence in particular, and theory of political action in general, were based on a regimen of self-control, the ultimate goal was to overcome the body's physical limitations, a fact that ultimately rendered the physiology of sex and gender irrelevant to the realization of truth, while allowing for the reconstruction of such purportedly asexual and apolitical roles as brother/sister, mother/son, father/daughter. If Gandhi's larger agenda was patriarchal in any sense, and I am sure the argument could be made that it was, it was patriarchal despite itself on the level of institutionalized ideological structures, but not on the level of biomoral substance.

By contrast, I am arguing, that the contemporary nationalist regimen of brahmacharya seems to go beyond the metaphysical limitations of Gandhi's experiments by postulating a substantial, incarnate, seminal truth. Although semen is inherently male, the brahmacharya postulate is that it is proto-sexual; its power derives not from the kinetic agency of masculine sexuality, but from the potential energy manifest in the essence of male substance. By locating truth in the male body, the contemporary brahmachari translates an ideology of domination into a particularly insidious form of biological determinism while, ironically, appearing to deconstruct the whole edifice of sex as such. Thus, truth becomes not just a male virtue, but something that only men can embody by virtue of who they are. Such a proposition has often been the substance of patriarchal myths of power and glory but, in the case of brahmacharya, one finds a version of that myth in which embodiment is virtual rather than putative, a myth in which gender emerges more powerful on account of being essentialized as a biomoral substance. In these terms, nationalism is not synonymous with the ideals of 'humanism', as Gandhi might have it, but with an exclusive form of truth that heroically animates the 'man in the body'.

> Brothers! Liberate our dear Mother India from poverty and resurrect her true power and glory! India's freedom is dependent on each and everyone's freedom, and everyone's freedom is achieved once the yoke of poisonous slavery has been cast off. We, like our forefathers, must achieve this end by controlling our semen. (Sivananda 1984:156)

The tragic contradiction—or perhaps ominous indictment—of such a heroic vision is, of course, that 'everyone's freedom' cannot be based on the seminal truth of biological determinism, no matter how fluid.

The question remains, however: what brings gender and nationalism together? What factors are involved in bringing about the transformation of one conception of the body into another? I have argued that postcolonial desire, and the history of sexuality in colonial India played an important part in this process. As a secret vice that permeated society, sex came to be regarded as a key to power and truth. What emerged was a discourse on sexuality that radically essentialized the practice of sex. To construct an opposing discourse to this essentialism required a degree of what I suppose must be called counter-essentialism, that is, the production of a theory of power and truth that could deconstruct the hegemony of sexuality at its most basic level. What the brahmacharya argument does is to effect this deconstruction on two planes: the proto-sexual level of semen, thereby relocating power to a more primary position within the body, and the utopian level of national harmony, where debauchery is preempted by the balanced integration of body and nature. The whole discourse of postcolonial desire that afflicts contemporary society is thus crushed, it is hoped, by the logic of an argument that both undermines and preempts the structure of modern sexuality in India.

Engendered Nationalism: Capt. J.N. Banerjee, Bar-at-Law, at the age of seventy.
The image appears under the dedication to 'Young Bengal' on page 3 of
Barbell Exercise and *Muscle Control*. Bishnu Charan Ghosh, B.Sc. and
Keshab Chandra Sen Gupta, B.A. Calcutta: Self Published, 1930.

3

Seminal Truth
A Modern Science of Male Celibacy

As indicated in the previous chapter, the practice of semen control (*virya nirodh*) has religious, social, political, and psychological implications. Although the literature on semen control and 'anxiety' is quite extensive, little attention has been given to what might be called the 'medical mechanics' of being and becoming celibate. Moreover, ethnographic studies of male sexuality in modern India have tended to ignore the vast self-help literature that exists on the subject (cf. Anonymous n.d.; Gotham n.d.; Hiralal 1983; 'Krish' n.d.; Mahindra 1985; Narayananda 1950, 1976; Saraswati 1982; J. Shastri 1970; K.J. Shastri n.d.[a], n.d.[b], n.d.[c]; Sivananda 1984). My purpose in this chapter, therefore, is to analyse and contextualize the self-help literature on brahmacharya (celibacy) as it relates to questions of health and identity in contemporary north India. I have done this through both a close 'ethnographic reading' of the literature and field research with the Bharatiya Yog Sansthan (Indian Yoga Society) in Delhi where a 'reading' of this literature is put into practice.

I will show that a male concern with celibacy is couched in terms of a discourse about truth. Although male sexuality is spoken of in moral and ethical terms that highlight the importance of 'self-control' and 'self-knowledge', I argue that brahmacharya is a concept that does not take the 'self' as its primary object. Celibacy neither presumes nor produces a natural, individuated self. Instead, it is a concept that refers directly to the constituent 'human' elements that produce and regulate life on a more primary, psychosomatic level. It is on this level, rather than on the intersubjective level of action or the psychic level of emotion, where truth is thought to be produced and strategically deployed. Consequently, the morality that brahmacharya speaks of is intimately associated with the precise regimen of health, which is codified more in terms of biology than ideology.

Theoretical Concerns

Primarily on account of Michel Foucault's work on the history of European sexuality, scholars have recognized that medical discourses of and about sex are discourses of and about power and knowledge and not just of and about identity, morality, and psychological health (Birken 1988; DeJean 1989; Gallagher and Laqueur 1987; Laqueur 1986; Martin 1991; Peiss et al. 1989; Weeks 1985, 1989). Needless to say, brahmacharya emerges from a history quite different from that which has produced medico-moral discourses on masturbation, fornication, sodomy, adultery, and so forth (cf. Foucault 1990a). Even so, the contemporary literature clearly demonstrates that many men in South Asia view sex as a medical problem and as a biomoral issue with strong religious overtones that must be scientifically analysed (cf. Carstairs 1957; Edwards 1984; Kakar 1982, 1990; Obeyesekere 1976; Spratt 1966). Moreover, as will become clear, the whole concept of brahmacharya has become medicalized in much the same way as have various aspects of sexuality in the West. One need only look at the striking correspondence between modern Indian injunctions against masturbation and Tissot's eighteenth-century text *On Onania or A Treatise Upon the Disorders Produced by Masturbation* (1781), Joseph Howe's medical analysis of the subject (1974 [1887]), or Henry Maudsley and Edward Spitzka's theories on masturbatory insanity (Gillis 1974; Hare 1962; Mather 1723; MacDonald 1967; Neuman 1975; cf.

Dyer 1889. For more contemporary appraisals see Barbach 1975; Calderone 1960; Dodson 1933; Demartino 1974; Masters 1967). Brahmacharya has, to some extent, developed as an encompassing apparatus for decoding masturbation and sensuality. Celibacy thus becomes an integral part of a medical regimen not only to restore health, but to exercise control over both public and private morality.

There is, however, an important qualification that must be added to this rather simplistic West-to-East comparison. According to Foucault, the subject of European sexuality is the self, and the problematic nature of sexuality refers directly to the health of the individual and his or her self-conception as an autonomous, free agent (1990b:6). Foucault speaks of the process by which the self is made a subject unto itself as the 'hermeneutics of the self' (1990b:6). I would argue that this primary element of European sexuality is overshadowed, if not altogether absent, in the modern discourse on brahmacharya. Despite all that has been said about mystical modes of ascetic and yogic 'self' control in South Asian society, celibacy is not a problem of 'self-knowledge' in the purely reflective, intersubjective sense of which Foucault critically writes. It is not about coming to grips with a particular, singular, public identity that emerges from the interface of psychology and biography. As expounded in much of the classical literature, brahmacharya is fundamentally about a knowledge of the transcendental Self, which is only partially realized in any particular individual, but this Self is categorically different from the sexually objectified secular self of Eurocentric discourse. Significantly, knowledge of the Self is not accessible to the brahmachari by means of a hermeneutic epistemology. Consequently, the scientific discourse on brahmacharya and the health regimens associated with masturbation and semen loss in India are radically different, while appearing in their formal guise to be very much the same as their European counterparts. The question of morality, which is ultimately common to both, is addressed in radically different ways: one as a hermeneutics of truth about the body, and the other as an embodiment of truth in somatic terms.

Issues of morality and health are directly implicated in the construction of the self. In the West the self has generally come to be regarded as indivisible—in an autobiographical and psychological sense—and therefore as the smallest common denominator of social facts. It is regarded as a singular, holistic unit that cannot be subdivided into smaller meaningful parts without compromising the integrity and health of the individual. In this regard, the agency of social action is always manifest on the level of intersubjectivity: the interaction of self with self or self with other selves (cf. Mead 1977). A concept such as this, which places the self in a position of autonomy and control vis-à-vis both social and biological facts, tends to dichotomize experience by reifying an incipient mind/body duality while magnifying the significance of autonomous individuality. As McKim Marriott (1992) has noted, these and other related issues tend to inhibit our ability to analyse other social systems that are predicated on radically different assumptions about the relationship between biological and social facts, and the substantial constitution of the self. Along these lines he has advocated the development of 'alternative social sciences' that allow for the construction of ethnoepistemology (1992). Specifically, Marriott has developed an ethnosociology of Hindu society in which he demonstrates that the individual is not primary or indivisible, but is, rather, the contingent, constituent product of more primary 'dividual' elements and processes (1976, 1977). Thus humours, elements, 'strands', and human aims—such things as phlegm, wind and bile; water, fire and air; goodness, darkness and passion; and advantage, coherence, attachment and release—relate to an integrated, fluid sphere of psychosomatic reality, the ebb and flow of which animate the self, and more significantly, the position of the self within particular social contexts (1990, 1991). In his formulation the person is a contingent, protean product of forces that fall on an intermediary plane somewhere among biology, psychology and sociology. Significantly, various identities are derived from the heterogeneous confluence of 'dividual' elements, thus giving any one person, as well as all people, a broader, more fluid spectrum of characteristic traits. The brahmachari simply tries to configure specific elements in order to reconfigure his 'true' identity. Following the spirit of Marriott's argument, I would suggest that a rigid Eurocentric concept of self, and the attendant sciences that take that self for granted, are inadequate for understanding the modern concept of brahmacharya. Rather than begin with the self, one must begin with semen in order to understand the constituent properties of the male brahmachari. Thus Marriott's formulations neatly counterpoise Foucault's critique of sexuality and provide a means by which to understand an aspect of sexuality in India without recourse to psychological models built on the problematic nature of the 'Westernized' self.

Although the concept of brahmacharya is certainly not new (cf. R. Gandhi 1982; Kakar 1981; O'Flaherty 1973), celibacy has been problematized in a rather unique way in late twentieth-century India. Much of this problematization has to do with a changing socio-moral climate of modernization and development: a feeling that the integrity of the individual citizen is being systematically undermined by an immoral and unhealthy life-style (Alter 1992a, 1993a). Young men in particular are thought to be susceptible to the consuming passion of modern pleasure. Underlying this pervasive, modern anxiety about the integrity of the male body is, of course, an even more fundamental fear of female sexuality. To an extent the whole concept of male celibacy, and the attendant discourse on self-control, is predicated on a powerful myth of female eroticism, a myth that not only animates the male subconscious, as Carstairs (1958), Kakar (1981, 1982), Kurtz (1992), Obeyesekere (1976), and Roland (1988) point out, but a myth that is enacted in ritual (cf. Bennett 1985; Marglin 1995; Wadley 1975), codified in day-to-day interactions (cf. Daniel 1984; Trawick 1990), and canonized in the classical religious literature as well (cf. O'Flaherty 1980). A great deal of work on female sexuality in India clearly shows how this male myth is historically constructed and perpetuated (cf. Chatterjee 1989; Mani 1987; Sangari and Vaid 1990). Among other things, it is becoming increasingly clear that 'female sexuality'—where issues of purity, chastity, honour, and auspiciousness have been traditionally juxtaposed with problems of lust and danger—is a highly contested arena that cannot be understood in terms that are often simplistically coded to a male ideology. As Oldenberg (1991) has shown, for example, the courtesans of Lucknow have developed practices that strategically contest the power of masculine virility.

It is also noteworthy that chastity among widows and female renouncers (Khandelwal 2004) may in some instances serve as a critique of masculine ideology, even though female chastity does not seem to be constructed in terms of a biomoral truth along the same lines as male celibacy (Khandelwal, Housner and Gold 2006). In any case, the 'traditional Hindu view' of sexuality is clearly a hegemonic myth of epic proportions. In fact, there is not one 'Hindu sexuality' but many different expressions and experiences of sexuality given one's position in the hierarchies of class, caste, and gender (cf. Nanda 1990; Reheja and Gold 1994). My concern, however, is with the contingency of the pervasive patriarchal, Brahminic view, examined, as it were, from the inside out. Along these lines I have argued elsewhere that a modern anxiety about the integrity of the male body, and a parallel anxiety about the integrity of India as a nation-state, have resulted in the extreme reification and polarization of gendered sexualities in north India, in part through the production of new generic concepts of hypermasculinity. The internalization of truth as semen—where 'real' selfhood is thought to be biologically located—is in many ways a radical, and some might say radically paranoid, attempt to control female sexuality by defining it as not only dangerous but as antithetical to truth.

It is noteworthy but not at all surprising therefore to find that the discourse on male celibacy is effectively and self-consciously silent on the subject of female bodies, while loudly evoking the danger of heterosexual sex and blaming women for erotic passions that men are not able to control. The insidious nature of the discourse on seminal truth is of course that it is insipidly gendered and almost pathologically male. Rather than elaborate on this point here, however, my concern is to show how truth—distorted, essentialized, and reified—can be powerfully embodied. In doing so I follow Cynthia Russett (1989) who has shown how the conjunction of sex and science in nineteenth-century England produced a truth about the natural inferiority and weakness of Victorian women—except that in the north Indian discourse on celibacy the problem is not so much one of engendered sexual distinctions based on the radical opposition of masculine and feminine traits as it is on a monistic, valorized conflation of 'man' and nature.

Context: The History and Ethnography of Seminal Truth

Although it is difficult to know how widely the literature on celibacy is read, and more difficult still to know the degree to which it is taken to heart, books that deal with the problems associated with male sexuality tend to have a wide circulation among urban lower-middle-class and middle-class boys and men. I found that young boys and men between the ages of sixteen and forty-five read this literature when they felt they were suffering from semen loss, or when they simply wanted to look and feel more energetic. This therapeutic cum public health dimension of brahmacharya emerges from a very specific and relatively modern history of yogic practices, and finds concrete sociological expression in various institutionalized yoga movements.

Many of the books on celibacy are written by Brahmin men. Moreover, many of the yoga centres where celibacy is propagated clearly reflect a Brahminical bias. Brahmacharya, however, appeals to men from a broad spectrum of caste backgrounds (cf. Alter 1992a). This may be due in part to the fact that there is a strong link between celibacy and the widespread devotional cult of Hanuman, which also cross-cuts many social hierarchies in north India (Alter 1993b). Furthermore, many authors of the self-help manuals affect a world-renouncer's persona and thus position themselves as nonpartisan critics of the socio-moral order. Nevertheless, the practice of brahmacharya has gained its greatest mass appeal, I would argue, largely through 'secularized yoga' as propounded by moral reformers on the one hand, and on the other by the numerous medical practitioners who prescribe yoga techniques to prevent and cure a broad range of mostly chronic diseases.

Beginning around the turn of the twentieth century, and taking institutionalized form in the early 1920s, there was what has come to be called a 'Yoga Renaissance' in India (De Michelis 2004). Pioneered by Sri Yogendra of the Yoga Institute of Santa Cruz, Mumbai (Alter 2006), Swami Kuvalayananda of the Kaivalyadhama Ashram in Lonavla (Alter 2004, 2007a), and Swami Sivananda of the Divine Life Society, Rishikesh (Strauss 2005), yoga was propagated as a scientific form of universal public health and physical fitness. The emphasis at these institutes, which have grown steadily in size and scope, is on the beneficial medical effects of *asanas*—various kinds of stretching exercises; *pranayama*—techniques of breath control; and *kriyas*—specific forms of personal hygiene. While the modern literature on yoga as a form of physical therapy slightly predates the establishment of these two institutes, the past seventy-five years has seen a virtual explosion in the number of books on yoga in general. Many select bibliographies run into thousands of entries. In the past thirty-five years or so, however, there has been a further proliferation of relatively cheap self-help guides in many regional Indian languages. I have collected approximately 200 in Hindi and English. While this literature does not always focus on the issue of celibacy—and is, to a high degree, ungendered on a practical level—brahmacharya is always explained as one of the key biomoral practices upon which yoga is based (cf. Kumar n.d.; Siddhantalankar 1983:260–269;

Yogeshwaranand 1985:24–34). Moreover, it is almost always explained in distinctly masculine terms, even when the majority of authors, who are men, try to address themselves to both men and women. Thus the contradiction inherent in 'seminal truth' is virtually ignored. The following typical example is taken at random from one of these books:

> Celibacy improves the condition of your semen. However much semen you are able to retain, you will receive in that proportion greater wisdom, improved action, higher spirituality and increased knowledge. Moreover, you will acquire the power to get whatever you want. (Yogacharya Bhagwandev 1992:15)

In conjunction with this literature on yogic practices, there has been a parallel growth in the popularity of naturopathy. While not quite as extensive as the yoga literature, there are hundreds of books that prescribe various regimens of natural diet, sun baths, soak baths, mud packs, and enemas for all kinds of illnesses. The popularity of naturopathy seems to be closely linked with Mahatma Gandhi's advocacy for this mode of popular, public health (cf. M.K. Gandhi 1948, 1949, 1954, 1965a). While many of the books on nature-cure make reference to Gandhi's dietary experiments, they also prescribe specific kinds of yoga therapy. Given Gandhi's own concern with the problems associated with semen loss (cf. M. K. Gandhi 1948:23–29, 1958, 1964a, 1965b:145–167; Gangadhar 1984), it is not surprising to find that many of the therapies prescribed in the literature on celibacy are elaborations of common naturopathy techniques.

The modern literature on celibacy clearly emerges out of these two discourses on public health since many of the men who write about celibacy have also written numerous books on yoga and naturopathy. In this regard it should also be noted that some of the 'scientific' literature on celibacy is written by men who teach and practise yoga as a form of spiritual self-realization. For men such as Swami Sivananda, Swami Yogananda Saraswati, Swami Jyotiramayananda, and others, 'seminal truth' emerges from the realization of divine consciousness as it is embodied in physical form, and as it is apprehended through the science of yoga.

Each in their own way, the pioneers of the yoga renaissance have popularized yoga as an international and transcultural form of more or less spiritual physical therapy. One distinctly modern yoga movement, the Bharatiya Yog Sansthan (hereafter BYS), however, has effectively redefined the way in which yoga discipline and naturopathy is taught, and I would argue that BYS has thereby established a context within which it is possible to understand the sociological dimensions of brahmacharya as a discourse about 'seminal truth'. Although I conducted field research in Delhi on BYS, conducted interviews with the founders, leaders and members of the society, and participated in its daily programme of yoga therapy, my concern here is to use the BYS as an example of how 'textbook' concerns about selfhood and semen come together in practical terms. I have therefore focused exclusively on those aspects of yogic practice that are concerned with the control of semen. (For a more general treatment of the BYS see Alter 1997.)

The BYS was established in 1968 by two young middle-class men from north Delhi who had become disillusioned by the rampant sensuality, tension and violence of modern life. Inspired by Mool Raj Anand, a moral reformer who advocated nonviolence, raw natural foods, and yoga discipline, they resolved to do something about the sickness of modernity and therefore began to do yoga asanas in a public park near their homes. Gradually they persuaded others to join them. The idea was that if everyone who was sick, angry, nervous, and consumed by desire practised yoga, society as a whole would become healthy, happy, peaceful and, above all else, moral and self-controlled. To this end, the single purpose of the BYS is to give free lessons to anyone who is interested in learning about yoga, health and hygiene. These lessons are conducted every morning at 5:30, free of charge, in public parks, where predominantly middle- and lower-middle-class men come together and participate in a form of 'mass-drill' type of yoga exercise routine. Members tend to be well educated. Many work in government service occupations or are employed as professionals in large private companies. A significant number own small businesses. In the past twenty-five years the BYS has grown into a massive movement with over 250 centres in twelve states. In Delhi alone there are 150 chapters with a registered lifetime membership of over 17,000. I would estimate that at least four times this figure participate semi-regularly in the hour-long morning sessions, monthly seminars, annual camps and yoga pilgrimages.

Although the BYS teaches yoga as a form of biomoral social reform that is far more encompassing than celibacy, the quarterly magazine *Yog Manjari*, published by the BYS, often contains articles that echo many of the basic principles and practical rules of celibacy (Chopra 1990; Maheshwari 1992; Navarya 1988; Sood 1985; Vashisht 1992). The BYS also does a brisk business selling enema pots and pumps, nasal hydrators, catheters, and various other equipment used by those who are trying to develop celibacy and total natural health. I have found through regular participation in the BYS regimen that many men talk with one another about the problems inherent in maintaining self-control—a discourse about seminal truth, which I also found expressed in almost identical form among wrestlers throughout India (cf. Alter 1992a). Both the wrestlers with whom I spoke and the members of the BYS articulated concerns about semen loss, truth and identity that were the same as those expressed in the more specific self-help manuals—a modern concern with the complex relationship between biology, selfhood, and society.

Brahmacharya

Brahmacharya is regarded as a lifestyle and not simply a condition of contingent abnegation. Those who advocate such a lifestyle do so in minute and exact detail, producing, to use Foucault's phraseology, the 'meticulous and patently documentary' grist for the ethnogenealogist's mill (1984:76). Above all else, brahmacharya means total control over the flow of one's semen. Without question it signifies an immunity from sexual desire. While denoting a specific condition, however, brahmacharya evokes a much broader range of meanings. One author in particular provides a detailed etymological analysis. The root *brahma*, he writes, means *brahmgyan*, which is 'that which is unchanging regardless of the circumstances and is the same for all humanity' (Saraswati 1982:89). It is synonymous with truth. The fragment *acharya*, he continues, means *acharan*, or behaviour and conduct. Behaviour, which in this context may be taken to mean a pragmatic regimen, is subdivided into three categories: diet, exercise, and work or business. Saraswati then explains that the conjunction *brahma-charya* means a 'truth diet (simple food), truth exercise (simple walking) and truth work (simple living). A person who eats simple food, walks or "goes simply", and lives simply is called a brahmachari' (1982:89). In an interview with one of the founders of the BYS I was told that the correct root was, in fact, not *acharya* but *chariya*, meaning literally 'to walk [the path of] truth'. Perhaps the best-known exemplar of such a person was Mohandas Karamchand Gandhi, whose autobiography, entitled *The Story of My Experiments with Truth*, may be read as a treatise on the relationship between celibacy and truth (1929; see also Alter 1996; Erikson 1969; Fox 1989; M.K. Gandhi 1948; Kakar 1990:85–128; Rudolph and Rudolph 1967).

Brahmacharya is therefore an inclusive way of life based on simplicity. The goal is to bring all faculties under control so as to embody truth. *Kama*, or lust, is the aspect of experience that is most unstable, and sexual desire in particular is thought to be volatile and dangerous to control (Daniel 1984; Edwards 1983; Kakar 1990; Kakar and Ross 1987; Obeyesekere 1981; O'Flaherty 1973, 1980; Spratt 1966). While desire is hard to control, one does not seek to control it on moral grounds simply because it is wrong. Sensual passion, of which sex is one manifestation, is not evil or sinful. It is one of the 'four aims of man' and therefore contextually legitimate. But it has generally come to be thought of as inferior and base when juxtaposed with the other three aims of *dharma* (right action), *artha* (advantage), and *moksha* (release, or non-attachment). Within the context of the brahmachari's regimen, however, *kama daman* (controlling desire) is primarily significant as a way to protect semen. That is, it is a psychosomatic defensive mechanism and not an issue of virtue or vice for which there is a single moral mandate. Nor, significantly, does the discourse on brahmacharya ennoble the three 'nonsexual aims of man' in order to debase the fourth 'sexual' aim. Neither is the brahmachari's simple lifestyle a spiritual or philosophical quest for knowledge. Controlling desire—regardless of how noble, advantageous or enlightening—is simply not an end in itself. It is a practical programme for healthy living by which means one's psychosomatic essence is channelled away from desire and towards an integrated experience of the plain and simple truth. In at least three separate discussions with senior members of the BYS, I was told that controlling desire is simply a means for realizing the sublime nature of truth. As one man put it, 'it is a matter of rechannelling the power of sex into pure consciousness.'

Semen and the Embodiment of Truth

The significance and power of semen is almost always explained in terms of diet and blood. As a number of scholars have pointed out, the truth and quality of food a person consumes is directly related to health in general by way of its particular influence on the flow, volume, or 'temperature' of body fluids (Khare 1976; Khare and Rao 1986; Zimmermann 1988). Food quality and quantity has a direct and measurable effect on the production and flow of semen. The process is as follows. When food is eaten it takes five days to become blood. Blood is then 'digested' for another five days, at which time it becomes flesh. During this time waste products are purged in various forms. After another five days flesh is made into fat, fat into bone, bone into marrow, and finally, after the last increment of five days and a total of thirty, marrow is made into semen. The whole process is akin to progressive stages of distillation and condensation. It takes one *maund* (about forty kilograms) of food to make two *tola*s (roughly a tablespoon) of semen. Therefore, calculated at a rate of 1.3 kilograms of food per day, it would take about one month to make the amount of semen (1½ *tola*s) spent in each ejaculation. Kakar (1990:119) outlines a similar physiology following Sivananda (1974) and Narayananda (1965), and points out the very common calculation that forty drops of blood produce, or are equivalent to, one drop of semen. Along these lines, Swami Sivananda asks his readers to consider the ignorance and egregious waste of energy involved in ejaculation: it is as though a person were to carefully nurture a beautiful garden in order to extract the essence of each flower only to then throw the sweet perfume into a dirty drain (1984:48). Wrestlers and others with whom I spoke in Banaras expressed similar sentiments. Rhetorically asking me to 'do the calculations', they would shake their heads woefully at the horrific arithmetic of passion. Although clearly embellished for effect, I think such statements must be taken at face value. Sivananda and others are not speaking of a metaphysical essence, they are speaking of the distillate of food and the condensed energy of organic matter. As B. K. Suri, a yoga therapist in south Delhi, explained in an interview:

> The problem with semen loss is ultimately a problem of the mind, and one must try to understand what that mental problem is, but a 'mental balance' cannot be achieved if one's blood is contaminated by various things. Therefore, to treat the problem one must analyse and regulate one's diet in order to get at the mental problem.

Although most authors note that semen is concentrated in the testicles and the various ducts that are part of the genitals, they also indicate that it is found in a reservoir in the head. It is thought to pool in the head and thus vitalize the brain and eyes in particular, and also as we will see below, the general physiology of skull, cheeks, and other facial features. More significantly, however, the authors agree that semen in fact permeates the whole body 'like oil in an almond; butter in milk; juice in raisins; scent in flowers; and fire in an ember' (Sivananda 1984:47). Consequently, as Sivananda graphically writes:

> To get even one drop of semen out, you must squeeze your body like a lemon. Just as milk is churned and butter drawn out of every molecule, in the same way semen is drawn out of every molecule of the body when a person is stimulated to the point of ejaculation . . . At the time of orgasm all of the body's nerves are violently shaken, and all parts of the body are jolted as if by the force of a train. (1984:47)

All authors regard ejaculation as seriously enervating, the result of which is not simply a reduction in volume but a chemical or physiological transformation of substance (see Lynch 1990 for an analogous example). Thus a person who has an orgasm is changed into a less-perfect form of his previous self—a dried-up lemon, or that which is left over when butter is taken out of milk.

If semen remains within the body, it is the essence of vitality, and many writers spare no hyperbole in their descriptions of a body glowing with the energy of semen.

> Semen! What a beautiful, sparkling word! When reflecting on it one's mind is filled with grand, great, majestic, beautiful, rejuvenating, and powerful emotions. (Shastri n.d.[a]:10)

Although Shastri casts his rhetoric in terms of adjectival poetics, it is clearly on a metonymic level that the word *semen* is embodied as the essence of life. Semen does not simply correspond to virtue on the level of a somatic analogy; it is what might be called a psychosomatic virtue wherein truth and beauty, among other abstractions, are given substantial form. Thus a celibate person is not only virtuous or great because of what he does (according to some behavioural standard) but because of what his body becomes as a virtual incarnation of semen. Many times while talking with yoga teachers and wrestlers, I found that there was an implicit connection made between physical beauty and celibacy. Often when those I spoke to had been at a loss for words to describe the quality of this relationship, they told me to 'look at the face' of Vivekananda, Buddha, or Mahavir and 'see for yourself that there is something . . . just something there'. A number of authors point out that a brahmachari is 'hammered full' of divine aura and that such 'hammering' has the effect of making the brahmachari's eyes shine with a special light, his cheeks glow like roses, and his expression absolutely devoid of desire or lust. As one yoga teacher put it, 'your cheeks will glow like Kashmiri apples'. Descriptions then move directly to touch on stance and physique: 'his chest is firm and his stride determined'; and then to intellect and ability:

> He is at the head of his class and wins in sports; he does everything he sets his mind to. With a single, well chosen word, he can silence others. With his melodious and influential voice he incorporates the good logic of wise men into his own discourse. (Sivananda 1984:58–59)

What is of particular importance here is the literal extent to which semen is implicated in shining eyes, glowing cheeks, a melodious voice, and the ability to work hard, debate well, and redact wisely; the extent to which a forthright stride does not simply signify courage but is a physiological manifestation common to courage and motility.

Semen is regarded as so powerful and universally manifest that it can cut through, or undermine, 'important' distinctions that are culturally constructed. For example, one author points out that an artificially 'light' complexion—affected through an effete preoccupation with style, and effected with powders, lotions and creams—cannot mask the basic poverty of a man who wastes his semen. Similarly, the power of semen is so great that it eclipses material poverty and low status, allowing one to 'feel love for a young man who radiates vitality' regardless of his circumstances (Sivananda 1984:59). The appeal here—fantastically exaggerated, to be sure—is to something more basic than status, wealth and institutionalized power. It is an appeal to a more somatic economy of value wherein all men are equal in terms of their ability to control the flow of their semen. Clearly there are echoes here of *tantric* and other ascetically inspired critiques of power, and it is noteworthy that both wrestlers and many practitioners of modern yoga are critical of various forms of social hierarchy (cf. Alter 1992a, 1992b). In an article in *Yog Manjari* that highlights the importance of brahmacharya for the younger generation, Dr R.L. Sood writes that *yama* and *niyama*, the fundamental principles of yoga practice, are a panacea for 'selfishness, distrust, intolerance, indiscipline, violence, hatred, envy, and cowardice' (1985:18–19).

It is precisely on this level that the institutionalized structure of the BYS effectively transforms the mechanics of celibacy and seminal truth into a crusade against the 'mental tension', sensuality, hate and violence of modernity. Despite its distinctly middle-class makeup, the BYS philosophy is structured around an ideal of universal brotherhood that builds on the essential, elemental nature of everyman. By quoting Sivananda, among many others, and publishing essays on celibacy in their quarterly magazine, the BYS is trying to effect socio-moral reform by linking the power of semen with an individual's ability to work hard, concentrate, be more productive, and most significantly, to do all this 'with peace of mind' in an atmosphere of 'brotherly love', as expressed in one of their popular slogans emblazoned on iridescent bumper stickers.

Semen is also associated with pedagogy and the power to teach, convince others of what is good, and make them appreciate and remember what they have learned. Pedagogy is an important factor in part because most authors who write about brahmacharya direct their comments to students aged thirteen to eighteen. In this respect, celibacy is regarded as an integral part of education insofar as it puts pupils in the right state of body/mind to learn. On at least one occasion the BYS awarded first prize in an annual essay competition to a fourteen-year-old boy who passionately articulated the need for celibate discipline in the competitively cut-throat environment of modern Indian education. The power to make students learn, however, is dependent as much on the instructor's control over his semen as on the control exercised by the students. Semen is thought to make discourse more powerful and to make it more significant and comprehensible. Thus words spoken by a celibate teacher—like the *mantra* spoken by a tantric guru—are eminently more powerful, regardless of their generic meaning and public character, than the same words spoken by hundreds of thousands of other non-celibate teachers. Sivananda points out that a person who hears something spoken to him by a brahmachari will remember it until his death (1984:60). Here again there is a conflation of truth (what the brahmachari speaks) and essence (what he is).

While discussions of semen's magnificent power quickly spiral up to virtually incomprehensible levels of abstraction, many authors provide detailed accounts of the symptoms that occur when semen is wasted. A number of these symptoms, such as spermatorrhoea, impotence, nocturnal emission and watery semen, are often regarded as illnesses in their own right and have been studied by psychiatrists and other medical professionals (cf. Edwards 1983:55–57) as well as by anthropologists (Carstairs 1957; Obeyesekere 1976; Nichter 1981). The more general symptoms associated with semen loss, on the other hand, enable one to get a clear idea of how semen affects overall health. What is particularly significant about these lists is the insight they provide on the logic of what constitutes a symptom or sign. A few examples may be drawn from Sivananda's list, which includes a total of thirty-three entries. Those who are afflicted by semen loss and overcome by desire are unable to make eye contact with older men, stick out their chests and impudently make a display of themselves in public, have a great desire for plays, novels, and other books about passion, and are not able to concentrate, focus, or complete any task. Blackheads appear on their once rosy cheeks. Their eyes appear sunken, and their jawbones separate so that their mouths hang open. They are not interested in productive work. They are anxious and worried; their hearts beat wildly at the slightest fright; a molehill of sadness appears to them as a mountain of sorrow. They have painful joints in their hands, feet, and whole body. They have backaches and headaches as well as pains in the chest. Their gums are swollen, and they have bad breath.

The symptoms on this list and others slide along a scale extending from discrete somatic functions (perspiration, spermatorrhoea, 'watery semen', indigestion and acne) through matters that are clearly socio-psychological (a lack of respect, anger, irritability, and general mood swings, laziness, and anxiety) to the other extreme where symptoms are no longer manifest in the individual body or its various parts, but in the body of society at large—the 'race' as a whole and the sorrow, slavery and social disgrace to which Sivananda alludes in both his first and final points. The whole complex of symptoms taken together is, in many ways, a catalogue of social and biomoral degeneration. Talking with members of the BYS, and reading issues of *Yog Manjari* published over the past thirty-five years, one gets a clear sense of how yogic discipline in general and celibacy in particular are designed to follow the same trajectory outwards from a person's most elemental being to the social whole that is engendered by truth. As Prakash Lal, the current president of the BYS, said in an interview:

> Our primary purpose is to bring about a reform of society. These days people are sick and unhealthy because they have a negative attitude towards everything; they are concerned with satisfying themselves; of taking things and trying to make themselves happy rather than with giving of themselves in order to make others happy. What the Bharatiya Yog Sansthan tries to do is to teach people to find happiness by making themselves and others healthy.

Various therapies that treat the symptoms of semen loss, among a host of other illnesses, figure prominently in the regimen of yogic treatments. Writing for *Yog Manjari*, one author outlines a two-hour regimen of yoga practices to transform the kinetic energy of sexual passion into the energy of 'true bliss' (Navarya 1988:16). Clearly then, brahmacharya and semen loss are not simply culturally conditioned expressions of some hidden anxiety about the self. Celibacy should be seen as a social theory and practical regimen of personalized public health: a medical response to a biomoral problem, which addresses sexuality head on. Consequently, the cultural construction of 'seminal truth' may, in fact, be read as a deconstruction of Eurocentric psychotherapy.

Sickness, Sex and Regimens of Health

Without a doubt, brahmacharya is both conceptually and practically opposed to 'the sickness of masturbation', for which it is prescribed as a panacea. The magnitude and seriousness of onanism is a direct consequence of the fact that masturbation and semen loss are symptomatic of one another, resulting in an accelerated downward spiral of health. Although masturbation is antithetical to brahmacharya, it is only the logical extreme of a whole series of lesser forms of arousal. Most of these are defined in hetero-normative terms and have to do with fantasies stimulated by pictures of, discussions about, or interaction with women (Sivananda 1984:15). Independent of orgasm and ejaculation, emotional arousal causes a degeneration of semen within the body, making it more likely to leak out. The yoga teacher of the Nehru Park chapter of the BYS in south Delhi brushed aside one student's anxiety about direct physical arousal, pointing out instead that mental and visual images were far more dangerous. And then, in the context of a discussion about arranged marriages, he and one of the members talked at length about how love was simply a strategic emotion employed in order to 'get' sex. The teacher went on to say that romance was not only dangerous, it was akin to obsessive madness; being purely self-centred, it served no practical, social purpose. Along similar lines, one man in his eighties, who claimed to have inspired the founders of the BYS, told me that as a young brahmachari in rural Haryana he was so fanatical that he moved out of his house in order to be out of sight of his sisters and mother, and would shut his eyes when going into the house to collect his meals from them lest they arouse in him even a hint of passion. The subtle effect of sensuality on semen, illustrated by these examples, is of particular relevance in understanding the association between masturbation and nocturnal emission.

Nocturnal emission, or *svapna dosh* (dream error), is given special consideration by all authors. Kaviraj Jagannath Shastri devotes his whole book to the subject, and because of its 'involuntary' nature, calls svapna dosh the worst of all 'personal diseases'. In the first part of his book, Shastri provides a detailed examination of the mechanics of ejaculation. He then has four chapters on 'the science of discharge'. Here Shastri catalogues the symptoms and causes of semen loss and arousal (n.d.[a]:26–29). Although in many ways similar to the list given by Sivananda for semen loss in particular (see above), Shastri enumerates forty-two factors that either cause or are symptomatic of nocturnal emission. Some of these factors are clearly physiological. For example, an infection of the penis may result in nerve stimulation leading to unconscious ejaculation (n.d.[a]:31). Urinary tract infections, indigestion, and constipation can all have the same effect. Shastri, however, also lists factors that are clearly psychological, such as tension and depression (n.d.[a]:34). Yet other factors are more enigmatic. For example, the pleasure of singing alone and narcissistic self-admiration—preening in front of a mirror—can cause night discharge; so can sitting too close to a fire in winter or carrying extra heavy loads (n.d.[a]:32–34).

It is important to note that Shastri and others make no distinction between the biomoral implications of sexual intercourse, masturbation and other overtly sexual acts on the one hand, and night discharge and other unconscious processes on the other. In other words, a loss of semen is a loss of semen regardless of how it happens. The primary issue is what happens to a person on account of that loss, not what he did to make it happen. Although nocturnal emission might be regarded as a purely physiological problem and therefore amoral and not implicated in questions of personal character, this is not the case. Indeed, nocturnal emission is more of a moral problem than masturbation since 'self-control' is much more difficult to effect when the problem is simply somatic and not also imperatively ethical. When Shastri's list is finally tallied, what is at issue is the hydraulics of flow and not erotic passion. Questions of who does what to whom, even in an onanistic sense, is finally not nearly as important as are the psychosomatic consequences of an action, be it conscious or unconscious. Consequently, in order to prevent an 'involuntary' loss of semen it is essential to develop a comprehensive regimen of health that goes beyond self-control to an unconscious, biomoral level where both body and mind are brought under control. This is a kind of introspective strategy that must be able to transcend the limits of visual surveillance and public confession: a strategy whose object is not simply the behavioural components of vice, but the psychosomatic elements of virtue. The discourse on brahmacharya does not seek to make public scorn of secret desire or mandate the parameters of 'natural' sex, since what is at issue is a political anatomy of health, and not, as in English boarding schools, academies and Anglo-American families, the parsimony of repressive propriety (cf. Foucault 1980, 1990a:28, 29, 104). Indeed, most authors make only passing reference to the family, the school, or other social institutions where sexuality might be regulated. Punishment is almost totally absent from the discourse on brahmacharya, and the rubric of failure is characterized more by private regret than public shame. It may be in part for this reason that Gandhi was able to speak so frankly in public about his problem with night discharge (cf.

Kakar 1990:103–108), and why Rakesh Chopra is able to write in a recent issue of *Yog Manjari*:

> If you have an erection, apply an *uddiyan bandh* [a common yoga 'bond' in which the diaphragm and stomach are pulled back toward the spine], recite *om* over and over, position your mind on 'high ideals' and do 20 breathing exercises. (1990:25)

Many books on celibacy provide comprehensive discussions of how semen loss can be treated. The primary concern is usually with the role of digestion and circulation in maintaining the body's overall balance and fitness. Whereas pure, healthy blood builds up semen, poor digestion can cause semen to flow out of the body. A number of authors, such as Saraswati, recommend yogic healing practices to improve digestion and circulation (1982:37–84). As with most other authors, however, Saraswati's perspective on medicine is highly eclectic. Treatments are drawn from Ayurvedic, Unani, homeopathic and Western traditions. Nevertheless, Saraswati most often subscribes to the holistic practice of yoga and naturopathy. He advocates a number of 'water cures' such as taking water in through the nose and spitting it out through the mouth (Saraswati 1982:37), as well as water-induced purges, enemas and soak baths, which remove waste from the body and thus help to purify and cool blood as well as promote good digestion. It is on this front where the much more extensive literature on naturopathy and yogic hygiene becomes especially relevant to the structure of seminal truth. Even in the literature published just by the BYS there are detailed discussions of the therapeutic rationale and method for all of the yogic kriyas (disciplines) and nature cures prescribed by Saraswati and others. Moreover, these are incorporated into the regular regimen of public health—where groups of forty or more people can be seen vomiting and cleaning their sinuses together, as preparation for doing *pranayama* (breathing exercises) and as a kind of generalized immunization against many kinds of illnesses.

Of all modes of promoting health, one of the most basic, and therefore important, is breathing. A tremendous amount of detailed information is provided by Saraswati and others on the proper way to breathe in order to prevent semen loss.

God has made [mankind with] two nostrils. The air which is taken in through the right nostril is heated, whereas that taken in through the left nostril is cooled . . . Every two hours and twenty-four minutes there is a change, and air is inhaled through a different nostril. If this rotation functions properly, there is very little chance of falling sick. However, a poor diet, a change in season, or an uncontrolled life-style can break the oscillating rhythm and lead directly to illness. (1982:28)

A 'sure fire' remedy for semen loss, developed along the lines of this respiratory physiology, is to lie down on your left side, plug your right nostril and breath in cool air for a prescribed number of minutes. This is a modified version of a common yogic pranayama that is, in turn, derived in part from a tantric interpretation of the *nadi*s (channels) in the subtle body. The left nostril is thought to be connected to the cool, lunar or *ida nadi* that, in Saraswati's modern interpretation at least, functions to cool desire and bring about peace of mind.

However primary, breathing is but one mode of preventative health care. Saraswati and others say that after urinating one should pull one's penis upright, as this helps to increase the overall volume of blood and decrease the chance of penile stimulation. Saraswati also advocates good posture, not because, using the metaphor of 'backbone', it signifies traits of good character and strong moral fibre, but because sitting up straight prevents semen from 'pooling' in cramped joints and bent limbs. One should sit cross-legged with a straight back and with one's genitals 'pulled up' in the manner of a horse. This promotes the best circulation of blood and the production of strong semen (1982:31–34). The ability of horses and other animals to retract their penises when not in use is taken as a model for emulation by many who write about brahmacharya. The fact that male genitalia 'hang down' is regarded as an unfortunate problem since the organs are always being stimulated through contact with skin and cloth. The closest approximation of penis retraction is to tie it up firmly in a *langot* (g-string), a practice so common among brahmacharis that a popular adage for celibacy is 'firm or tight of g-string'. Similarly, one of the single most important asanas in yoga, the *siddhasana*, which is done by crossing one's legs and sitting erect, is said to effectively control desire since the heels of one's feet 'pinch' or hold the penis and scrotum from above at the pubic bone, and from below at the perineum. One modern yoga teacher claims that this asana is so effective in controlling desire that it should not be excessively practised by householders.

Celibacy and Life

Although most authors prescribe specific remedies for the symptoms of semen loss, they all argue vehemently that prevention is better than cure. And, as we have seen through the example of the BYS, many authors advocate a specific regimen of activities that immunize one from desire. As Sivananda points out, the most important aspect of such a regimen is discipline.

> Nature is systematic. Nothing happens without a reason . . . in order to live in tune with nature one must live systematically . . . Many people live a chaotic life with no particular time to sleep and wake; bathe and eat; live and defecate. A set schedule or regimen can make a foolish man wise, a sick man healthy, a weak man strong, a miserable man happy, and a despicably low man highly exalted. (1984:145)

From the point of view of one concerned with the relationship between sexuality and everyday life, it is interesting that the mechanics of discipline associated with celibacy are spelled out in such minute and comprehensive detail. Rather than a discourse that makes sex into a much talked about secret, the discourse on brahmacharya 'writes' a particular sexuality into the public interstices of everyday life. To be sure this is not an erotic sexuality. It is more of a banal or quotidian sexuality that is focused on the microphysics of personal health. Sexuality is integrated into everyday life so that control can be effected over the ebb and flow of a person's biomoral essence. For the brahmachari, sexuality is an open, pervasive and public issue. It constitutes his whole identity. In and of itself this is not particularly unique, however, since monks of various orders are also defined in large part by their chastity (Brown 1988; Foster 1984; Lea 1884; Massyngberde 1967). What distinguishes the secular brahmachari, however, is the non-exclusive, non-secretive, non-mystical, public health nature of his regimen.

Space does not permit a full catalogue of the ways to make one's semen resilient. But typical articles in *Yog Manjari* outline standard lists of 'do's and don'ts' with regard to sleeping, studying, relaxing, defecating, drinking, and above all, eating (Chopra 1990; Navarya 1988; Vashisht 1992; cf. Saraswati 1982:21–24; Shastri n.d.[a]:52; Sivananda 1984:103–104). Food is important to the brahmachari insofar as it promotes the balanced development of the three humours—phlegm, air and bile—and establishes a balanced equilibrium between the three *guna*s (psychosomatic strands): sattva, rajas and tamas (Shastri n.d.[a]:43). Together, the three humours and the three strands comprise the primary coordinates of health (cf. Khare 1976; Marriott 1991).

In general, all authors advocate various forms of yogic breathing and isometric exercise, but they emphasize the simple and natural exercise of walking. On this count, Sivananda's extended discussion of footwear provides a striking example of the extent to which sexuality is demystified and decoded in terms of a physiology of psychosomatic fitness.

There is an important connection between the genital organs and the sinew which runs along the side of the big toe. If that sinew were to break, a man would die within an hour. When one wears sandals and the toe grip presses down on that sinew, it has the effect of pressing down on desire.

Now, filthy shoes destroy life. Heat, cold and illness enter through the feet and through the head. Anyone who has worn shoes knows how much they smell . . . They are stylish to look at, but disease and sin lie beneath their surface attraction . . . [On the other hand,] sandals impart peace and stability to one's defective feet . . . But not just any old sandals which might hurt your feet; they should be light and pleasing. In any case, be they good or bad, what is of utmost importance is the shape and texture of the toe grip. It should be wide and feel good. (1984:147)

The list of rules for structuring a daily regimen is as extensive as it is compulsively detailed. It includes the proper way to wash out one's eyes and genitals; techniques and methods for fasting, walking, devotion, 'friction' baths, socializing, studying, and sitting; and recommendations on how to dress, conduct business and work. These rules are not articulated as discrete entities from which one might pick and choose, but as a complex plan. Everything a brahmachari does must be part of this plan. There is no room for random action and no time for doing nothing.

Freud would undoubtedly have had much to say about the brahmachari's compulsive behaviour in general and about his pedantic obsession with shoes and toes, to say nothing of masturbation and defecation. But a psychological interpretation of a brahmachari's lifestyle, based on an analysis of his public and private life, would have little of consequence to say about the role of power in a public discourse about sex that seeks to demystify and reform precisely that which can be made to appear seductively mysterious in the rhetoric of another discourse. To paraphrase the master himself, sometimes a shoe or a big toe is just that, particularly when its relationship to the genitals is physiological and not symbolic.

Conclusion

There can be little doubt that the literature on brahmacharya falls within the domain of what Foucault calls a *scientia sexualis*: a discourse on sexuality conceived of as a scientific inquiry into the *facts* about sex (1990a:53–73). As Foucault writes, sexuality is implicated in a matrix of power that is primarily concerned with the relationship between a subject and truth (1990a:56). Revelations about sex are the media through which a person knows him or herself, and is known by others. In the history of European sexuality there is an implicit connection between what is done—the various acts of sex, in all their detail—and truth, but a connection that is only effected when it is spoken about, or when one speaks about speaking about it, or when one is overcome by the guilt of not having proclaimed the truth about what was really done. The disciplinary mechanics that are effected through this 'confessional discourse' tend to be in the form of rules and regulations for and against various kinds of sex. What is at issue in terms of the truth about self and sex is who does what to whom, and when, how and why he or she does it. Sex involves someone else, and the intricacies of sexual interaction constitute the discursive parameters of truth.

In contrast to this Eurocentric discourse, the discourse on celibacy in north India seems to be marked by an absence of confession in any form, and an almost total silence on the interactive, 'kinetic pleasure' of sex as an act. Although various authors, teachers of yoga, and members of the BYS 'talk' at length about the mechanics of sex, they neither presume nor advocate that the truth about sex be sought by those who engage in it, talk about their encounters, desires, and transgressions. The sexuality with which they are concerned is not at all dialogic on this level. As we have seen, they are concerned with a truth about 'sexuality'—the *brahm* of brahmacharya—that is physiologically coded to the body as a biomoral organism, but this is not a truth that emerges out of discourses that produce meaning, per se. Nor is it a truth that defines a person in terms of revelations about what was or was not done—adultery, fornication, sodomy or masturbation. It is a truth that is eminent in the fluid that these acts cause to flow: a truth that is, to a large extent, independent of whatever moral value may be attributed to these acts.

As we have seen, the truth of sex is only contingently restricted by the individual body and the individuated self. It is in this regard, I think, that the question of truth in the discourse on celibacy differs most fundamentally from the truth of Eurocentric self-knowledge. The history of European sexuality seems to have resulted in a location of truth in the individual. The discourse on brahmacharya, in contrast, locates truth on a plane that is at once greater than and less than the individual per se. Hence, the mode of discipline for the brahmachari is more elemental—in the sense of dealing with blood flow, saliva secretions, the temperature and depth of bath water, and which side of the nose to breath through—and more universal in the sense that one's blood flow and semen production is directly implicated in a kind of truth that is also the 'natural order of things'. Thus an organization such as the BYS is able to reform society and 'enlighten mankind' by training men how to simply sit and breathe properly. In the place of the confessional, and its panoply of secular heirs, which seem to extract truth from sex, the 'science' of brahmacharya in modern India seems to have produced a regimen where embodied truth tries to speak for itself: a shift of concern from secrets about the body and its passion to questions about what the body secretes.

A regimen such as this has serious socio-political implications. Even though the disciplinary mechanics of celibacy—and their presentation as scientific facts—break truth down into criteria that appear to have no bearing on power, the whole regimen of semen control is, in fact, informed by what might be called a masculine imperative. Although the men who practise and write about celibacy in north India are not burdened with the weight of a Victorian legacy, their frankness and candour on the subject of sex is seductively misleading. Their public discourse on seminal truth effectively 'silences' all other claims regarding the legitimate place of sex and sexuality in social life, while purporting to establish a universal moral mandate for public health. Seminal truth is, therefore, a tremendously powerful—and insidiously destructive—construction of masculinity in modern India. Anxiety about the fluid nature of truth notwithstanding, the regimen of celibacy enables men to passively usurp the most elemental criteria of public power. It is not that women, among other critics, are denied a voice in this discursive field, for brahmacharya's gendered pretensions can be easily criticized from an ideological, political, and cultural angle. What I have tried to show, however, is that 'seminal truth' dislocates power and knowledge away from public discourse where 'ideas' about the self might be at issue, and relocates it, through science, to the private parts of male physiology, thereby defining 'universal truth' in terms of a highly specialized—not to say reified—biology; a truth that has considerable public appeal among a group of powerful people: urban middle-class men in the 'Hindu sphere' of north India.

Jor: Akhara Bara Ganesh. Varanasi, 1988.

4

The Celibate Wrestler
Sexual Chaos, Embodied Balance and Competitive Politics

Introduction

Although clearly a sport, the practice of wrestling in India (*pahalwani*) as a 'performing art' is a complex matter of self-development played out on a public stage where the embodiment of balance enables a wrestler to improve himself and become both powerful and successful. Elaborating on this theme, my purpose in this chapter is to analyse the problematic interface in Indian wrestling between sexual energy and celibacy. While potent energy and self-control are intimately related to one another, a delicate balance must be maintained between them. In this regard, I will provide an interpretation of why and how physical, aesthetic and socio-moral balance are important to the wrestler, and how embodied balance figures in the wrestler's critique of national politics. I will show how specific wrestling techniques and practices provide a kinaesthetic grammar—a material morality—for structuring the wrestler's problematic sexuality, and how this structured sexuality helps map out the political terrain of the Indian state.

By referring to wrestling as a 'poetics of movement' or a 'kinaesthetic grammar', I do not mean to imply that moves and countermoves somehow serve as basic metaphors for the struggle of life—wherein, one might say, there are issues and problems with which one must grapple. Wrestlers in India do not conceive of the body as lexical or analogic in this sense. It is not simply, to adapt Levi-Strauss's phrase, something through which they think about larger, complex questions of order and disorder. Nor is the body simply an outward, corporeal sign which reflects the more primary health of the 'inner man's' state of mind. Both of these formulations presume an incipient disjunction of mind and body, and therefore simply impose analytic frameworks which extract meaning, as it were, by 'decoding' bodies which are presumed to have a binary structure.

As McKim Marriott (1976, 1990) and others have pointed out, 'Hindu' notions of the self in general, and the body in particular, lend themselves imperfectly to analytic formulas which are conceived of in terms of binary distinctions between ideas and biology: mind and body (cf. Daniel 1984; 1988; Trawick 1990). Structure, substance and meaning are inextricably fused together in notions of somaticity, and in order to understand how a person 'feels' about something on an emotional level—such as sexual desire—one must often start by asking questions about health and fitness. Along these lines, in slightly different yet complementary ways, both Marriott and Daniel have developed interpretive models for the analysis of 'Hindu' society which emphasize the importance of equipoise or balance. Marriott argues that the 'Hindu' universe is best understood in terms of a tripartite scheme in three-dimensional relief (1990: 16). The constituent aspects of the world—elements, humours, psychosomatic strands—can be charted on a graph based on a set of basal themes or processes which underlie all categories. Marriott's scheme is highly detailed and very sophisticated, but what is of particular relevance to this discussion is the way in which balance is conceived of as a point at which the constituent properties of the world converge in a perfect state of equilibrium (ibid.: 29). While this state of perfect balance is, in some sense, cognate with the mystical ideals of salvation in various articulations of philosophy, Daniel, writing about Tamil experience in particular, has shown that a concern with intersubstantial compatibility—what to eat, when to bathe, and where to build a house in order to negotiate contingent balance—concerns many people on the mundane level of daily life (1984:6–8). In these terms, well-being is understood as a process of negotiating a complex set of relationships between oneself, one's body and the world: a complex set of relationships which wrestlers conceive of primarily in terms of sex and the power of sexuality. Although the wrestler's complex physique is coded in terms of many of the specific categories delineated by Marriott, here my concern is strictly with the wrestler's sexuality as it relates to the problem of negotiated psychosomatic balance.

The wrestler's concern with celibacy and balance is worked out in terms of a discourse about health and a structured programme of physical fitness. However, the wrestler's concept of fitness and health is dependent both on what I am calling the grammar of his regimen and the poetics of his movements as well as the socio-political environment in which he lives. This socio-political environment is often destabilizing to the extent that it is erotic, violent, materialistic and unhealthy. In seeking to achieve perfect health the wrestler must negotiate his way through a somewhat chaotic world animated by the metaphoric codes of power and passion and structured by the metonymic function of sexual fluids.

The Wrestler's World and the *Akhara*

Modern Indian wrestling, known variably as pahalwani, or *mallayuddha*, derives from two sources: an indigenous form of the art which dates back at least to the time of the great war described in the Mahabharata (c. 900 BC), and a Mughal form of Persian wrestling brought into the subcontinent by Babur's army in the sixteenth century AD (Mujumdar 1950; Raghavan 1979; Rai 1984). These two forms—and some say a third in the form of classical Greek wrestling introduced by Alexander's soldiers in 327 BC—mingled over time to produce a uniquely Indian martial art. Indian wrestling is technically very similar to Western free-style wrestling. Although there are fundamental differences in some basic rules—the length of a bout and the criteria for a pin, for example—the techniques and various moves employed are virtually identical.

While wrestling in northern India is a popular sport in both rural and urban areas, it is difficult to tell precisely how widespread and prevalent it is. In the city of Banaras, where I conducted a year of field research, there are roughly 150 active gymnasia. Of these only six or seven are organized. According to at least one source, there are four or five hundred small gymnasia in the larger Delhi metropolitan area; but, again, only five or six with a large, established membership. Until recently, though to a lesser extent, gymnasia were to be found in many large villages in the districts of Ettawa, Gazipur, Gorakhpur, Banaras and Baliya in central Uttar Pradesh; Kolhapur and Sangli in Maharashtra; Jabalpur in Madhya Pradesh; throughout Punjab, and in many other regional areas as well. Despite its popularity in these areas, wrestling is not a highly visible sport—most of the activities associated with practice and training take place early in the morning, and there are very few permanent venues where public competitions are held.

While many of the large gymnasia are now located in urban areas such as Lucknow, Allahabad, Delhi, Meerut, Mathura, Banaras and Patna, most wrestlers feel that their art is aesthetically and morally rooted in a rural way of life. An akhara (gymnasium), where most wrestling activities take place, is the geographical and social space which defines this rural ethos. Ideally an akhara is out in the open, near a body of water, and in the shade of some trees. The main feature of every akhara is the wrestling pit, which is, in fact, not a pit at all but a soft earthen platform raised about twenty centimetres above ground level and roughly ten to twelve metres square. The pit is usually located within a pavilion of some kind so that it remains dry in wet weather. An exercise area of hard packed earth is located near or around the pavilion. Every akhara also has a water source, usually a well, and at least one temple or shrine dedicated to Lord Hanuman, the tutelary deity of many gymnasia (Alter 1993a).

In most cases an akhara is under the direction and management of a particular guru (master teacher), and membership in that akhara is a function of one's affiliation to him. However, membership and participation in akhara activities is not rigidly controlled. Most wrestlers speak of an akhara as a public place where anyone interested in wrestling may go and engage in exercise or practice. However, a serious wrestler is always clearly affiliated with a particular guru.

Men and boys of almost any age practise wrestling with various degrees of commitment and rigour. The most disciplined practitioners of the art, and those who thereby define the archetype for all wrestlers, are usually between the ages of eighteen and twenty-five. Although wrestlers come from many caste backgrounds, various regional caste groups tend to produce more wrestlers than others: Jats in western Uttar Pradesh and Haryana, Yadavs and Rais in eastern Uttar Pradesh and in west central India.

The akhara serves as a focal point for the wrestler's daily regimen, which begins at about four in the morning and continues until eight or nine in the evening. Needless to say a wrestler is not engaged in rigorous physical training for the full duration of each day. However, as wrestlers define preparation, everything they do—eating, sleeping, resting, walking, talking, defecating, as well as practising moves and countermoves or doing various types of exercises—is geared towards integrated self-development. It is in this sense that each twenty-four hour period is the cycle of one holistic work-out, and that wrestling is an all-encompassing way of life bent on effecting psychosomatic equilibrium.

Sexuality and the Daily Regimen

Elsewhere I have written about the wrestler's way of life as it relates to concepts of health and fitness in general, and morality, renunciation and politics in particular (Alter 1992a, 1992b, 1993b). A characteristic feature of this way of life is that it is precisely regimented. Gurus give their wards very specific instructions on what to do and how to do it. To become a successful wrestler one must do three things which require a great deal of commitment and concentration: exercise and practise hard; respect, revere and obey one's guru; and be a devotee of Lord Hanuman. On a more general level one must be absolutely celibate since practice, obedience and devotion are rendered meaningless and ineffectual by sexual passion. Consequently the whole regimen of wrestling is keyed to the principle of celibacy.

Although wrestlers do a variety of exercises, the two that are most important to their *vyayam* (exercise) regimen are *dand*s (jack-knifing push-ups) and *bethak*s (deep-knee bends). Typically, wrestlers do hundreds and sometimes over a thousand of each in the course of an evening session. These exercises develop shoulder, chest, thigh and lower back strength in particular. Elsewhere I have discussed the particular merits of each exercise in detail, noting that dands and bethaks shape both the character of the wrestler as well as his physique, since exercise is very closely linked to moral, ethical and spiritual development (Alter 1992a:103–5). However, dands and bethaks are also directly implicated in the production and control of semen. As Atreya points out, 'all manner of illnesses associated with semen are cured by these exercises' (Atreya 1974b: 21).

> All of the diseases associated with semen are cured by doing pure *dand*s. . . It is for this reason that character radiates out from a person who does these exercises. His body shines with an aura of vitality (Atreya 1974b:19).

While there are many reasons why dands and bethaks promote good health in general, they seem to be directly related to semen by way of their effect on the circulation of blood through particular parts of the body. In the physiology of various medical traditions in India, semen is regarded as a pure, condensed distillate of blood. What dands and bethaks seem to do is facilitate the process by which food is transformed into semen through blood. At least one important component of this process is breathing. While doing dands and bethaks it is imperative that a wrestler breathe through his nose, and that he breathe deeply in rhythm with each movement. Breathing is particularly important because it allows for the regular and systematic elimination of waste from the body, which in turn ensures the purity of both blood and semen (Atreya 1974b: 21). Breathing through the nose is crucial because it cools the blood, and generally keeps the body in a state of equilibrium.

Although the physiological connection between semen, blood and exercise is clearly worked out in the wrestler's regimen, there is also an important symbolic association between dands, bethaks and sexuality. A dand is done by first assuming a position on all fours with one's buttocks raised into the air and arms extended straight in line with one's torso, rather like the *adhomukha shvanasana* depicted in image six. One then dives down just above the ground between the plane of one's hands, finally arching up while thrusting one's hips down towards the ground while extending one's arms straight. The hips are then cocked back up to the original position in order to start the manoeuvre over again. Dands are done quickly, at a rate of about forty per minute, giving the impression that a wrestler is thrusting his hips up and down in a manner which resembles intercourse.

Although wrestlers take their regimen very seriously, there were a number of occasions during my field research when someone would make some kind of joke about this correlation. These jokes were usually subtle and involved only slight code-shifting. For example, when a wrestler started breathing through his mouth rather than his nose, another wrestler would imitate his heavy breathing, but make it sound more like the ecstasy of passion than the exertion of exercise. Significantly, breathing through the mouth rather than the nose means that one has, to a degree, lost control of one's body at a critical stage of self-development. Whenever a young wrestler would start gasping for breath he would be soundly rebuked by his guru. Also, when a wrestler would show off by doing his dands at a vigorous pace, others would ask, with a glint in their eye or a half-smile, whether or not he was 'having fun yet'. Sometimes this would entail a play on words. Wrestlers often use the term *masti* or *mast* to describe the feeling of invigorated bliss which accompanies a particularly hard work-out. A wrestler who is charged with energy and ready to take on anyone or do anything is also spoken of as *mast*. Significantly, mast can also mean intoxicated with passion, or, in more colloquial terms, simply 'horny'—a modern, 'high-class' brand of condoms is called by this name. Therefore, there is ample opportunity for wrestlers to strategically confuse the meaning of the term in order to make a joke at someone's expense. This may simply involve the expression on a person's face—a wink and a knowing tilt of the head—when he directs a comment or asks a question about someone's mood or state of mind.

A far more common way of joking about sexual energy in the akhara is to make reference to the number of children a person has fathered. This only works, of course, for those few active wrestlers who are married. However, for these hapless fellows any sign of weakness, exhaustion or imperfection in their regimen is often met with some kind of sarcastic comment about where their energy is being misspent.

On other occasions non-wrestlers who were associated with wrestlers in one way or another would use dands and bethaks as a way of joking about their own sexual prowess. For example, older men who spend their leisure time at the akharas I worked in would often vigorously do a dand or bethak in order to demonstrate their youthful virility. When talking with one old man about age and health, he pointed out that he had no teeth. But then he flashed open his lungi (loincloth), thrust his hips at his ribald compatriots, did a few vigorous bethaks and said something to

the effect that 'teeth or no teeth', he still had what it took. In a
similar vein, the following example is apropos. While in Banaras I
became friends with the non-wrestling son of a well-to-do senior
wrestler. My friend was somewhat of a self-proclaimed Casanova,
although his libertine exploits were largely the product of his
concupiscent imagination. One day I asked why he didn't wrestle.
His mischievous response, typical of his general disposition, was
that he did; but that he 'visited the night akhara'. By which he
meant, of course, that he engaged in grappling of a different kind,
with a different sort of partner: the dark, passionate antithesis of
the wrestler's daily routine.

Serious and self-righteous wrestlers would be shocked by the
attitudes and behaviours described above, and all of the examples
I have cited involved friends of wrestlers who only occasionally
frequented a gymnasium, or 'wrestlers' who were somehow on the
fringe and not committed to the regimen as such. In any case, it is
obvious that dands and bethaks signify an important component
of all wrestlers' sexuality, and that on this symbolic level there
is also a fine line between the inherent balance of control, the
control of balance, and the potential chaos when the metonymic
production of sexual fluids threatens to translate too easily into
a metaphor for kinetic sex.

A wrestler's diet is also explicitly associated with the problem
of controlled sexuality: of maintaining a balance between the
production of semen which enhances strength, and the enervating
tendency of semen to flow out. In addition to regular fare,
wrestlers eat large quantities of almonds and ghee (clarified
butter), and drink large quantities of milk. High in fat and
calories, a diet such as this gives the wrestler the necessary energy
he needs to wrestle and exercise. In addition to this obvious
fact, however, it is also important to note that milk and ghee in
particular are thought to 'digest' smoothly into blood and semen.
According to many wrestlers, milk and ghee already share many
of the primary chemical features of semen, and therefore are
easily, efficiently and directly assimilated as such into the body. As

I have noted elsewhere, milk, ghee and almonds are also directly associated with semen on the level of myth, ritual, folklore and common speech (Alter 1992a). Thus, when a wrestler consumes half a litre of ghee—which many are wont to do—he is well aware that what he is doing has sexual significance on a number of different levels.

A wrestler's dietary regimen is most significant, however, in terms of its relationship to a larger scheme of balance. In terms of Ayurvedic medicine, as well as general folk concepts of psychosomatic health, all organic matter including primarily food and people is comprised of three qualities, or strands: sattva (clarity and calmness), rajas (passion and aggression), and tamas (dullness and lethargy). These three forces work against one another in a dynamic tension which produces, or animates, the psychic, emotional and physical nature of the individual. A person who is tamasic, for example, is stereotypically dark, heavy, and slow-witted, whereas a person who is sattvic tends to be fair, energetic and wise. Insofar as one is able to manipulate these qualities, the goal of a wrestler is to have more sattva and less rajas or tamas. The most expedient way of doing this is to structure one's diet to exclude anything which produces agitation, aggression, passion, dullness and lethargy—meat, spices, salt, certain kinds of oil, sour foods, eggs, various types of lentil, and a host of other things as well—and to eat those things which are sattvik by nature, namely, milk and ghee. To be sattvik by nature is to be in control of oneself and to be in a perfect state of good health.

In an article on the place of ghee in a wrestler's diet, Dr Shanti Prakash Atreya elaborates on the balanced, sattvik nature of the wrestler who regularly eats a quarter kilogram of ghee. He points out that sickness in general is a condition of imbalanced forces within the body, and that ghee is able to effect a rebalance of elements, humours and the 'four human aims' in order to make a person healthy:

Only such a person is content and happy. He exudes divine happiness and love, and feels compassion and affection for everyone. Under whatever circumstances, he remains composed and calm. As one who has renounced worldly concerns, a wrestler must eat a sattvik diet. (Atreya 1984: 23)

Ideally, then, the body/mind of the wrestler becomes more and more balanced as it moves further and further away from the chaotic world of sensual preoccupation. In addition to being sattvik, however, ghee has other properties which also have a direct bearing on semen. As Atreya continues:

Ghee alone produces resilient semen, strength and energy. Unlike eggs [for example], which enhance passion and thereby cause semen to flow, the semen which is produced by ghee stays in the body for many years. One of the best things about ghee is that it enables one to easily control one's thoughts (Atreya 1984: 23–24).

Celibacy and Balance

In addition to exercise and diet, wrestlers concern themselves with a whole series of ancillary regimens which contribute to the body's equipoise and the critical balance of semen. Gurus often give their wards specific instructions on how to maintain celibacy. Prescriptions refer to the care of one's hair, dental hygiene, the quality of bedding and position of one's bed, and the weight, fabric and style of clothes to be worn during a particular season of the year. Some gurus are far more specific than others, and there is a fair degree of variation from one akhara to another. Likewise, some wrestlers are far more disciplined and doctrinaire than others in their interpretation of a guru's dictum. Regardless, the point is that wrestlers talk as though they could go through life without making a single arbitrary decision or engaging in an irrelevant act. Everything from the temperature of bath and drinking water to the firmness of a bed can be brought within the purview of disciplined self-preparation.

In a book on the subject of brahmacharya, Shastri locates the primary problem of sexual desire in the unconscious mind (Shastri n.d.b). As discussed in the previous chapter, latent sexual urges result in either night discharge, which is dangerous by virtue of being involuntary, or masturbation which is regarded as flagrantly carnal on account of the deliberate, conscious and self-absorbed nature of the act. Shastri provides a detailed list of 101 ways to avoid the path which leads from sleep and idleness to self-abuse. The details of this list are interesting in their own right for what they say about concepts of psychological health. However, the list as a whole is also of interest insofar as it indicates a particular concern for detail, and an attempt to 'grammatically' structure the vast imponderabilia of daily life. A few items on the list are fairly obvious: to not sleep close to, or intertwined with, another person; to not look at pictures of naked men and women; and to not talk about sex or intercourse. Other items on the list refer more specifically to hygiene: the injunction not to use the same water with which one cleans oneself after defecating to wash one's genitals; to wash the tip of one's penis with clean, cold water every morning and evening; and to not use oil on one's genitals. A number of prescriptions concern sleeping. For example, one should not lie down until one is ready to fall asleep. Do not sleep with your head covered. Do not sleep naked. Upon waking, immediately get up and out of bed. There are also a host of other features which relate to specific situations. One should eat honey instead of sugar or sweets, for example, and not make a habit of riding a horse or a bicycle. One should bathe only in cool water, and never warm oneself by a fire.

Since 101 is an auspicious number which to some extent implies an infinite progression, Shastri's list is inherently partial and contingent. The principle of infinite enumeration is more important than any set of delimited guidelines, no matter how comprehensive. In accordance with this principle one can, quite literally, live one's life not simply as a passive, defensive celibate, but as an aggressive brahmachari whose compulsive quest for equipoise is all-consuming. It is on this level in particular that the wrestler's sexuality becomes politicized. In his quest for equipoise, the wrestler structures his public identity around a spectrum of moral coordinates such as honesty, non-violence and humility which define the basic parameters of citizenship. As we will see later, institutionalized politics undermine the power of balanced sex upon which this citizenship is founded (cf. Alter 1994).

One may look at the rules and recommendations for achieving public celibacy as a kind of sexual grammar by means of which wrestlers, and many other young men and boys, make sense of their embodied feelings. Significantly, sexuality is not subverted or repressed by this grammar; it is structured. As one wrestler told me, repressed desire only leads to more complex problems. The wrestlers' strategy, so to speak, is to link sex with all aspects of social life—mundane and magnificent alike—and then to confront sexuality in this public arena where it is less likely to get tangled up in the dark, private corners of an adolescent mind. In this way, unchecked desire, the chaos of sex, is not isolated as a purely moral or psychological problem for which the individual is held responsible. Nor is a cure effected through some form of therapy which unlocks the mysteries of the mind. Sexuality is turned into a complex, public problem of syntax wherein the images responsible for bringing on night discharge, or the fantasies which spawn masturbation, may be edited out by rearranging elements of daily life—more baths, less food, a harder bed, looser clothes, and an evening walk in the company of like-minded friends, for example (Alter: 1994). One's guru is responsible for mandating the specific details, and, as one wrestler pointed out, 'you must not so much as urinate without your guru's permission.'

Structuring one's sexuality is a problem of considerable magnitude if one recalls that what is at issue is the health of the whole person, and not just his psyche. It is significant that a person who suffers from semen loss shows obvious physical signs of falling apart. As Shastri points out, his face is yellowish, he angers quickly, does not smile, tires after the slightest work, cannot tolerate the sun, has a burning sensation in his feet and hands, and shakes uncontrollably (Shastri n.d.:31–35). Clearly, the alternative to disciplined celibacy is a dramatic erosion of psychosomatic health. As long as a series of precise rules are followed, good health, energy and balance can be maintained. For the wrestler in particular the problem is magnified. His fitness demands a large store of semen, and yet a large store of semen is dangerous on account of its inherent instability. A wrestler must be able to find and constantly maintain precarious balance at that critical point where the power of sex may be turned away from the chaos of passion and into disciplined strength and skill (see Alter 2002).

Daw, Pech, Pantra: The Poetics of Fluid Movement

At this point it is necessary to move from the literal semantics of psychosomatic health to a figurative plane of balance and the poetic structure of wrestling moves and countermoves. The 'art' of wrestling, I will argue—as distinct from the regimen of training and diet—blends an aesthetic concern for competitive balance with the wrestler's more general concern with psychosomatic equipoise and seminal balance: a convergence wherein the literal and figurative meaning of 'fluid movement' is ultimately the same.

Moves (*daw*) and countermoves (*pech*), in conjunction with various stances (*pantra*) are conceived of in terms of absolute rules of balance and movement broken down into grips, trips, flips, twists, slides, feints and parries. Every aspect is equally important and the precise accuracy of combined elements determines the success or failure of a move's application. Although it is possible to explain how a particular move is executed, the minute complexity of speed, balance, counterbalance, leverage and so forth defies description. Anyone who has tried to wrestle is aware of the disparity which exists between the comprehension of a move in principle and its application in fact. Even after a great deal of practice it never works every time, even for the most accomplished wrestler. But when it does work, it appears as though every single movement fits together perfectly. It is in this illusive and ineffable sense that the aesthetic of wrestling is poetic, for success depends more on inspired improvization than on the cold, hard diction of strict rules of procedure, no matter how detailed.

Moreover, a move, described as such with a clear beginning and end, is a decontextualized fiction: an idealized fragment that really only exists in a wrestler's imagination. Whenever two wrestlers grapple, every move is cut short, aborted, or transformed by a countermove. Similarly, a stance is only balanced until one's opponent feints or parries, at which time one must take that precarious step from one point of balance to another. This is the nature of competition; but the dynamic tension produced through aggressive confrontation generates movement which is radically different in form and structure from the idealized move which is imagined by an individual wrestler.

With this in mind, it is necessary to make an important distinction between competitive wrestling, known as *kushti*, and practice wrestling, known as *jor*. Jor means to exert force, and it is the term used exclusively to describe non-competitive wrestling practice which takes place between the members of an akhara. The idea behind jor is to build up strength, agility, stamina and skill by wrestling with a number of different opponents for an extended period of time. I often watched as wrestlers engaged in jor for one to two hours under the supervision of their guru. Although exercise is derived from the application of moves and counter moves, the idea in jor is to 'trade moves' with one's partner. A wrestler engaged in jor must structure his defensive manoeuvres in tandem with his partner's offensive strategy. After offering a modicum of resistance, he must let himself be thrown, pushed or tripped. Since collusion overrides competition, winning or losing is not at all at issue. What is at issue is balance, and the aesthetic appeal of a move properly executed.

Properly done, jor looks very much like a vigorous dance. Each distinct movement is marked by what preceded it and what must inevitably follow. Though improvised, action is smooth, rhythmic, and above all else, intelligible. Doing jor and watching jor are both aesthetic experiences from which wrestlers derive a great deal of satisfaction. Many times a crowd would gather around as a well-matched pair of young wrestlers traded moves with one another. This aesthetic dimension of jor must, I think, be viewed in relation to the wrestler's more inclusive regimen. The kinaesthetic rhythm of jor evokes the precision of the wrestler's celibate lifestyle. In both domains, balance is a premium and loose ends are anathema. Total control is an absolute necessity. With no pun intended, it must be said that wrestlers are constantly grappling with their sexuality when practising jor. That is, the moves and countermoves they employ engender both a somatic and aesthetic sense of balance.

Like many of the vyayam exercises discussed earlier, jor promotes the flow of blood and other bodily fluids to various parts of the body. It contributes directly to the production of semen. Moreover, when wrestlers practise jor they say that the earth from the pit, which covers their saturated bodies from head to toe, draws excessive heat out of their bodies, and thereby absorbs and neutralizes the agency of passion. However, jor ignites the seminal fire of psychosomatic energy known as ojas, thus creating a radiant aura of power-shining eyes, glowing skin and a kind of electric sparkle which is thought to emanate from semen. The earth pit provides a cool environment where the wrestler's sparkling body may reach a critical state of embodied power without actually running the risk of self-destruction: a state of balanced opposition reflected in the common adage used to describe wrestlers—diamonds of the red earth.

Jor also builds resilient character. Although wrestlers fight with one another in a combative, competitive sense, they are eminently non-aggressive when it comes to social and personal relations outside the akhara. Many wrestlers now lament the fact that their art has been used to advance self-interest by way of threats and intimidation. This is particularly so in the context of modern communal politics and Hindu nationalism where, in popular perception at least, there has tended to be an easy translation of pahalwani into *goondagiri* (thuggery) based on the loose equivalence of physical violence and strength (see Kakar 1996). It is probably also true that some men who have developed their bodies through the discipline of wrestling have been seduced by the kind of rank status which can be achieved through strongarm tactics. As we will see later, the somatic codes inherent in the practice of wrestling allow for an easy but very dangerous 'slippage' from chaste self-control to what might be called virulent, vulgar virility. In any case, the ideal among wrestlers is to be totally selfless and humble, and not let prowess translate into pride. A 'hot-headed' person is unable to control himself and is apt to replace precision and poise with anger and brute force. Jor teaches one to be passive, humble and calm. It does this in two ways. On the one hand, a skilled wrestler knows exactly where he stands, so to speak, and his self-confidence translates directly into the noble virtues he is meant to embody. On the other hand, however, his virtue is a function of the psychosomatic balance he has achieved. In other words, the energy of semen produces the virtues of celibacy, and since celibacy and exercise promote the development of semen, the wrestler is animated by the power of a virtual conundrum wherein personality has a clearly physical dimension. Wrestlers would often use the English word 'personality', in conjunction with various positive Hindi adjectives, to denote the moral physique of an energetically virtuous person who comports himself in a particular way.

Wrestlers explain that to learn the art of wrestling is to learn how to present and carry oneself both in and out of the pit. In this regard a great deal of importance is placed on stance. Ideally a wrestler should assume a position in the pit such that he is practically rooted to the ground. Outside of the pit this balanced rootedness is affected in a stylized form of comportment. Wrestlers have a slow, methodical walk, but a spring in their step. They hold themselves erect with shoulders squared, arms slightly splayed, and necks stiffened. In conjunction with a radiant physique, this style of comportment has a clear aesthetic appeal which makes people turn their heads and take notice.

In sum, jor and celibacy are linked together not simply through the metaphor of balance, but through the details of a regimen—a kinaesthetic grammar—wherein a balanced stance and fluid movement contribute both literally and figuratively to a balanced disposition and an attractive personality. As we shall see, the symmetry of this relationship is fractured when wrestling becomes competitive.

The *Dangal*: Sex and the Chaos of Competition

*Dangal*s (competitive wrestling tournaments) vary greatly in terms of both pomp and circumstance. Weekly neighbourhood or village tournaments represent the most basic form of competition. Large, national bouts are characteristically more bombastic, dramatic and expensive. Irrespective of size, all dangals follow a fairly predictable schedule, beginning with bouts between junior contestants, and culminating with the prize fight of two well-known champions. Bouts last anywhere from a few minutes for junior contestants to more than half an hour for the senior competitors. They continue until one of the wrestlers wins by causing his opponent's shoulders to touch the ground simultaneously, or until the set time limit elapses and the contest is declared a draw.

Dangals are dramatically public events. Although in some cases tickets are sold for large dangals, in most cases a tournament is open to any man who wants to come and watch. Small weekly tournaments often attract a thousand or more spectators, while large, publicized dangals attract as many as twenty or thirty thousand from different districts and states. Some large dangals go on for two or three days until the roster of bouts—sometimes numbering near one hundred—has been gone through.

The nature and aesthetic of competitive wrestling in the dangal are quite different from that of jor. Where jor is based on a principle of structured balance, competitive wrestling, known as kushti, entails uncompromising resistance and the trickery of feigned complicity. Half the game is to leave oneself apparently vulnerable to a particular move in order to draw one's opponent into a position where a move may be successfully applied on him. Whereas in jor each move is elaborated and often embellished by virtue of the fact that the two wrestlers are working together, kushti is a drama of truncated moves and failed attempts. There is certainly a sense in which kushti has an aesthetic appeal. However, the aesthetic is clearly not one of balance and harmony. It is more an issue of superiority, and ultimately the imbalanced hierarchy of success and failure which spectators appreciate. For example, crowds 'go wild' when a wrestler has his feet kicked out from under him and he flies through the air to land in that most vulnerable of all positions: *chita*, flat on his back. Significantly, success of this kind is based purely and aggressively on a level of individual skill which renders an opponent utterly helpless. A move perfectly executed signifies consummate skill; but skill from which the cooperative, balanced tone of jor is conspicuously absent.

As a place where disorder and chaos often prevail, the dangal is a context within which the wrestler's sexuality becomes particularly problematic. The tournament dramatically ruptures an otherwise precisely ordered and clearly articulated way of life. The word *dangal*, which also means unruly crowd, is cognate with a number of other words which suggest disorder: *dang* (perplexity, fear); *dangal* (mutiny); and *dangi* (riotous). A palpable tension permeates many dangals whenever two well-known wrestlers compete, and although dangals are usually well organized, there is always an underlying sense that the whole affair may degenerate into a free-for-all. Disputes are not at all uncommon. On a number of occasions I have seen a dangal fall apart when a wrestler's entourage—his akhara cohort and various fans and friends—stormed the arena to protest a questionable decision, or when tempers flared over a particularly egregious foul. Police are often on hand to prevent any minor conflagration from escalating and getting out of control.

Although wrestlers often claim that dangals are inherently peaceful and controlled, evidence would suggest otherwise. While conducting research in Banaras and other parts of north India I found that weekly tournaments in some towns and cities had been cancelled due to inter-ethnic tension. Wrestlers often lament this fact, for it cuts against the grain of their non-sectarian ethic, but the fact remains that a structured defeat can very quickly spiral into an unstructured conflagration between winners and losers (Alter 1992a). This can have drastic consequences in an environment where Hindus and Muslims, who often compete against one another, are already at odds. I will have more to say about the political implications of this later.

The tension inherent in some dangals is symbolically coded in all tournaments. Although wrestlers enjoy competitive wrestling, there is also a deep ambivalence on the part of many towards what the dangal signifies. For many wrestlers, fitness and health has become an end in itself, and jor in the akhara is simply the primary manifestation of a larger natural order. For them, jor, vyayam and *khurak* (diet) are their own reward. In a dangal there must be a winner and a loser, and the asymmetry of this fact often grates on the nerves of the wrestler whose psychosomatic self is dependent on harmony. I was at first often surprised to note the degree of satisfaction with which wrestlers would respond to a bout that was drawn. It was almost as though they were relieved, on an aesthetic, affective level, that balanced parity won out over hierarchy and conflict. A draw is an appropriate ending which does not need to be resolved by the imposition of a dramatic conclusion. The issue here is not simply the possible ignominy of defeat. Surely, no one likes to lose; but the egoism of success is no less difficult to reconcile with a body/mind which derives strength from the kind of passive humility which both jor and a drawn bout evoke.

I think it is logical to assume that kushti evokes the chaotic nature of kinetic sex—at least from a common perspective wherein sex as an aggressive, hierarchical and dangerous act can substantially transform one, usually for the worse. Although success and failure, winning and losing, have a great deal to do with this on a purely analogic level, there is also a significant way in which the balanced production of semen is destabilized by competitive wrestling. Unlike jor, kushti develops as a series of aborted moves and countermoves; feints and parries which, for the most part, are ineffective. Although wrestlers try to maintain their balance, they are, more often than not, off balance. In other words, the whole dynamic of kushti undermines the principle by which wrestling as an art is conceived of as a fluid chain of improvised movement. The encounter of two men who are bent on taking advantage of one another's weaknesses inevitably results in a degree of chaotic confusion.

It is intriguing that the word most commonly used for being pinned in a wrestling tournament is *chita*, which means, in other contexts, to be supine. Curiously, the word *chita*, used as a noun rather than an adjective, means mind or intellect. In this regard it seems to be virtually synonymous with the word *chitta*, which has a clearly psychological meaning in ayurvedic and yogic theory. In common usage, chitta means mental processes or thought and understanding. However, as Sudhir Kakar has pointed out, the technical meaning of chitta comes closer to the Western psychological concept of id:

> Chitta is . . . the part of the psychic organization which represents the elemental, instinctual drives of the organism . . . . Thus, if Freud described the id as 'a chaos, a cauldron full of seething excitations' [Freud 1965 [1933]], the concept of chitta can be evoked through similar imagery. (Kakar 1980: 22).

Unlike the id, however, chitta 'strives towards its own transformation' into a balanced state of one-pointed synthesis, moving from a state of dark confusion towards a condition of bliss wherein 'I' and 'Other' merge in perfect harmony (Kakar 1980: 23). As Kakar points out, the chaotic nature of chitta is animated by sexual instincts, and a cultural recognition that those instincts are extremely hard to bring under control (ibid.: 24). Irrespective of whether or not there is an etymological connection between chita and chitta, the sexual chaos denoted by the latter is a good indication of what the former means in the context of competitive wrestling. A wrestler who loses his balance and is flipped onto his back has had more than his ego bruised; he has, quite literally, had his 'id' exposed—and the same is true, to a lesser extent, for the wrestler who pinned him down, for the nature of competition is such that it moves both wrestlers away from the psychosomatic ideal to which they aspire in other arenas. This makes particular sense if one remembers that the primary strategy of the brahmachari is not to overcome his natural urges—either in the sense of repressing desire or finding a wholesome outlet for pent-up energy—but to coordinate his body with the bio-social world. The discordant environment of the dangal is dangerous because it brings the essence of sexual energy so close to the surface without any sort of attendant mechanism for control. To be pinned simply peels away the last vestige of an elaborate cultural construct which plays with the dangerous power of sex.

Ayurvedic medicine is directly concerned with long life, and the act of sex is explicitly associated with factors which reduce one's lifespan. Ejaculation is, therefore, both a medical condition which leads to death, as well as a symbolic expression of death and dying. Sex brings together, in a single powerful event, the exaltation of pure pleasure and the terrible realization of ultimate mortality. Winning, too, is like ejaculation. There is a moment of tremendous exhilaration, and then the contest comes to an abrupt end. At best the career of a champion wrestler is short-lived and fitful. It is a career which moves from tournament to tournament, and climax to climax, as the iconic case of Gama illustrates (see Alter 2000a), a career which ineluctably ends in defeat. As such it directly cuts against the grain of the balanced, cyclical akhara regimen which keeps the wrestler young and healthy.

It is in relation to this natural, inevitable mortality that the heroic identity of the competitive wrestler is undermined by the significance of sexual meanings over which he no longer exercises control. In the moment of his success he embodies the chaos of all instinct, and in particular that dimension of sexual desire which threatens the order of all culture on account of its purely egoistic self-referentiality. Those who come to watch wrestling tournaments are at once fascinated and disturbed by the iconic, enigmatic heroism of a champion wrestler who embodies radical ideals of individual potential in a context where such ideals are highly problematic. When sex is added to this picture the heroic wrestler becomes a narcissistic anomaly whose self-referentiality cannot be sustained as a source of strength and inspiration (see Alter 2002).

Although the sexual implications of wrestling are obvious on the level of practice, where semen is regarded as basic to strength and skill, the issue of sexuality is usually coded in much more covert and oblique terms in the dangal milieu. In a few cases, however, the issue of sexuality is made explicit.

When engaged in the competitive bouts, wrestlers wear tight-fitting cotton briefs called *janghia*. Janghia are clearly phallic, not only because of their function to support and hold up the genitals, but because 'holding up the genitals' is a metaphor for celibacy and controlled passion. Janghia are designed such that they are skin-tight, and wrestlers often require the aid of one or two helpers to pull them on and tie them up. Red, which is often associated with sexual energy, is the preferred colour for janghia material. When a wrestler has won a number of bouts, and feels that he is invincible, he will take off his janghia, put one finger through a leg hole, and strut around the pit swinging it over his head. This is a universal statement that he is willing to take on any challenger. Swinging one's janghia in this manner does not happen very often. On the few occasions that I witnessed it, however, it evoked a dramatic response from those who were watching the tournament. Wrestlers I was with felt that it was a statement of extreme conceit, and were, to an appreciable extent, disturbed by the blatant disharmony and imbalanced egoism which the act implied. They were also disturbed, I think, by the powerful and not too subtle sexual symbolism of an act which almost made explicit what they were uncomfortable with on an implicit and personal level: the kinetic proclivity of seminal power to degenerate into passion.

As pointed out, wrestlers occasionally joke obliquely about the sexual implications of dands. At one regularly held, Sunday afternoon dangal in particular, numerous jokes were made at the expense of a past-his-prime wrestler who had fathered eight children. This man played the role of jester in the dangal arena and thereby helped diffuse tension. Whenever he entered the pit he would often do a quick set of fifteen or twenty dands in a kind of burlesque parody of his own physical prowess. The crowd, familiar with these antics, would respond with mock admiration. As one man put it, referring to the hapless old wrestler pumping away beside the pit: 'he has already fathered eight children, and just look, he is still going strong!' Everyone laughed uproariously. This comment brought down the house, I would argue, because it made explicit fun of an implicit set of very serious concerns.

Mother India and Dangal Politics

As intimated, some of these serious concerns about sexuality are played out in public contexts which are explicitly politicized. Dangals are almost always sponsored by political organizations such as municipal boards, village panchayats and regional parties, or highly politicized economic associations like the Jaycees (Junior Chamber of Commerce) trade unions and various affiliated merchant organizations. On many occasions local, regional and sometimes state-level politicians are invited to attend dangals in order to enhance the prestige of the organizing body. In addition to MLAs and other politicians, DFOs, BDOs, DSPs and almost anyone else who is recognized by the authority of an acronym is invited, given a seat of honour, garlanded, and asked to distribute prizes to the successful wrestlers. In other words, on one very obvious level dangals are stages upon which men grapple over the political power inherent in prestige. As everyone I asked said, a person organizes a dangal, humble or lavish, in order to publicize his name, enhance his status, and either win votes—which is often the case—or influence those who bestow favours.

For their part wrestlers almost unanimously criticize and lament the fact that competitive wrestling has become politicized in this way. In their view *rajniti*—power politics—is an inherently corrupting force which casts a shadow over competitive bouts. Although in part this has to do with the question of whether or not a bout has been fixed, the nature of what might be called rajnitic action goes much deeper. Many wrestlers feel that power politics further undermines the already precarious balance between celibate power and lust, and I think no small part of this has to do with the fact that there is a very close correlation between sex and politics whenever power is at issue. For although the wrestler's 'power' might seem to be of a different order than that of the politician, the two are, on a bio-moral level, almost identical. Both the wrestler and the politician are, ultimately, concerned with self-development, albeit by different means and with radically different objectives in mind. Where the politician is able to play himself off—metaphorically speaking—the wrestler's self-control, thus nominally taking on the bio-moral attributes of celibacy and strength, the wrestler, unfortunately, is compromised by the mechanics of a kind of political action which is, again, metaphorically speaking, akin to the agency of aggressive sex.

There are also indications, however, that the connection between politics and sex is more than metaphoric. When I spoke with many wrestlers in Banaras about their non-wrestling activities, I was often told that they did not engage in politics. Politics is inherently immoral, I was told, since it requires deceit.

Deceit agitates the body, thus contributing to the tendency of semen to flow out of the body. It is not surprising, therefore, to find that politics and wrestling only come together at the dangal where there is a great deal of ambiguity and confusion about the 'proper' relationship between power and sex.

As I have written elsewhere, the art and practice of wrestling are directly related to a kind of public critique of modern Indian politics wherein the moral, economic and administrative state of the nation is regarded as inherently corrupt. Many wrestlers claim that the nation's moral economy is thoroughly bankrupt and in need of radical reform: a kind of reform which must be effected on the level of the individual body. The basic idea is, in effect, to turn everyone into a balanced wrestler so as to root out the primary agency of corruption and rebuild the nation from the ground—or should I say semen—up. Although this connection between the sportive body and political action is often regarded by those who are prejudiced by Eurocentric rationalism as having little practical efficacy, it is a connection which makes perfect sense in terms of the wrestler's holistic concern with bio-moral balance. In the wrestlers' view there can be no distinction between ethics and exercise, and they refuse to believe that politicians can be reformed on a purely ideological level. To do good, they must embody goodness, and wrestlers, perhaps more than others, are profoundly sceptical of rhetoric and platitudes. Conversely, the agency of corruption afflicts the body, and it is for this reason that Indian wrestlers, unlike their Western European counterparts, speak the language of politics in an idiom of physical fitness. Borrowing from the lexicon of various Hindu somatic philosophies, therefore, I would argue that the blatantly politicized rajasik dangal—with all it represents in terms of aggressive individualistic hierarchy—is a primary negative inspiration for the wrestler's sattvik nationalist discourse on political reform: which brings us to Mother India.

When a dangal is finished, wrestlers quickly put on their clothes and leave, but after the vigorous routine of jor and the exertion of doing hundreds of dands and bethaks, they take a great deal of pleasure in simply sitting in the akhara earth (see image 1). This kind of relaxation, which functions to cool them down before their reintegration into public social life, is often spoken of in highly sensual terms. The wrestler and the earth are thought to exist in dramatic symbiosis such that the properties of one flow in and out of the other and many wrestlers expressed a sense of deep embodied satisfaction when describing the sensation of being covered, head to toe, with earth. In fact it can be said that when a wrestler, radiant with the energy of exercise, is enveloped by the cool, pure earth, he is able to achieve that elusive state of perfect balance towards which he strenuously strives. It will come as no surprise that akhara earth is spoken of in unambiguously maternal terms, and that when wrestlers exercise in their gymnasium, they speak of this as playing in their mother's lap. When describing the emotional pleasure of their regimen, wrestlers often use the imagery of maternal care with particular emphasis on notions of comfort, protection and security, in addition to the more obvious theme of nourishment.

From a psychoanalytic perspective it is perfectly logical for those who seek the balance of pure celibacy to recreate a non-erotic environment of maternal love. What strikes me as noteworthy, however, is that the maternal akhara is more than a subconscious fantasy. It becomes the agency of moral reform. In their critique of corruption, wrestlers often contrast the environment of modern politics with the natural environment of 'mother earth', and in this respect the akhara is regarded as the microcosm of a pure nation. Elsewhere I have elaborated on the utopian nature of this political discourse (Alter 1993), but here I would like to clearly articulate, in conclusion, what might be called the sexual politics of balanced national reform.

Although 'Mother India' has become a powerful symbol in contemporary nationalistic politics, many wrestlers subscribe to an image of Mother India which is at radical odds with the kind of xenophobic chauvinism which the popular, militant usage conveys. In the militant discourse of Hindu nationalism, Mother

India has come to represent the holy land upon which Ramraj is to be founded. It is in this regard, I think, that young militant nationalists—and conservative ideologues—feel that her virtue and purity must be aggressively defended against alien men who are not the sons of her soil. By contrast, the wrestler's conception of Mother India has very little, if anything, to do with religious ideology per se. As I have pointed out, this conception is most certainly political, but not at all concerned with ethnic, linguistic or communal issues. One reason for this is that wrestlers perceive the problem of politics as running much deeper than ideology. Moreover, for them there is a tangible, metonymic connection between earth and mother. Consequently, when they speak of Mother India they are not trying to evoke any sort of political rhetoric. That is, they are literally talking about earth as a nurturing, protective mother whose natural agency is intrinsically political to the extent that it can effect energized, celibate balance. As a result the wrestler provides a dramatically different perspective on national reform than that of the militant Hindu. From the wrestler's perspective, everyone must empower themselves—and thereby the nation—by returning to their mother's lap. But she does not need to be aggressively protected or militantly 'purified', since her virtue is substantial and all-pervasive, and not just contingently and metaphorically meaningful as in the hagiography of 'modern' traditionalism. If one may extrapolate from this, I think it is fair to say that in the view of many wrestlers, the militant Hindu attitude simply amplifies the inherent violence in all politics by calling to mind the dangerous relationship between power and sex. In this regard it is ironically logical that in contrast to akhara equipoise, and in spite of what most wrestlers wishfully say, many dangals do, in fact, degenerate into violent chaos.

Conclusion

In the Banaras area, and many other parts of northern and western India, wrestlers celebrate their art on Nag Panchami by cleaning their gymnasium, adding fresh earth to the pit, invoking the protection and blessing of Lord Hanuman and organizing dangals. Above all, however, it is on this festive occasion that wrestlers symbolically enact the more pervasive religious folk ritual in which milk is fed to snakes. As I have argued elsewhere, this ritual is saturated with sexual significance which goes well beyond the simple symbolism of seminal milk and phallic snakes (Alter 1992a: 136–66). Nevertheless, the act of feeding milk to snakes may be interpreted as the opposite of ejaculation, and, therefore, as a ritualized code for the wrestler's celibacy. It is in the context of this graphic, allegorical code that one explicitly politicized dangal in particular became dramatically problematic.

Usually dangals are organized on neutral ground, but on Nag Panchami things tend to get somewhat blurred. Akharas sponsor ceremonial 'contests' wherein it is not exactly clear whether what is going on is jor or kushti and this can lead to a great deal of confusion. At one ceremonial dangal at Akhara Bara Ganesh in Banaras, Lallu Pahalwan, the guru, had staged an elaborate affair to which a local Member of the Legislative Assembly and his retinue had been invited. The coterie of politicos were seated on a raised dais overlooking the pit and all of the senior members of the gymnasium were dressed in formal, new clothes. The pavilion was festooned with mango leaves and freshly painted with images of jumping monkeys, flowers, and wriggling snakes drinking from bowls of milk. The area around the pavilion was packed with hundreds of spectators while the younger members of the akhara were all standing in or near the pit.

When I arrived on the scene the ritual blessing of the fresh, new earth had just been completed and the dangal was about to commence. However, much to Lallu Pahalwan's obvious dismay, no one but the most junior boys seemed willing to extend a challenge. I had come with a number of the senior wrestlers from Akhara Ram Singh, a rival gymnasium. Upon seeing us, Lallu Pahalwan and some other senior personnel immediately came over and tried to get at least one of us to enter the pit and extend an open challenge. They were obviously agitated. The three wrestlers I was with seemed to be at a loss as to what to do. Finally they refused. However, the crowd closed in behind us and we soon found ourselves standing on the edge of the pit. Here Lallu Pahalwan tried to force the issue by introducing us to the MLA. At this point there was no alternative but to ritually 'salute the pit' and thereby open ourselves up to a challenge. However, no challenges were proffered, and the eager crowd began to get restless while Lallu and his cohort seemed visibly distressed. At this point, the wrestlers I was with seemed very anxious to leave, but the crowd was unrelenting. It was impossible to move. Lallu made one final effort by appealing directly to me—as a somewhat naive stranger—to put on a 'demonstration' bout with one of the senior wrestlers from Akhara Ram Singh. Fortunately, my timid hesitation was definitely overruled when those I was with told me in no uncertain terms, and obvious disgust, that we were leaving. As this chaos continued, a well-known local wrestling patron, who was also an honoured guest, stood up to the microphone and began to make a speech. As we fought our way through the crowd, I heard him commenting on how wrestling built character and instilled a sense of moral purpose among those who steadfastly committed themselves to the discipline of exercise and practice. Having previously told me of how this leading patron was a double-talking power-monger, one of the wrestlers I was with sarcastically lampooned his remarks and then, as we left the akhara, called him a mother-fucking bastard (*harami, ma chod*) under his breath.

In using this common expletive, I do not think that my wrestling friend was trying to be literal, yet in the context of Nag Panchami, where the integrated imagery of mother's milk, earth, and phallic snakes freely mix, he was, perhaps, not too far off. In any case, the events at Bara Ganesh seemed to graphically demonstrate the extent to which the ritual of politics is at odds with the drama of celibacy. One cannot, it seems, confuse akharas and dangals or kushti and jor without also confusing poison and milk.

Wrestling thus has a great deal to do with a single vector in the larger field of constituent categories: the problematic energy associated with sexuality. For the wrestler the trick is to harness the latent and potential energy of sexuality without igniting the fire of passion: to become super virile but to remain absolutely celibate. Exercise in general, and practice wrestling in particular, contribute to the production of semen and the maintenance of a fluid balance in terms of both somatic and semiotic codes. The akhara, regarded as the substantive essence of mother earth, maintains this fluid balance and also defines the geopolitical parameters of a pristine, elemental maternal state. In this regard the dangal is a dystopic drama of classical, masculine hierarchy in which sex and politics threaten to undermine the integrity of both embodied balance and celibate action.

Vajikarana. Dangal Poster, 1930s.

Dwipitapashu—Hawaii Nude Yoga Retreat: Jared Sam in Downward Dog (*adhomukha shvanasana*). Dennis Dehler in Reclining Warrior (*suptavirasana*). Photographer: Michael Salita

5

Uninhibited Modifications of the Mind
Yoga, Sex and the Politics of Knowledge

Yoga is the inhibition of the modifications of the mind.
(*The Yoga Sutras of Patanjali* 1:2. I. K. Taimni's translation)

Kama is the enjoyment of appropriate objects by the five senses
of hearing, feeling, seeing, tasting, and smelling, assisted by the
mind together with the soul. The ingredient in this is a peculiar
contact between the organ of sense and its object, and the
conscious pleasure that arises from that contact. (*The Kama Sutra
of Vatsyayan*, 24. Sir Richard F. Burton's translation)

Orientation

The question of who controls knowledge, and what counts
as control, is both a quintessentially contemporary question
that shapes the reality of postcolonial understanding and
intellectual history, as well as a problem at the heart of yoga.
Since the body is also at the heart of yoga—as a problem and a
fluid point of orientation—this chapter engages the politics of
postcolonial knowledge with reference to the moral materialism
of embodied action.

In January 2004 the Bhandarkar Oriental Research Institute
in Pune was attacked by a group of angry, violent men. The men
were reacting to what they regarded as a gross mischaracterization

of Shivaji, the great seventeenth-century Maratha king, and the alleged complicity of the BORI in this academic transgression. While the incident is undoubtedly complicated and, in its own way, a call to arms, it raises a simple question that extends beyond the reverberation of opposition: What is the relationship between perception, representation and truth; between the mind at work and the objects it works upon? In relation to the answer to this question, what is truth and true knowledge?

Violence—encompassing both hatred and sorrow born from the delusion of compassion—is an act of extreme reification. As such it is like sex. The *Gita* links them together on a number of different levels, and anchors both in the nature of the body. Among other things, violence and sex produce the illusion that, at an opposite extreme from the embodied act, there is an ideal moral and ethical standpoint based on experience and value: perfect celibacy and non-violence as against absolute, unrestrained lust and violence. Both directly and through contrast, violence produces nothing but the delusion of value in fact; lust, nothing but desire; illusions of definitive truth based on discrimination mirrored in contrast.

> When a man lacks lust and hatred
> His renunciation does not waver.
> He neither longs for one thing
> Nor loathes its opposite:
> The chains of his delusion
> Are soon cast off. (*Bhagavad Gita* 5:3)

Another way to this understanding, expressed in Sri Krishna's response to Arjun's confusion, is captured in the relationship between two representations of history that correspond to the question of lust and hatred within a rubric of sex and masculinity: Chandrashekhar Azad, freedom fighter and militant revolutionary, as he is made to look in the image at the end of this chapter, and the bloody image of Chandrashekhar Azad's dead body—as well as his body in fact—as it was put on public display in 1931 by the British police after a violent confrontation in Alfred Park, Allahabad.

Although the history of yoga is a relatively innocuous topic, at least when compared to the events of 2004 in Pune and 1931 in Allahabad—or any other Kurukshetra, for that matter—there are powerful groups and institutions that have a significant stake, both in terms of financial investment and professional reputation, in representing yoga as a timeless icon of Indic civilization, and in representing the truth about yoga with reference to enlightenment in general and the enlightenment of certain sages in particular. Therefore, pointing out, in the grounded tradition of Lokayata scepticism—and with hubris that extends across space and time— that Transcendental Reality does not exist, that enlightenment is a product of the human imagination, and that the truth about yoga is in the multiple histories of that imagination at work in the material world, can be perceived of as a threat and can incite violence. Alternatively, on a battlefield where the enemy is a close cousin, where the pursuit of academic knowledge is akin to the politics of ashram enlightenment, one can all too easily become confused and lose heart.

While being a purely academic question, the problem of representation and truth is also, in essence, a question at the centre of yoga: both in the most abstract sense as well as in the more specific manifestation of a discourse on violence and reality at the heart of the *Gita*. The problem is perception and misperception. The question is how to know truth. The answer to the question—both academic and yogic—is through detachment: through selfless action. Action is the answer.

The problem addressed in the *Gita*, allegorized across many planes of experience, is about being seduced by the warp of illusion and by the question of whether to act or not act in terms of the self interest of righteousness and its fruits: to confuse the pursuit of knowledge—which is a moral duty—with the reflections of definitive, imperative truth in the modifications of the mind. The *Gita* provides a solution to the paradox of righteousness;

and the lesson of this solution has implications for social theory, as theory charts a course of action in knowledge. It is a lesson that has been calcified in the disinterested objectivism of battle-hardened science, but that also takes shape in the recursive logic of intellectual discrimination born of other duties: knowledge of what is real in relation to what is not, recognizing that what is real is always reflected in that which is not.

In a word—and in relation to the way in which the fact of violence makes illusion transparent—academic research is its own best defence against ignorance; although it will rarely, if ever, function as a defence against specific individuals and groups. I realize that this does not address a number of problematic issues, such as ethical responsibility to individual informants: to all relations on the battlefield. It relies, perhaps too heavily, on the kind of vindication that only a very long stretch of history can provide. As such it does not provide a ready answer to the question of how to respond to the kind of direct confrontation that some of my fellow academics have faced. Nor does it provide specific insight on how academic institutions should respond to the politics of self-interested intellectual nationalism. But it does provide a solid, proactive point of reference for the formulation of answers to the sorrow born of the doubt in these very questions.

Having foregrounded—and resolved, at least within the fluctuating modifications of my own mind—some issues in the politics of knowledge, what I would like to do is simply engage in some critical thinking about yoga and the modern history of its development in relation to sex and sexuality.

Sex, like violence, is intimately linked to morality and character—of individuals, groups and 'civilizations'—thus making the question of yoga's relationship to sex a more fraught political issue than the question of yoga's relationship to other things. In any case at the outset it must be made very clear that sex—and the problem of sex in relation to the body—is what yoga is all about. This is not a matter of interpretation, psychological or otherwise. It is not allegorical. Yoga is concerned with the problematic literalism of sex, sexual fluids and the relationship between sex, death and immortality that is woven into the structure of embodied guna.

Yoga as Such

Yoga is an interesting phenomenon for a number of reasons. First, it is a form of embodied philosophical practice that has come to signify the profundity and historical depth of Indic civilization, both in the popular imagination as well as in many encyclopaedias and reference works. Second, it portends the ways and means of Universal Truth, and is therefore cognate with religion. Third, although cognate with religious belief and practice, enlightenment—the realization of Universal Truth—is an experience that is not dependent on God; it is thought to be the natural expression of our true, organic nature. Fourth, yoga remains inherently mysterious and arcane, even when putatively demystified and subject to rational, objective exposition. Fifth, and finally, yoga has become a virtual *sine qua non* of postmodern globalization, being open to almost endless, radically divergent, dislocated interpretations. In many ways the unassailable esoteric nature of yoga is what makes it good grist for the mill of globalization. Mystery, almost by definition, invites constant, multidimensional interpretation, and *arcanum* has endless market value. However, there is latent tension in how the scope and breadth of globalization relates to history, and specifically to the kind of history that evokes, in various ways, Indic civilization.

Given the fact that yoga is both archaic and postmodern, but also given that it must have a history—or various histories—of development and change through time, how does one articulate a general truth about yoga, other than the somewhat evasive—and politically problematic—academic truism that there are multiple truths. The position of radical relativism in which all roads of interpretation lead away from Rome to diverse points of equivalent meaningfulness is not very insightful, interesting or imaginative.

One way to approach the problem of critical generalization is to take a set of radically divergent interpretations and work towards a synthesis. For example in *Yoga: Immortality and Freedom* (1990) Mircea Eliade declares unambiguously—and with the backing of 364 pages of text, 65 pages of notes and 800 sources—that the practice of yoga should never be 'confused' with physical fitness and gymnastics. B. K. S. Iyengar has made a career precisely—and strategically—out of this confusion. His book *Light on Yoga* (1993) documents, in 544 pages supported by over 600 photographs of him doing yoga, how one can achieve perfection in the athletic performance of asana and pranayama.

One could say that one of these men is right and the other wrong; that they are both wrong—which is a classic academic move—or that they are both right, just talking in different ways about different kinds of yoga being practised in different contexts. In conjunction with this, however, there is the problem that Eliade is, among other things, a Western academic, and Iyengar is, among other things, a Brahmin disciple of an iconic adept with tangible skills whose training in yoga is based on years and years of practice. They both speak with authority, but with very different kinds of authority, and, for the most part, to different audiences. This compounds—and politicizes—the problem of generalization.

A contingent solution—to deploy another standard academic move—is to make the question more interesting and focus on the categorization of experience: What is physical fitness, as different from something else, and why is it such a contentious issue in the history of yoga? To answer this entails deconstructing Eliade's bias, which reflects deeply entrenched ideas—going back to athletic philosophy and the moral problem early Christians had with skanky Greek gymnasiums—about the unequal and disarticulated relationship of body to mind. It also entails historicizing Iyengar's practice within the framework of a larger history in which yoga is understood to be a reflection, both physical and metaphysical, of the desire for immortality and freedom, and not a manifestation of immortality and freedom as such.

Having elsewhere examined the question of physical and metaphysical fitness (Alter 2004, 2007b), I would like to focus here on radically divergent, contradictory interpretations of sex and sexuality in the practice of yoga, so as to both reflect on the politics of knowledge—who makes what kinds of claims, why and on the basis of what authority—as well as to problematize sex and sexuality.

Sex as Such in Relation to Yoga

The two contradictory positions are 1) that practitioners of yoga should not engage in sex, and that the practice of hatha yoga helps to promote celibacy; and 2) that the practice of yoga increases virility, promotes sexual pleasure and should be engaged in to this end (Filliozat 1991: 327–339).

For some readers this will immediately bring to mind a modern classic in the field: *Asceticism and Eroticism in the Mythology of Siva* (1973). In this book O'Flaherty points out that Lord Shiva embodies a paradox. He is the paradigmatic ascetic and iconic yogi, completely chaste and free of desire, and yet also passion incarnate and the deified essence of virility. One of the clearest and most powerful symbols of the paradox is Lord Shiva's erect phallus, which symbolizes both the ascetic retention of semen as well as impassioned, unbridled eroticism (1973: 9).

Following O'Flaherty's argument it would be possible to bring my analysis to a quick, unceremonious and simpering conclusion: yoga is as Maha Yogi does. But there is a problem. Quite apart from whether or not it 'really works', yoga does not resolve into symbolism, nor is it governed by the logic and structure of mythology. It is a form of practice, and this grounds it in the temporal domain of experience, in the material world of the senses, and ultimately in history.[1] A dynamic, meaningful and powerful paradox in the Pine Forest hermitage (see Doniger 1973) is a problematic contradiction in everyday life.

One position, arguably the most defensible, is the claim that the practice of yoga must be based on celibacy. In the scheme of *ashtanga* practice, brahmacharya is counted as the fourth of the five principles of restraint. There are numerous references in texts ranging from the classical to the early modern and modern period that define brahmacharya as abstinence from sexual activity. Based on this Eliade points out that:

> The practice of these restraints . . . does not result in a specifically yogic state, but in a 'purified' human state, higher than that of common humanity. This purity is necessary for the later stages. Through it, one suppresses one's egoistic tendencies; through it one creates new centres of experience. Sexual abstinence is practised to the end of conserving nervous energy. Yoga attaches the greatest importance to these 'secret forces of the generative faculty', which, when they are expended, dissipate the most precious energy, debilitate mental capacity, and make concentration difficult. (1990: 50)

In physiological terms brahmacharya represents the most general logic of yoga philosophy and practice: cessation, the end of transformation and the embodiment of immortality. Semen is understood as central to both physiological transformation and aging as well as procreation and the flow of existence through time from birth to death. Reversing the flow, through breath control, transforms semen into the nectar of immortality. As David White explains,

[1] There are also other, somewhat tangential problems that cannot be explored here but are important to keep in mind. Primarily, what is the historical relationship of yoga as such to Shiva as a deity, given that the former ante-dates a large percentage of art and literature associated with the latter? When do their paths cross, so to speak?

In *hatha yoga*, the principle motor behind the transformations of mundane semen into divine nectar of immortality—and of mundane mind (*manas*) to a state beyond mind (*unmana*)—is a pneumatic one . . . When the breath is stable, mind and semen are stabilized; but more important, when, through breath control (*pranayama*) the base of the medial channel is opened, the same breath causes the reversal of mundane polarities. Rather than descending, semen, energy and mind are now forced upward into the cranial vault, effecting total yogic integration (*samadhi*), a reversal of the flow of time, immortality and transcendence over the entire universe. (1996: 45)

Thus celibacy is a powerful metaphor, an essential technique as well as the agency of an extremely vital, elemental substance. To be celibate both represents and produces immortality.

A second position on the relationship of sex and sexuality to the practice of yoga finds expression in the tantric literature dealing with *maithuna* or so-called ritual sexual intercourse where the yogin and the yogini engage in the cosmic act of creation. The logic of maithuna is closely linked to the physiological logic of yoga, except for the fact that sex is enacted in order to reverse the flow. As Eliade put its:

We must not forget that *maithuna* is never allowed to terminate in an emission of semen: *bodhicittam notsrjet*, 'the semen must not be emitted', the texts repeat. Otherwise the yogin falls under the law of time and death, like any common libertine. In these practices, 'sensual pleasure' plays the part of a 'vehicle', for it produces the maximum tension that abolishes normal consciousness and inaugurates the nirvanic state, *samarasa*, the paradoxical experience of Unity. As we have seen earlier, *samarasa* is obtained by the 'immobilization' of breath, thought and semen. (1990: 268)

Clearly this is a very cryptic, thumbnail sketch of a ritual with many possible meanings based on forms of practice that can only be superficially glossed as 'mystical eroticism'. Beyond this, there is a rich and elaborate history associated with the role of the yogini in tantric rituals, as these rituals are specifically concerned with the flow, mixing and consumption of male and female sexual fluids (White 2003). However, the question of ejaculation is critical. In the hatha yoga literature there is a technique, alluded to by Eliade, called *vajroli mudra* whereby semen is, in fact, ejaculated, mixed with rajas, and then reabsorbed both by the yogin and yogini (see White 2003: 82, 215; Feuerstein 1998: 233–34). This takes the logic of reversal past the point of orgasm, and effects a more complete conjunction of opposites than is achieved in the form of the ritual referred to by Eliade. In any case, what remains most important is the logic of reversal, union and immobilization as linked to sexual fluid as it flows both within and between bodies.

In *Kiss of the Yogini*, David Gordon White provides a detailed analysis of ritualized sex in the mediaeval period, and in *Tantra: Sex, Secrecy, and Power in the Study of Religion* (2003) Hugh Urban writes about the modern discourse of sexuality in the Orientalist scholarship on South Asia. Both of these works provide critical perspectives that are relevant to understanding the relationship between yoga and sex at different points in time. Based on White's argument there would seem to be no question but that hatha yoga developed between the ninth and fourteenth centuries as a form of practice directly linked to the subtle hydraulics and symbolic significance of ritualized sex. Asana and pranayama are not very often mentioned explicitly in the context of maithuna, but the two domains are clearly linked together in terms of contextual overlap.

Although the historical development of hatha yoga from roughly the fourteenth century to the twentieth is difficult to trace, it is clear that by the early twentieth century there was concerted effort by a number of different reformers to dissociate the practice of asana and pranayama from sex and magic, which simply underscores the probable association beyond the purview of modernist reform. Nevertheless, hatha yoga also has a history of development in which asana and pranayama are linked to health and healing on the one hand and physical fitness and martial arts on the other. Much more research needs to be done on the history of this development over the past eight or nine hundred years, but at the very least it can be said that it is a history in which the meaning, significance and expression of sex has been subject to twisted logic.

Shifting from a mediaeval to a modern and postmodern frame of reference, Urban's analysis shows how the exotic, erotic spirituality of tantrism influences the discourse on sexual liberation and self-realization. With respect to tantra—mediaeval or New Age—sex is a constituent element of practice. That is, it goes without saying that tantra involves sex. Thus Urban can take it for granted that sexuality is central to Pierre Bernard's Tantric Order in America, Alister Crowley's sex magic, and Omar Garrison's *Tantra: The Yoga of Sex* (1964). Similarly his analysis of Chogyam Trungpa, Swami Muktananda and Bhagwan Shri Rajneesh focuses on the way in which they exploit sex.

My concern is with a closely related but somewhat more problematic case, since it involves a discourse on sex in practice that is fraught with contradiction and elision. It involves a very specific genre of literature: self-help books that seek to show how asana and pranayama can improve sex (Antiyappan 2001; Chetananda 1977; Haich 1972; Jacquemart and Elkéfi 1992; Kapur 1977; Lalvani 1997; Moore and Douglas 1970; Noelle 2003; Volin and Phelan 1967). This literature must be interpreted in the context of a far more pervasive popular literature in which asana and pranayama are explicitly dissociated from sex and sexuality.

In the early twentieth century a number of individuals in India began to experiment with the techniques of hatha yoga and demonstrated that these techniques had clearly defined health benefits and were not mystical and arcane or associated with magic and occult sexuality. Men such as Swami Kuvalayananda and Shri Yogendra (see Alter 2004, 2007a) followed in line with Swami Vivekananda's attempt to sanitize and modernize Hinduism (Alter 2006), but focused almost exclusively on the practice of asana and pranayama. To some extent Kuvalayananda and Yogendra had to work against the larger, more pervasive discourse of tantrism, which so easily encompassed—and 'tainted'—all forms of yoga, both in India and elsewhere. Yogendra in particular travelled to the United States in the early 1920s where he actively engaged with the moral discourse on muscular Christianity and developed his own brand of simplified asana physical education in direct opposition to the teachings of Pierre Bernard, Alister Crowley and other self-proclaimed practitioners of tantric yoga (Alter 2006). Part of the problem faced by the early advocates of asana and pranayama as 'good clean' physical fitness was that the mediaeval literature on hatha yoga—which was being translated and published at about the same time—invokes sex and sexuality rather explicitly, although in complicated ways.

In any event, Kuvalayananda and Yogendra were tremendously successful, and it is possible to trace, from about 1920 up to the present, the development of an ever-expanding form of yoga that is almost—but not quite—secular, and concerned with the promotion of holistic health, psychological fitness and general well being. Most of this kind of yoga is based on the physical performance of asana and pranayama supported by a loosely configured philosophy that emphasizes peace, purity, nonviolence and self-discipline. In this context the principle of brahmacharya serves a vital function in the moral discourse of yogic practice—the perfect counter to swirling scandal associated with secret orgies, 'filthy' rituals and the exploitation of credulous disciples by perverted god-men. In other words, the history of hatha yoga's normalization in the twentieth century is closely linked to the construction of celibacy as a moral ideal.

One of the most outspoken early proponents of celibacy and hatha yoga was Swami Sivananda who founded the Divine Life Society (DLS) in Rishikesh. His writing on the subject fits directly into a genre of literature on celibacy in general that grew rapidly and was closely associated with nationalism and masculinity from 1920 onwards (Gupta 2002: 69–72). Although Swami

Sivananda was, quite obviously, concerned with questions of spirituality, his teachings on asana and pranayama are in keeping with the general twentieth-century trend towards secularization and demystification. However, his synthesis of hatha yoga and Vedanta within the framework of the DLS—itself inspired by Vivekananda's Ramakrishna Mission—established a model for the development of a number of other organizations that have sought to combine the practice of postural yoga with meditation and spirituality (see DeMichelis 2004). It should be pointed out that organizations that fit this model, such as Swami Rama's Himalayan Institute, the Bharatiya Yog Sansthan and Swami Gitananda's Ananda Ashram in Pondicherry are significantly different from the ones established by Bhagwan Shri Rajneesh and Swami Muktananda—as well as those associated with Aurobindo and Vivekananda—insofar as they are based on the practice of hatha yoga and tend to emphasize the importance of celibacy. Despite the tantric orientation of its founder Swami Satyananda Saraswati—who was Sivananda's disciple—the Bihar School of Yoga also reflects the model of the Divine Life Society with a similar perspective on the importance of brahmacharya.

Although clearly having a spiritual orientation, it is also important to note that the publications of the Divine Life Society, the Himalayan Institute, the Bihar School of Yoga and Ananda Ashram all reflect the way in which hatha yoga has been linked to health and healing since the turn of the century. In this context celibacy is understood to reflect good sexual health and fitness. The principle of vitality and vigour expressed in the classical literature—*brahmacarya-pratisthayam virya-labhah*, as Patanjali puts it (II:38)—is translated into a discourse in which celibacy does not so much aid in the practice of asana and pranayama as take on discrete physiological importance in the context of self development. In these terms it fits into a conservative modern discourse on the dangers of venery, in particular masturbation.

It is in the context of these developments that I would like to consider a small book first published in 1973 called *Yoga and Sex*. The primary author is Pandit Shiv Sharma, probably one of the most well-known Ayurvedic physicians in India and a vocal advocate for a purist tradition of indigenous medical practice from the 1930s through to the early 1980s. In his view Ayurveda is a science unto itself and should not be subject to Western scientific testing. Between 1938 when he was elected president of the All India Ayurvedic Congress and his death in 1982, Sharma dominated the debate on how Ayurveda would be taught and practised. In 1967 he was elected to Parliament and ultimately 'had himself appointed as Chairman of the Ministry [of Health's] Central Council for Research on Indigenous Medicine, and dominated national policy through the 1970s' (Leslie 1992: 182–183). He was, obviously, a very powerful man, who spoke with a great deal of authority. As Charles Leslie has pointed out, Pandit Shiv Sharma was also an interesting and complex character whose advocacy for traditionalism was as much a function of his modern, cosmopolitan orientation and lifestyle as it was a function of his knowledge of, and faith in, the classical medical literature (1992: 182). This paradox is clearly reflected in *Yoga and Sex*, as well as other texts of this genre, to the extent that it begs the critical question of relativism: at what point does an authoritative cultural construction such as Shiv Sharma's stop making sense?

Sharma clearly states in the introduction that *Yoga and Sex* was written in response to the so-called sexual revolution of the late 1960s and 1970s. As far as I have been able to determine it was the first book in what has subsequently become a discrete sub-genre describing how to perform asana and pranayama in order to increase sexual stamina, potency and pleasure—a fact that would certainly have Sivananda rolling over in his *samadhi*.

Although Shiv Sharma's book provides a description and discussion of thirty different postures and techniques—as distinct from 'positions', although we will get to those as well—and provides a point-on-point analysis of the sexual benefit of each, it also contains a lengthy introduction in which yoga sexuality is theorized. The book is a wonderful example of how meaning can be logically manipulated and, in the context of the larger body of literature on yoga, forces a key question in the politics of knowledge—must we take Sharma seriously?

Before taking this question on directly, it should be noted that apart from Sivananda's conservative position, echoed by a large number of writers on the subject, there are others who, for various reasons, have taken a less rigid position on the question of celibacy. Here the best example is probably B. K. S. Iyengar. In the introduction to his book *Light on Yoga*, first published in 1966, Iyengar provides a commentary on each of the branches of ashtanga yoga and says the following about brahmacharya.

> It is thought that the loss of semen leads to death and its retention to life. By the preservation of semen the yogi's body develops a sweet smell. So long as it is retained, there is no fear of death. (1993: 34)

So far, so good. But then Iyengar changes registers. Citing Shankaracharya he defines *brahmacharya* in strictly etymological terms that elide the question of sex—'the self-discipline by means of which one realizes Brahman'. Following this he writes:

> Brahmacharya has little to do with whether one is a bachelor or married and living the life of a householder . . . It is not necessary for one's salvation to stay unmarried and without a house . . . Without experiencing human love and happiness, it is not possible to know divine love. Almost all the yogis and sages of old in India were married men with families of their own. They did not shirk their social and moral responsibilities. Marriage and parenthood are no bar to the knowledge of divine love, happiness and union with the Supreme Soul. (1993: 34–35)

Iyengar combines the etymological definition of brahmacharya with reference to the final verse in the *Sivasamhita* which states that a 'lordly householder' can even achieve success in yoga provided he practises in secret and has no attachment to his wife, his children or his duties. It is relevant to note that the *Sivasamhita* provides the primary reference for the 'sweet smell' of the yogi's body (III:29), and also points out—in terms that will become even more relevant as we consider Sharma's discourse on sexuality—that that practice of yoga produces a 'strong appetite, good digestion, cheerfulness, a handsome figure, great courage, mighty enthusiasm and full strength.' (III: 32).

Lest all of this be given too liberal an interpretation, the verse immediately following states, unambiguously, that yogis must renounce the companionship of women (III:33) and later that women are one among a long list of 'worldly enjoyments'—such as beds, dainty dishes, dancing, singing and riding on elephants and horses—that are impediments to practice (V: 3). It says nothing about men keeping company with men—except in the general sense of 'renouncing all company' (V: 184), but my guess is that this reflects an unconscious heterosexual bias.

In any case, Iyengar articulates what might be called a moderate position on brahmacharya that locates practice in the home, leaving unanswered the question of how to reconcile love and happiness with the sickly smell of post-coital fear-and-trembling-that-leads-to-death. This is important to keep in mind because it helps to illustrate two points: the way in which renouncing sex invokes sexuality and the highly problematic logic of compromise.

Pandit Shiv Sharma is uncompromising in his logic of absolute synthesis:

> Yoga elevates and spiritualizes sex itself. The added ecstasy of the spirituality attained through Yoga much enhances the physical thrill of sex. The orgasmic explosion is intensified and post-coital tranquillity acquires an element of the divine. (1991: 8)

Sharma does not try to avoid the obvious problem with which he is faced when making this claim. He states, directly, that his book is not written for those who have chosen the rigid and austere path of 'renunciation, asceticism and transcendentalism' (1991: 11). However, the claims he makes for a productive synthesis of yoga and sex are clearly argued in terms that take yoga seriously and reflect a great deal of knowledge about its practice. His overarching argument is that yoga and sex are, in fact, analogous. Beginning from a point of etymological kinship—the word 'yoga' is derived from the root 'yuj' which means to join and is found in the word *samyojnam* which means sexual intercourse—Sharma points out that when practised properly, both yoga and sex produce pure love, oneness, truth and spirituality, as well as longevity, alertness, radiant health, contentment, serenity and tranquillity (1991: 13).

Within the bracket of this arch, Sharma structures the logic of his synthesis of sex and yoga with reference to two arguments. First, yoga produces mental strength, emotional maturity and self-control, which allows for uninhibited sexual expression. Second, on a more explicitly physiological plane, the performance of asana and pranayama improves the function of the nervous system and effectively harmonizes the relationship between sympathetic and parasympathetic actions, and between the involuntary nervous system and the somatic nervous system.

The coordination between the sympathetic and parasympathetic actions is understood to be particularly important since the latter, connecting from the lower lumbar through the pelvic nerve, is responsible for producing dilation of the sex organs and maintaining vasocongestion, and the former, connecting from between the twelfth thoracic and the third lumbar through the lumbar splanchnic nerve, is responsible for ejaculation and the rhythmic contractions that produce an orgasm, this being a relatively exceptional case in which the two systems work in synch.[2] The location of nerve centres along the spine is important

[2] The terms 'erection' and 'ejaculation' tend to be used in much of the popular literature, but the physiology of sexual arousal is largely the same regardless of how the genitals are configured by the structure and ratio of chromosomes.

since the performance of asana and pranayama is thought to exercise these centres in very specific ways. One of the results, to use an example that once again raises the problematic question of relativism, is heightened sensuality.

> Masturbation can relieve tensions arising from apparently non-sexual causes, but Yoga can almost always play this role just as well. It can safely be said that Yoga will, in the first place, divert the mind from masturbation, and that masturbation, when wanted and carried out, will be more pleasant as the orgasm will be comparatively more ecstatic in a body made healthy by Yoga where the tissues are bound to be more alive and responsive. (1991: 24)

How the subtle physiology of *nadi* conduits is linked to the gross physiology—but unconscious action—of the autonomic nervous system is a subject that has concerned a large number of people interested in secularizing, modernizing and medicalizing yoga, foremost among whom was Vasant G. Rele. In the late 1920s, he was probably the first person to correlate the *sushumna* nadi with the vegus nerve and *chakra* centres with the spinal nerve plexuses. His book *The Mysterious Kundalini: The Physical Basis of the 'Kundali(Hatha)yoga' in Terms of Western Anatomy and Physiology*, published in 1927, is still in print. Although most research conducted in India since the 1930s does not posit a simple or direct correlation between the chakras and the plexuses, the visual model that was first developed by Rele has powerful popular appeal and persuasive force. Given that they overlap almost exactly in anatomical space with the sympathetic and parasympathetic nerve plexuses associated with the sex organs, the *muladhara* and *svadhisthana* chakras take on specific significance.

Following on this Sharma develops an argument whereby techniques that are used to control the urge for sex are used to develop sexual control and fitness by exercising—in one way or another—the two chakra centres. This is clearly stated in his discussion of the benefits of each of the asanas described in the book, but is most clearly apparent in two asanas: *Stambhanasana*, translated by Sharma as the 'semen retention pose' and *Goraksasana*. With regard to *Stambhanasana* Sharma writes:

> Yogic experts are unanimous in their praise of this Asana as being very effective in toning up the sex centres. It is therefore practised by both the recluse for the effective sublimation of the sex urge and by the family man for the strengthening of the sex centres for better sexual performance.
>
> The pose also tends to control morbid, excessive sexual desires bordering on mania and helps counter the deleterious effects of sexual excesses . . . It is considered the best Asana for the cure of premature ejaculation and the thinness of seminal fluid. The regular practitioners of this Asana will notice that it thickens the consistency of the seminal fluid . . . In general it improves the tone of the entire body and is equally beneficial for the male and female. (1991: 83)

In the case of the *Goraksasana* the physiological manipulation of the chakra centres is more obvious, but the effect exactly the same. Here the heels of the feet are turned under and behind the genitals so that they press upwards on the perineum. It is used by adepts to control the urge for sex, but can be used to promote sexual fitness, stamina and control to the end of giving greater, longer-lasting pleasure and producing 'strong, healthy, intelligent' progeny.

As David White has shown, the so-called chakra system of subtle physiology has a complex history of development that has been open to numerous interpretations, but since the eighth century one relatively common line of interpretation clearly links all the chakras to sex and sexuality through symbolic association with yoginis and the serpent power of *kundalini*. As he puts it,

> [T]he phallic emblem of Siva, the lingam, is often sculpted with a coiled serpent around its base, whose spread hood serves as its canopy. This is a particularly evocative image when one recalls

that the *kundalini* is figured in the classical hathayogic sources as sleeping coiled three and a half times around the internal lingam, with her head or mouth covering its tip. When the yogi awakens her through his practice of postures and breath control, she pierces the lower door to the medial *susumna* channel and 'flies' upward to the place of Siva in the cranial vault. (2003: 233–234)

It is important to note, however, that White begins the analysis that leads up to this conclusion with reference to the inherently magical nature of yoga, and the concern of mediaeval yoginis with 'supernatural enjoyment' (2003: 220). The literalization of kundalini in the vegus nerve and her 'deflection' through the sympathetic and parasympathetic nerve plexuses linked to erection and ejaculation at the *svadhisthana* chakra is, if not magical, most certainly an interesting twist.

It is interesting to note that although Sharma firmly advocates the free and open expression of sexuality, his book is not very graphic. It is, in fact, very clinical in terms of describing how to perform asanas and then discussing the benefits of each. It is also virtually impossible to 'read' eroticism into the format of presentation in which a man with long hair, a long beard and wearing tight shorts, and a woman in a bikini with neatly tied-up hair—are pictured on opposite, facing pages performing the same asana. Nevertheless, Sharma makes passing reference to an issue that has, subsequently, become an erotic icon in books on yoga and sex. After briefly commenting on the way in which boredom can undermine the desire for sex, he points out that:

[t]he Kamasanas (different sexual postures) are analogous to the Yogasanas. Some physicians advise middle-aged couples to avoid attempting different sexual positions as they may lead to spraining of muscles, but the problem would not arise in the case of people already accustomed to Yogic positions. (1991: 25)

In the modern imagination kamasana and yogasana come together in the performance of the iconic *yub-yam* or Shiva-Shakti 'postural position' of sexual intercourse: Shiva with *linga* erect seated in a cross-legged asana with his consort seated on his lap with her legs entwined behind his back. And here it is possible to identify a number of subtle shifts in signification that directly extend the slippery logic of sexual control and the control of sex into the domain of athletic intercourse.

As one might guess, in the contemporary literature this allows for advocates of yoga and sex to embrace and interpret the *Kama Sutra*, particularly the chapter dealing with coital positions. If you do an image search on Google for yoga and sex you will see what I mean. One, reflecting homoerotic posturing, appears at the beginning of this chapter as image six.

Ellen Barrett, a very well-known yoga trainer, has published a book entitled *Sexy Yoga: 40 Poses for Mind-Blowing Sex and Greater Intimacy*. After describing and interpreting the location and importance of the 'root' and 'sacral' chakras, she writes:

> Blend the study of the *Kama Sutra* and the practice of hatha yoga and voila—Sexy Yoga is born. Not only is it stunning how relevant the 2000 year old love manual is in today's world—it is fascinating how similar the sexual positions are to yoga postures . . . [M]any of the advanced sexual positions illustrated in the *Kama Sutra*—with their extreme flexibility and body awareness—could never be realized without a steady yoga practice. (2005: 10–11)

Her book then illustrates how a man and a woman can have intercourse while performing specific yoga, or yoga-inspired, postures: man in *ustrasana* woman in *halasana*; man in *shavasana* woman in *virasana*; man in *padmasana* woman in *gorksasana*, and so forth. Barrett's blending of the *Kama Sutra* and hatha yoga is based on an assumption that the athleticism of the former—reflected in Khajuraho and Konarak temple sculpture—is entirely dependent on the practice of the later.

This raises the obvious historical question.

If one dates the emergence and development of hatha yoga to the five-hundred-year period between the eighth and twelfth centuries, and note that Orissa is proximate to those areas of eastern South Asia where the Natha Siddhas are said to have been active, it is conceivable that the practice of asana may have inspired coital intercourse techniques depicted in temple art such as that of the thirteenth-century Sun Temple at Konarak. However intriguing, the evidence is circumstantial, coincidental and equivocal. To the best of my knowledge the first modern interpretation along these lines was made by Kanwar Lal in his book *The Cult of Desire: An Interpretation of the Erotic Sculpture of India* (1967).

A critical problem with this line of reasoning has to do with terminology. In the literature on sex, coital positions—as distinct from intercourse—are called *ratibandha* not *kamasana*. As far as can be ascertained, kamasana is a seductive neologism. The root '*bandha*' is used in hatha yoga to signify so-called locks in which prana is forcibly held at chakra centres before being channelled in various ways. In an extended sense the control of sexual fluids and their strategic ejaculation during intercourse fits with the lock-and-release structure of pranayama. But the problem of terminology also extends to postures.

One might look at the temple art at Konarak and assume that if a man is standing on his head having intercourse with one woman while fondling two others that he is performing a *sirsasana* or headstand posture. However, without accurate terminology describing this particular form of *utthita sanghataka maithuna*—standing group sex—sirsasana is not a sirsasana by any other name. A headstand or any other posture becomes an asana only in the context of hatha yoga; beyond that any formal correspondence is purely coincidental. Moreover, as Alex Comfort points out, in a wonderfully laconic introduction to the *Koka Shastra*, 'I have yet to see an Indian posture-book which exactly corresponds with literary erotology' (1964: 48). So a bandha is no more a bandha by any other name either. When you get right down to it, there is only a very superficial correspondence between the graphic temple art and asana techniques—both involve twisting the body into somewhat 'unnatural' positions.

Focusing on the erotics of sexual athleticism, Barrett's book connects two different tangents in the historical development of hatha yoga, one mediaeval and the other quite modern: sexuality and athleticism.

But this is not at all to say that there was no relationship between the elements of these tangents at some earlier point in time; just that the connection is probably not manifest in what would seem to be most obvious—the twisting and turning of bodies. Rather the connection is most directly manifest in the symbolism of sex, and the way in which the iconography invokes tantric principles in general and the ritual of yogini sex in particular. Comfort—whose interpretation may not be quite accurate in its one-replaces-the-other logic—points out that there is a discernable historical development from the erotic iconography in Sakta and Pashupata shrines through to later Orissan mediaeval architecture. His conclusion points to a direct historical connection, but probably overstates the extent of change:

> Hand in hand with this the ritual erotism, as we see it depicted, has more to do with love and pleasure and less with magic and ascetic practice—instead of esoteric and ferocious it becomes joyous and popular. (1964: 50)

In any case, Comfort's position is that the 'sexual Golden Age' to which all of the erotic literature refers must predate 'tantric sexual yoga' because the literature 'contains no reference to its chief doctrine, the "absorption" of energy from women while avoiding ejaculation' (1964: 51).

Oriented as it is towards tantric ritual rather than eroticism as a literary genre, David White's interpretation is probably more accurate (2003: 140). He acknowledges that the libertine kings and feudal chiefs of the twelfth century were concerned with sex for the sake of pleasure, but that a close reading of the erotic scenes—which depict 'condemned poses' such as *rajapana* and orgiastic scenes with ascetic preceptors (see also Lal 1967)—seems to indicate that a ritual component extended well into the so-called 'sexual Golden Age', even though tantric *sadhaka*s ought not to be confused with the *nayaka* dandies described by Vatsyayana. In any case, the *ratishastra* literature read in conjunction with a historical analysis of late mediaeval Orissan temple art provides a clearer—but still obscure—perspective on what White refers to as the symbolic sublimation of the 'hard core' Kaula practice, than it does on a—necessarily—more literal reading of the art and literature with regard to the question of postures as such.

Quite apart from, but still related to, the question of sex and athleticism is another theme that seems to connect hatha yoga and the *Kama Sutra*: animals. In the *Gherandasamhita* it is said that there are as many postures as there are 'species of living creatures in this universe' and that many of these—such as the snake, eagle, bull, peacock and lion posture—reflect the form of the animal in question (II:1 Pancham Sinh's translation). Eliade interprets this with reference to the fact that yoga developed out of shamanic beliefs and practices, since shamans transform themselves into animals—which takes us back to the iconic image of the horned ithyphallic 'proto-Shiva' depicted on a terracotta seal surrounded by a number of different species of animal.

In the *Kama Sutra* the embodiment of animal forms is also important. The opening sutras of chapter one, part two, have taken their place in the history of sexuality—or at least in the post-colonial history of erotica—by comparing men and women to animals based on the size of their genitalia and establishing a table of equal and unequal unions based on the relative compatibility or incompatibility of their sizes. Vatsyayana's concern here is to distinguish between high and low unions.

The more directly relevant reference to animals, however, has to do with the model they provide for how humans might engage in intercourse. After describing the cow congress—which has also taken its place in the history of modern sexuality—Vatsyayana makes note of an important point that is often ignored:

In the same way can be carried on the congress of a dog, the congress of a goat, the congress of a deer, the forcible mounting of an ass, the congress of a cat, the jump of a tiger, the pressing of an elephant, the rubbing of a boar, and the mounting of a horse. And in all these cases the characteristics of the different animals should be manifest by acting like them. (1993: 114–115, Richard F. Burton's translation)

If the practice of yoga was, strictly speaking, a ritualized performance of myth, it would be possible to elaborate on the formal correspondence between the *Gherandasamhita* and the *Kama Sutra* by pointing out, with reference to Daniélou (1962:42, see also 2001), that Shiva created the diversity of life through yoga by assuming the form of every being, and then reintegrated this diversity into himself while assuming a *siddhasana* posture. It is in this posture that 'his erect phallus is swollen with all the potentialities of future creations', the penultimate expression of urethral suction. However, the fetishistic sexual zoology of the *Kama Sutra*, as quite different from mediaeval Orissan zoophilia, seems to be mimetic of the act, with full sound effects, whereas the enactment of animal postures in hatha yoga is mimetic of form. And two *kukkutasana* do not make for a species specific *ratibandha*. In other words, it is possible to develop a line of interpretation that does not resolve into an ithyphallic siddhasana, or into any asana at all.

With this in mind perhaps the last partisan word should be given to Kalyanamalla, author of the sixteenth-century *Ananga Ranga*, a treatise on erotics commissioned by Ladakhan, a Lodi nobleman: Sex is 'equal if not superior to the pleasure of union with the Infinite, the bliss of the ascetic and the mystic' (I.VIII, in Prasad 1983).

Conclusion: The Babble of Nonsense

So, what are we dealing with: confusion, strategic confusion, meaningful elaboration or a case in which mythology has repeated itself as history through a combination of misunderstanding and unconscious structural elaboration? Regardless, modern history has twisted the cultural logic of yoga by forcing it to conform to the structure of dualism and categorical opposition. The practice of yoga in this context does not produce knowledge, but rather reproduces the contingent 'babble of nonsense', to adapt one of my favourite phrases from the *Hathayogapraipika* (IV: 113). It is difficult to say when the 'babbling' began, but in theory it must be at that point in time and space when semen and rajas flowed out, but not back in, and the *yub-yam* was performed as an exotic, athletic lap dance.

With respect to the politics of knowledge, here is the problem: If you dismiss Ellen Barrett's *Sexy Yoga: 40 Poses for Mind-Blowing Sex and Greater Intimacy* as post-colonial New Age nonsense, then you have set an analytical course where you must somewhat arbitrarily decide when, and in whose domain, an interpretation is legitimate and has authority. Is Kalyanamalla, writing for a Muslim nobleman, to be taken seriously? Is Pandit Shiv Sharma? What about Eliade? If you are going to draw lines, where and by whom are they drawn? Alternatively, if I may pervert the anthropologist Clifford Geertz's perspective on relativism, one must conclude that it is nonsense all the way down to the most elemental fluctuation of the mind. On one level this conclusion is exactly right. But the academic challenge is to be able to engage the paradox of truth in reflection; to take Barrett, Sharma and others seriously enough to include them all within the gambit of a critical analysis that does not fall into the trap of trying to answer the illusive question: to have lots of mind-blowing sex or to have no sex at all so as to embody immortality and transcend consciousness. However you answer that question, in point of fact your answer will be wrong.

And so, as academics, our analysis is, by definition, at odds with the claims made by everyone from Patanjali up through Gorkshanath and Matsyendranath and Swami Sivananda and Swami Rama to B.K.S. Iyengar, Pandit Shiv Sharma and Ellen Barrett. It is a steadfast academic position to take; and it is a position that is as challenging—albeit with reference to politics rather than yogic athleticism—as any you will find in the *Sivasamhita*, and as stimulating, with reference to the range of possible interpretations that the modification of the human mind can generate, as those found in the *Kama Sutra*.

Although one must always acknowledge that the 'facts' of history are contingent on the range of present knowledge—and that mythology is read into history all the time—it is highly unlikely that any significant historical connection can be found between the positions described in the *Kama Sutra* and asana and pranayama—except for the fact that they are all concerned with yoga. The word itself simply means union.

When fractured interpretation and disjointed history make it difficult to produce a synthetic analysis, sometimes the only significant generalization is in the literal meaning of a specific, but rather imprecise, signifier. In any case, in the domain of words, where the constantly modified relationship between sense and object is inherently political, etymology is king and critical philology the only way to resolve the problem of relativism and incompatible interpretations.

Chandra Shekhar Azad

Chandrashekhar Azad: Prachand Shakti.

6

Gymnastic Asana—Competitive Yoga
Physical Philosophy, Sex and the Problem of Perfection

We can distinguish at least two orientations, different yet convergent, in [the] emphatic valuation of the human body and its possibilities [in Hatha Yoga] . . . But perfection is always the goal, and . . . it is neither athletic nor hygienic perfection. Hatha Yoga cannot and must not be confused with gymnastics. (Eliade 1990: 228)

Semen is the raw material and fuel of every psychochemical transformation the yogin, alchemist and tantric practitioner undergoes, transformations through which a new, superhuman and immortal body is 'conceived' out of the husk of the mortal, conditioned, biological body. (White 1996: 27)

Introduction: Sport, Athleticism and Sex

Despite pervasive stereotypes that would suggest the contrary, athleticism and sport are complex cultural activities with historical roots in religious ritual, ascetic self-discipline, philosophical training and various articulations of sex, sexuality and embodied self-expression. Given the pervasiveness of modern sport as a global cultural phenomenon, and the complex and powerful ideological significance of embodied concepts like work, labour, exercise and strength, it is difficult to understand the correlation between athletic self-development and competitive sport with reference to meaningful cultural differences, and in anything other than modern physiological terms. Functional anatomy and the sciences of physiology and biochemistry—to say nothing of that bugaboo, evolutionary psychology—have served to further amplify an increasingly reductive correlation between a specific conception of fitness and a particular manifestation of success and perfection.

Unto themselves, sport and sex are deceptively two-dimensional in the sense that the former is often conceptualized as a desire to win—and the embodied enactment of that singular desire based on self-discipline aimed at physical perfection—and the latter to desire pure and simple and its sensory gratification. While athleticism, sex, philosophy and asceticism need not have any correspondence, the commonplace congruence of sex and athleticism can be reduced down simplistically to the calculus of 'animal attraction'. In abstract terms it is possible to conceptualize sport as completely distinct from sex and any articulation of sexuality, yet an analysis of sport must engage with the way in which three different dimensions of sex—physiology, kinetics, and desire—are integral features of many significant historical developments in the arena of competitive athletic self-development. In essence the inherent complexity of sport and sex unto themselves is further complicated by their coupling.

In many respects the analytical issue may be conceptualized with reference to how sex is reductively reified in terms of embodiment when physiology, kinetics and desire all line up to produce 'the beast with two backs', but how various independent, disarticulated aspects that anticipate the reified act are not unto themselves, necessarily, 'sexual'. Given the relative significance of sexuality on a number of different registers—psychological, moral, biological and social—the paramount 'problem' of desire, and the control of desire, tends to structure our understanding of the physiology and functional anatomy of sex. However, there is absolutely nothing intrinsically or exclusively sexual about a penis. It is more often involved in the excretion of urine than in the ejaculation of semen, and in the case of the latter far more often in relation to many different expressions of power and incidental pleasure than in terms of purposeful procreation. With reference to other parts of the body, visible and invisible, large and small, the problem is even more pronounced and problematic. Along these same lines, and in terms of both functional anatomy and physiology, athleticism is interesting and important precisely because it deconstructs aspects of embodiment that otherwise are conceptualized as 'lining up' in a particular way to produce a sexual experience.

Viewed in terms of a history of athleticism, yoga is particularly interesting for the way in which it articulates a relationship between selfhood and physiology that is, in many ways, very similar to an ancient Greek ideal of embodied philosophical fitness: an ideal that involves sex explicitly but is neither intrinsically erotic nor concerned with the problem of pleasure. In light of this, the staged performance of postural yoga as modern sport is not gross anathema—a perverse post-modern parody of ancient subtle wisdom—but rather a clear expression of a very long-standing paradox: how the perfection of the mortal body anticipates, but never produces, immortality, and the structural correlation between sex, the reproduction of life, and the inevitability of death. To the extent that these issues are manifest in athleticism, self-development and sport, modern competitive yoga may well be regarded as the penultimate—if not by any means perfect— articulation of a key problematic in classical Greek philosophy.

The history of modern yoga is shot through with many contradictions, and advocates for various forms of practice have often expressed ambivalence about the way in which the inherent physicality of postural yoga can undermine a philosophy of practice oriented towards ostensibly 'higher' ideals and metaphysical principles. In its most extreme articulation a modern philosophy of yoga holds that to achieve transcendence one must be free from desire, including the desire to be free from desire, and that the material world, including the body, is an illusion. And yet, at another extreme, an alchemical view of transubstantiation holds that embodied immortality can be achieved, and magical powers acquired, by means of both subtle and gross physiological self-discipline.

The mediaeval literature makes this goal quite clear, and, although the formulations are esoteric, arcane and mystical, a desire for embodied immortality is, intuitively, a very logical response to the inevitability of ageing and death conceptualized as a bio-cultural problem: a problem of physiological change, and consciousness of that change. At still another extreme, postural yoga manifests a phenomenological reality that directly involves the manipulation of the gross body. By this I mean that when an adept instructs a novice to perform a *mullabandha* and thereby 'reverse the flow of the *apana*'—which, as the subtle agency of excretion, is naturally inclined to manifest as gross flatulence—the novice presses his anus with his heel and constricts his *sphincter ani externus*. This prevents him from ageing and becoming, so to say, just another old fart (*Hathayogapradipika* 3: 60–64). A consideration of postural yoga must not lose sight of the fact that practice crosses the semiotic spectrum. In doing so yoga involves the nostrils, tongue, eyes, stomach, urethra, sinuses, lungs and intestines along with many other parts of the body and their denotative functions.

In any case, in all of its permutations—philosophical, physiological and phenomenological—yoga is concerned with perfection and perfection involves the body in general and the physiology of sex and the flow of sexual fluids in particular.

Like many forms of embodied activity concerned with perfection, postural yoga requires training and constant practice. In performance it can articulate various degrees of accomplishment and skill as well as levels of personal achievement. As in the case of gymnastics, yoga manifests an aesthetic of balance, an economy of movement and a concern with precision along with a specific form of embodied self-discipline that is reflected in physiological poise and flexibility. Quite apart from whether it is appropriate to do so or not, there is no question but that one can compare the performance of a specific asana executed by several different people and draw the conclusion, based on standardized, objective criteria, that one is done better than the others: this is the essence of competitive sport.

Given its metaphysical, mystical and magical underpinnings, yoga might seem to be categorically at odds with sport. However, on another level—one where a phenomenology of the youthful body is transcendent—its classification as such is completely unremarkable. If one examines the history of sport there have been any number of quite radical shifts in what counts as appropriate for inclusion in the category, and what can be contrived as competitive. Who among us is not bemused by 'quaint' images of tug-of-war and croquet in the historical documentation of the 'modern' Olympics, and is not similarly horrified—notwithstanding the aesthetics of embodied power reflected in statues found in the Uffizi gallery—by Greek descriptions of the no-holds-barred, anything-goes, fight-to-the-death *pankration* of the seventh century CE? And there is nothing intrinsically 'competitive' about gymnastics, as late nineteenth century German Turners pointed out.

In any case, if the pankration is at one extreme of the spectrum of sportive possibility, yoga is very likely at the other. As such it reflects an uneasy synthesis of modern physical fitness and conceptions of transcendent enlightenment, as these conceptions are linked to powerful ideas about an individual's attitude towards the world, and human attachments to it. Certainly since the end of the nineteenth century, many who sought to modernize mediaeval hatha yoga have collapsed metaphysics and physical fitness in order to change the semiotics of internalized sexuality into externalized forms of moral materialism.

With this in mind, a materialist history of yoga in general, and postural yoga in particular, provides an interesting point of entry into the history of sport and self-development on the one hand, and sexuality and self-control on the other. My argument in this chapter is that yoga competitions and advocacy for the inclusion of yoga into the modern Olympics—based on its radically disarticulated gymnastification—brings the question of 'sport' itself back around to a central problematic in the history of athleticism: the relationship between sex, substance and the embodied self as a social being.

In terms of analytical method and narrative form, considerable licence is taken from the fact that the history of yoga is anything but linear and bounded by 'tradition' and that yoga has been taken to mean radically different things by different people over the course of many centuries. The idea of traditional, ancient yoga is very much an artifice of modernity, and the artifice clearly involves complex, but ultimately contradictory, claims of authenticity. Consequently, the logic of my argument in this chapter reflects—rather than takes issue with—the historically suspect logic by means of which yoga as a philosophical tradition of South Asia, that took shape in the mediaeval period as embodied magic, is presented as an authentic 'ancient sport'.

Using arguments from which I derive significant interpretive licence, and from which I take considerable analytical latitude, advocates continue to make a case for the inclusion of asana gymnastic routines into the modern Olympics, and for the official recognition of rule-bound competitive yoga under the rubric of an international sports federation. The anti-parsimonious pastiche of post-modern synthesis aside, the real irony—as distinct from several artifactual ones—is that modern competitive yoga instantiates a configuration of sex and self-discipline, as well as the knotty problem of *eros*, that is characteristic of the quest for perfection in both ancient Greek athletics and mediaeval South Asian alchemy.

Exercise, Erotics and the Embodiment of Fitness

The Scythian [Anacharsis] observes that each of the Greek cities has a designated place in which they go mad every day—the gymnasium. (Martin 1996: 138)

Recently there has been considerable interest in the study of the relationship between sport and sexuality in ancient Greece (Dickie 1993; Guttmann 1996: 15–37; Loraux 1990). Guttmann and most others point out that the gymnasium was an intensely erotic environment, the fact of denoted nakedness evoking a range of feelings and desires. The 'young but fully grown body, moulded by gymnastics to the peak of its power' was most certainly the object of desire. The naked body was, as Guttmann points out, 'erotically charged when in motion', and clearly the gymnasium was a place where bodies were set in motion (1996: 18).

Beyond this, the athletic body was thought to be charged with sexual power (Keuls 1993), and here, as Loraux points out (1990), Heracles is the iconic, classical male athlete. In the logic of paradigmatic interpretation, the 'sexually powerful body' was measured in terms of what might be called kinetic sexuality and the calculus of sexual exploits, and this continues to be a very common motif, almost to the point that the enumeration of sexual conquests has become iconic of heroic masculinity. In conjunction with this, scholars have noted that it was in the gymnasium that the naked body was on display. And although there is nothing intrinsically sexual about a naked body, contextualized nakedness allowed for the body to become the object of desire, even when it was not erotically engaged. There is no sense in which the ancient gymnasium was purely and simply hedonistic. But exercise in the gymnasium increased both eroticism and sexual power and the intimate reciprocality of this relationship produced an escalating scale of desire.

To a large extent this interpretation is legitimate. But it draws attention away from an alternative interpretation that is more directly focused on the body as a whole. Sexuality—in the kinetic, erotic and ultimately moral and ethical sense—may, in some ways, be regarded as a derivative of exercise, which, unto itself, was designed to produce physical strength. Sex is directly relevant to strength and exercise, but not simply in terms of erotics. In this regard it is important to make a distinction between wrestlers and boxers as well as other athletes whose training regimens were extreme and produced 'heavy muscularity' on the one hand, and, on the other, the fit, healthy and balanced—as well as beautiful—body of the *palaestrita*. Quoting Margaret Walters (1978:14), Guttmann points out that palaestrita were 'boys, youths or young men who were adept at the exercises of the gymnasium and whose bodily beauty and grace of movement marked them . . . as shining examples of the physical ideal at which the gymnasium . . . aimed' (1996: 18). The body of the wrestler and the body of the palaestrita were not different in kind; they were different in degree, and the question of degree was calibrated, at least to a large extent, if not exclusively, with reference to what might be called the physiology of sexual fitness.

In an important way the physiology of sex—arousal, coitus, orgasm, and ejaculation—was directly linked to questions of health and fitness, and it is noteworthy that in his study of sexuality in classical Greece, Foucault is far less concerned with erotics than he is with the way in which sexuality was regulated and how this regulation was linked to dietetics, health and physical fitness, although he does not use the term physical fitness as such. With this in mind it becomes clear that erotics is only one aspect of sexuality, and a derivative one at that. The gymnasium was less an environment for the expression of erotic desire—as separate from sport and athleticism as such—and more a place where the problem of fitness and health engaged directly with the problem of desire.

As Foucault points out, the key problem with regard to sex in classical Greece was not whether it was good or bad as such, but what effect it had on one's own health and on the health of the children so conceived. Most certainly in medical texts, but also, it seems, in more general works, the basic principle was that one should abstain from sex as much as possible in order to promote health and strength. Diogenes Laertius along with Pythagoras claimed that sex dissipated strength. In the Aristotelian framework sex was recommended only in the case of 'pressing need', since the act itself was like doing to the body what is done to a plant when it is uprooted from the soil (Foucault 1990b: 118). It is noteworthy that the pathology of ejaculation is explained in detail with regard to the body as a whole. Aristotle theorized that the ejaculation of semen over-cooled the brain by drawing away the body's natural heat. Others, working with an understanding of the way in which the body produced semen from marrow, identified the spinal cord as vulnerable. Perhaps the most comprehensive treatment of the subject is in a Hippocratic text, *The Seed*. As Foucault points out,

> [In this text] [t]he sexual act is analysed, from start to finish, as a violent mechanical action that is directed toward the emission of sperm. First, the rubbing of the genitals and the movement given to the whole body produce a general warming effect; the latter, combined with agitation, gives the humor, diffused into the whole body, a greater fluidity, so that it begins to 'foam' (*aphrein*), 'in the same way as all other fluids produce foam when they are agitated.' At this stage a phenomenon of 'separation' (*apokrisis*) occurs; the most vigorous part of this foaming fluid, 'the most potent and the richest' (*to ischyrota to kai piotaton*) is carried to the brain and the spinal marrow, descending its length to the loins. Then the warm foam passes to the kidneys and from there through the testicles to the penis, from which it is expelled by means of a violent spasm (*tarach*). (1990b: 127)

Ejaculation was conceptualized as a whole-body process, just as semen was understood to be the potent extract of all the body's fluids.

Plato, Aristotle and Hippocrates offer different explanations for how and from what semen is produced within the body, but there is general consensus that it is precious, and that ejaculation is a kind of fluid drain on the body as a whole. Foucault paraphrases Aristotle as follows:

[It] is understandable that the discharge of . . . semen constitutes an important event for the body: it withdraws a substance that is precious, being the end result of a lengthy distillation by the organism and concentrating elements which, in accordance with nature, might have gone 'to all parts of the body', and hence might háve made it grow if they had not been removed from the body. (1990b: 132)

Ejaculation thus not only causes weakness, but stunts growth and development. And yet, as is quite obvious, the act of sex is necessary: it is the basis of life that extends beyond the bounded body of a single person. The tension between life and death manifest in the act of sex itself points to the cycle of life and death and to ideas about immortality, albeit somewhat different ideas than those articulated in the Pythagorean tradition. As Foucault puts it:

For Aristotle and Plato alike, the sexual act was at the point of junction of an individual life that was bound to perish—and from which, moreover, it drew off a portion of its most precious resources—and an immortality that assumed the concrete form of a survival of the species. Between these two lives, the sexual relation constituted, as Plato says, an 'artifice' (*mechane*) that was designed to join them together so that the first might, in its own way, participate in the second; this *mechane* provided the individual with an 'offspring' of himself (*apoblastema*). (1990b: 133–134)

To define the physical act of sex as an artifice is significant on a number of different levels. Quite apart from prefiguring the fetishism of Freudian interpretation, it anticipates the artifactual relationship between life and death in yoga, and the physiology of sexual power that is at the heart of yoga.

Before turning to an analysis of yoga as a kind of meta-physical fitness training, it is relevant to consider the training of Greek athletes, as this training involved a very specific and regulated form of what Foucault refers to more broadly as the 'exercise of existence' and the management of pleasure as a tool for self cultivation.

In many respects, the male Greek athlete seems to most clearly embody the principles of Galenic medicine, at least to the extent that his physical fitness reflects a theory of sexual physiology. Insofar as medicine was very much akin to philosophy in the classical period, it is possible to appreciate the intersection of philosophy, medicine and sport at this time. But it is also possible to see how the later development of sport and the refinement of medical knowledge combined to extract the body from philosophy by reifying it as a thing unto itself, reflecting physical strength and beauty on the one hand and physical health on the other.

Plato among many others makes reference to the way in which some athletes, while involved in training, practised sexual abstinence, and that this abstinence could be extreme. There is, needless to say, a degree of contradiction and ambivalence underlying this formulation: abstinence is good, since one's ability to retain semen—and to embody the power thereby derived—would seem to have no limit and increase in value directly in proportion to volume, but too much abstinence is bad if combined with other kinds of excess. In this instance citing Plato's praise for the chaste Olympian Iccus of Tarentum, Foucault makes the following remark, which is consistent with the inconsistency of the Greeks:

Men could—in certain cases at least—retain all their semen; far from causing them harm, strict abstinence on their part would preserve their force in its entirety, accumulate it, concentrate it, and carry it finally to a higher level. (1990b: 120)

If semen itself had value as a tangible, fluid reservoir, the pathologizing of sex was profoundly physiological and linked to substance rather than to the question of moral or immoral behaviour. Of note in this regard is not just the practice of abstinence, but the way in which the loss of semen through nocturnal emission was regarded as pathological on account of being involuntary and beyond self-control. Beyond this, the pathologizing of sex in medical terms involved 'the involuntary violence of tension and an indefinite, exhausting expenditure' (Foucault 1988: 113, see also 105–116). Philostratus explains that athletes must gradually rebuild their strength—particularly their endurance and breath—after losing their semen, and must get rid of the excess perspiration that seems to result from this as well. As Scanlon points out, Galen—in what is a beautiful example of pre-Freudian pragmatism—advocated the use of 'flattened leaden plates' placed over the groin to prevent nocturnal discharge. How this mechanical procedure was supposed to work is not clear. Another technology known as the 'dog's leash' (*kunodeseme*) was used to tie up the foreskin, apparently to crimp erections and, by extension—or, in fact, the lack thereof!—prevent arousal and ejaculation. Thus, the extreme form of the athlete's training reflected the particular pathology of sex:

> For as soon as the act takes place, it is, in its unfolding, regarded as intrinsically dangerous. Dangerous because it is a wasting of the precious substance whose accumulation nevertheless incites one to commit it—it allows all the life force that the semen has concentrated to escape. (Foucault 1988: 112–113)

Extreme abstinence is a solution; although it can also be regarded as exacerbating the pathology of sex by enhancing desire through extreme accumulation. Absolute chastity is, therefore, a contingent and rather problematic solution in terms of a calculus that is purely physiological.

What is most interesting about this is that it produces two levels of apparent contradiction. First, how does one reconcile the fact that gymnasiums were places for sexual liaison—eros as such—with the ideal of athletic chastity? Secondly, and perhaps more significantly, how does one make sense of the fact that Plato and Aristotle, among others, applauded the practice of strict sexual abstinence among athletes while they criticized athletic excess in general—for abstinence is, in fact, precisely a form of negative excess. The locus of the problem seems to have been in the way in which excessive training offset the balance between body and soul, involved an exaggerated concern for oneself, and, correspondingly, a shirking of civic responsibility. In this there was a definite parallel between athletic and valetudinarian excess. Both were

> characteristic of those who, in order to keep from losing their hold on life, tried their utmost to delay the term that had been appointed by nature. The practice carried the danger—moral but political as well—of exaggerating one's care of the body (*peritte epimeleia tou somatos*). (Foucault 1990b: 104–105)

In other words, an excess of physical training was seen as a kind of embodied self-absorption: a doomed attempt to become immortal. Whereas the act of sex was conceptualized as an artifice of immortality, athletic excess, including absolute chastity, was unnatural and contrived: artificial rather than an artifice.

As Foucault's work makes clear, for the early Greeks sexual behaviour was problematized in terms of 'its quantitative gradations' (1990b: 45), and, in many ways, the gymnasium marks a locus point of two possible extremes. From the perspective of a history of sexuality that is concerned with the development of ideas about propriety and impropriety, as well as the whole apparatus of Christian morals, the 'eros' end of the spectrum is most interesting and telling. It is this that most scholars seek to explain, even when they rightly focus on the broader techniques of the self and the physiology of sex. After all, is not the 'problem of pederasty'—and more broadly 'homosexuality'—the subtext if not the liet motif of this entire history? Clearly it is important to focus on the kinetics of sex in order to understand the development of moral and spiritual injunctions against acts and behaviour. But to focus on kinetics alone—or chastity alone, for that matter—is to forget that the gymnasium brought two opposing principles into a single gambit. The athlete embodied two extremes, and a key problem for the Greeks was how to make sense of sex as a physiological act linked to the problem of fitness.

Immortality, Sex and Death: Intimations, Imitations, Limitations

> Press the heel of the left foot firmly against the perineum, and the right heel above the male organ. With the chin pressing on the chest, one should sit calmly, having restrained the senses, and gaze steadily into the space between the eyebrows. This is called *siddhasana*, the opener of the door of salvation. (*Hathayogapradipika* I: 37)

Although framed in terms of esoteric concepts and arcane references, hatha yoga is concerned with the embodiment of supernatural power. Power is embodied by stopping the flow of consciousness, breath and semen. Once the flow of these substances is arrested, a person achieves immortality—an embodied experience of unchanging timelessness. As David Gordon White has persuasively argued, the psycho-chemistry of hatha yoga is based on a complex theory wherein a phenomenology of sex, sexual physiology and sexual reproduction is systematically extended into the domain of subtle experience to explain how the body can be perfected. Of central importance here is the way in which yoga involves the destruction of oppositions and the instantiation of a series of 'refusals' that result in the reintegration of symbol and substance on the level of embodied practice. In other words, hatha yoga involves the manipulation of semen in terms of ejaculation, channelled flow and transubstantiation as well as a manipulation of what semen means in terms of immortality and the unending cycle of mortal reproduction, as these meanings are a function of coital and cosmic union experienced as one and the same thing.

While many aspects of yoga involve concrete, explicit physical acts such as the placement of the heels in *siddhasana*—a point of singular importance—it is essential to keep in mind the fact that yoga is predicated on secrecy and secret insights. As the *Hathayogapradipika* puts it, in terms that are at once evocatively suggestive and unambiguously denotative:

> A yogi desirous of success should keep the knowledge of Hatha Yoga secret; for it becomes potent by concealing and impotent by exposing. (I: 11)

Although secrecy is a general principle in the practice of yoga, it is not so much a secret that is designed to be kept as one that references a set of practices that cannot be easily or readily understood on their own terms; that is, they are mysterious and arcane as well as hidden, and exposure does not so much reveal the secret as dispel—with reference to flaccid factuality—the powerful erection of a mystery. Secrecy takes on its most powerful significance with reference to the physiology of ejaculation commonly associated with kinetic sex and orgasm, although the emphasis is on fluid flow rather than sensory experience—it is substance, direction of flow and transubstantiation that matters.

Svatmarama, the author of the *Hathayogapradipika*, points out on a number of occasions that asana, pranayama, mudra and bandha are important and necessary aspects of practice that lead to ultimate success and final perfection—the term *siddhi* being used most frequently in the text to denote supernatural or magical 'success'. Although on one level it can be assumed that Svatmarama's intent is for a practitioner to engage in a comprehensive regimen of practice that involves the whole spectrum of techniques, and that the sequence is structured developmentally—like a staircase leading to the pinnacle, as the first *sloka* puts it—it is also clear

that each asana, pranayama exercise, mudra and bandha intimates
the ultimate achievement of immortality. The terminology most
often used is that a procedure 'destroys' or 'conquers' either death,
poison, disease or old age. For example, *Viparitakarni* is described
as follows in the chapter on mudras:

> Place the head on the ground and the feet up into the sky, for a
> second only the first day, and increase this time daily. After six
> months, the wrinkles and grey hair are not seen. He who practises
> it daily, even for two hours, conquers death. (3:80–81)

Here perfection, as in the case of siddhasana or 'perfect' pose,
is not calculated in terms of formal accomplishment involving
balance, stability and form, but in terms of duration, incremental
graduation and effect. The actual technique that is described is
rather vague on a whole range of different points, although clearly
it is what would be described today as a headstand. As a headstand
the mudra is unambiguous in terms of how and for how long it is
performed. Similarly it is a gross metaphor for the subtle process
by which the normal flow of things—time, breath, semen—is
reversed and, more generally, the way in which 'yogic techniques
invite to one and the same gesture—to do exactly the opposite of
what human nature forces one to do' (Eliade 1990: 96).

One means by which to avoid the knotty problem of what
postural yoga is meant to achieve, and the question of what
relationship achievement has to reality, is to focus on methods,
techniques and practices, as these are rooted in the material being
of the body, irrespective of what happens to it. This procedure
does not reduce yoga down to a set of generic exercises, since
each asana and pranayama technique is not only based on a
theory of physiological transformation intended to have a
specific effect or set of effects on the subtle body, but also entails
the manipulation of the gross body in very precise and varied
ways. Here clear examples can be drawn from the late mediaeval
literature where techniques that are said to have esoteric results and

produce magical powers, are described in terms of very mundane 'gymnastic' procedures, albeit procedures that are, for the most part, not commonplace or easy to perform. Covering a range of issues, the following are drawn from Pancham Sinh's translation of the *Hathayogapradipika*, a late seventeenth century text.

Taking the posture of Padamasana and carrying the hands under the thighs, when the Yogi raises himself above the ground, with his palms resting on the ground, it becomes Kukkutasana. (1:25)

Having assumed Kukkutasana, when one grasps his neck by crossing his hands behind his head, and lies in this posture with his back touching the ground, it becomes Uttanakurmasana, from its appearance like that of a tortoise. (1:26)

Having placed the right foot at the root of the left thigh, let the toe be grasped with the right hand passing behind the back, and having placed the left foot on the right thigh at its root, let it be grasped with the left hand passing behind the back. This is the asana explained by Sri Matsyanatha. It increases appetite, and is the instrument for destroying the group of the most deadly diseases. Its practice awakens the Kundalini, stops the nectar shedding from the moon in people. (1:28–29)

Place the palms of both the hands on the ground, and place the navel on both the elbows. Balancing thus, the body should be stretched backward like a stick. This is called Mayurasana. This asana soon destroys all diseases and removes abdominal disorders, and those arising from irregularities of phlegm, bile and wind, digests unwholesome food taken in excess, increases appetite and destroys the most deadly poison. (1: 32–33)

One of the interesting and important features of hatha yoga is that because practice is rooted in the three-dimensional gross body, in some respects the problem of perfection in performance comes down to the question of how well the elbows are placed on the navel; how well the left hand grasps the right toe; how well balanced the stick-like stretched-out body is, and so forth. In other words, it comes down to the physical body, as any number of aesthetically beautiful representations of lithe bodies in journals, manuals and websites is clearly meant to illustrate. The destruction of disease and the awakening of kundalini, like the appearance of a tortoise, or a peacock or rooster, is at least one step removed from the elements of precise *tableau vivant* positioning reflected in each posture. In any case, the gross phenomenology of the body implicated in performance in some sense defines the limitations of meaning while at the same time intimating a whole range of possibilities and possible meanings that extend beyond the body.

Yoga Gymnasiums and Sport: Perfection with a Twist, a Wink and a Nod

> The Yogi should practise Hatha Yoga in a small room, situated in a solitary place, being four cubits square, and free from stones, fire, water, disturbances of all kinds, and in a country where justice is properly administered [and] where good people live . . . . The room should have a small door, be free from holes, hollows, neither too high nor too low, well plastered with cow-dung and free from dirt, filth and insects. (*Hathayogapradipika* I: 12–13)

Reading the literature on classical Greek physical philosophy as practised in the gymnasium, and as reflected in sport—and reading about the 'sexual' relationship between adolescent athletes and adult trainers in particular—one cannot help but be struck by the complex synergy of erotic attraction, desire, intellectual passion, aesthetic stimulation, deep affection and bawdy humour, as well as by a number of interesting questions that emerge concerning what is and what is not appropriate in terms of what should or should not be done with respect to everything from body parts to parts of speech. In conjunction with what is explicitly written on this subject, black-on-red Attic vases and other forms of artistic representation clearly show how many aspects of sex, sexual relations, and derivatives thereof, were performed in the palaestra.

Aside from the fact that both were self-consciously located 'in countries where justice is properly administered', the isolated, one-roomed hut for the performance of fifteenth century hatha yoga is by no stretch of the imagination anything like a fifth century Greek palaestra. Nevertheless, modern yoga is most often practised within, or with reference to, institutionalized structures that have historical roots in the classical Greek gymnasium.

With the phenomenal global popularity of various forms of yoga, it goes without saying that the studied isolation of a cow-dung plastered forest hut has given way to luxuriously appointed urban aerobic studios, fitness clubs and health spas. Anyone familiar with the intimate social dynamics of yoga in these settings will immediately appreciate the parallels between the gestures of pederastic courtship in the palaestra and the posturing and positioning that is commonplace in contemporary practice. It is not surprising that, in conjunction with run-of-the-mill liaisons, hook-ups and dalliances, there has been some concern expressed recently—by yoga's Greek chorus, so to speak—about the ethical propriety of senior teachers becoming intimately involved with young, impressionable students, and about the responsibility yoga instructors have to protect students who may not appreciate being 'hit on' while attempting a downward-facing dog or some other asana. While there may be self-righteous adepts who claim Athenian moral high-ground for their yoga studio or school—and attempt to institute rules of enforcement—it is more likely that the truth is closer to a Spartan reality, with the added complexity that same-sex Spartan desire manifest as pederastic pleasure in the modern aerobic studio is complicated by equally uninhibited sexual attraction between men and women of all ages.

Although yoga is now practised as a full-fledged sport, and, as we will see, it is possible to infer sensuality and erotics in the performance of asana—and here reference to Hot Yoga© is particularly apropos—the gross physicality of postures as such means that the integral aspects of physiology that elsewhere find expression as sex—orgasm, *vajroli* ejaculation and *maithuna* embrace—are not at all manifest in the performance of a competitive asana routine. Obviously the whole thing can become an expression of sexuality on any number of different levels, since the encumbrance of desire runs deep, and meaning thereby readily imputed. But it is very important that the two dimensions not be conflated and confused. To the best of my knowledge no one has integrated the *khechari mudra* into a gymnastic routine, although the criteria for adept accomplishment—the kinetics of a sexual embrace that does not end in ejaculation—are very clearly defined in the *Hathayogapradipika* (III: 42). Conquering death and controlling the physiology of sexual fluid flow is not the measure of success in competitive yoga. But, in a very significant sense, yoga as sport reminds us of the importance of this configuration of complex things in the physiological athleticism of *askesis*—physical, moral and spiritual exercise.

It is difficult to know when, how and where postural yoga was first engaged in competitively, but since the structure of training entails improvement over time it is logical to assume that to get better and better one must engage in self-critical and comparative, if not necessarily judgemental, evaluation: am I performing a *siddhasana* as well as my teacher's other students? Despite philosophical ambivalence if not outright antipathy to the question, the fact that yoga brings about a transformation in consciousness and produces very specific kinds of power suggests an inherently comparative frame of reference: adept x is more adept than adept y. Along these lines the concept of *mahayogi*—great adept—manifests a calculus of penultimate Olympian perfection embodied by the ultimate Himalayan sage.

In any case, formal yoga competitions are a relatively recent phenomenon, but have been held in India since the mid-1950s with both national and regular state-level competitions established soon after independence. One of the most noteworthy articulations of yoga sport was in the 1970s by Swami Gitananda, then patron of the Pondicherry Yogasana Association, head of the International Centre for Yoga Research and Education and founder of the well-known Ananda Ashram. A second and probably better known individual who is directly associated with competitive yoga is Bikram Choudhury. Under the auspices of Bikram Yoga®™ he established the Bishnu Charan Ghosh Cup in 2003.

Apart from these individuals, the International Yoga Federation (IYF), administered from central offices in Uruguay, is a broadly defined umbrella organization modelled on the federation structure for competitive international sports. This organization now sponsors national competitions as well as the World Wide Yoga Championships that have been held for the past seventeen years in a range of different countries including India, Italy, Portugal, Argentina, Uruguay and Brazil. Along with a number of other bodies, the IYF is lobbying for the inclusion of yoga in the Olympic Games. Although there are many interesting and important dimensions to the formalization of yoga gymnastics by Swami Gitananda and the IYF, I will focus here on the legacy of Bishnu Charan Ghosh.

Notwithstanding recent litigation on the question of trademarks and embodied intellectual property rights, Bikram Yoga®™ is in fact unique in instantiating and institutionalizing, as well as literalizing—at least from the outside in—the generation of heated energy associated with 'forceful' hatha yoga. Although the rationale for Hot Yoga©, a precise series of twenty-six postures done in a room heated to around 104 degrees Fahrenheit, is that it produces greater flexibility, and induces healthful sweating, the theoretical correlation between heat and other bodily fluids is clearly outlined in the mediaeval literature.

Through heroic efforts of mental concentration and physical exertion, the yogi now initiates a controlled rising of his seed, the heat of his solar fires, and his breath along the medial channel . . . .

This heat, concentrated within the infinitesimal space of the medial channel, effects the gradual transformation of 'raw' semen into 'cooked' and even perfected nectar, *amrta*; it is this nectar that gradually fills out the moon in the cranial vault such that, at the conclusion of this process, the lunar orb, now brimming with nectar, is possessed of its full complement of sixteen digits . . . . This transformation of semen into nectar wholly transforms the body, rendering it immortal. (White 1996: 40–41)

Bikram Yoga®™ as such is no more or less 'erotic' than any other form of postural yoga. However, Hot Yoga© may be understood as an externalized literalization of a structural theory at the heart of postural yoga, and it is but a small step from semiotics to hot and heavy erotics. To be sure, the latter, like all that is fetishized in yoga, is a matter of interpretation. But Bikram Chaudhary, never shy in making any number of claims, is reported to have done exactly what one might expect someone in his position to do, and to do it—as he claims, in the abstract—with Olympian calibre, marathon stamina.

Bikram Choudhury's orientation towards competitive yoga was established by his guru, Bishnu Charan Ghosh. Ghosh, who died in 1970, was an interesting and colourful character cut in the mould of early twentieth century strongmen and body-builders such as Eugene Sandow, Bernarr McFadden and, much closer to home, Professor Ram Murti Naidu. Born in 1903, Bishnu Charan Ghosh was the younger brother of Mukunda Lal Ghosh, better known as Paramahansa Yogananda, founder of the Self-Realization Fellowship and author of the highly regarded, popular and influential book *Autobiography of a Yogi* (1946). The younger Ghosh was raised in Calcutta where he established The Ghosh College of Physical Education, now known as the Ghosh Yoga College under the Vice-Principalship of his daughter, Muktamala. The College was founded at a time when a number of other institutions for the promotion of indigenous physical education and athleticism came into being (Alter 2006), most notably the

Hanuman Vyayam Prasarak Mandal in Amravati (Alter 2007a) and the College of Physical Education established by Swami Kuvalayananda in Lonavala, Maharashtra (Alter 2007b).

Although the precise details are not clear, based on Bikram Choudhury's expression of debt to Bishnu Ghosh, it seems that the more worldly and down-to-earth younger brother of Paramahansa Yogananda combined physical fitness, the development of muscular strength, and the performance of asana and pranayama in a way that few others have ever done. Bishnu Ghosh's emphasis on the development of physical strength reflected in postural perfection is not completely unique by any means, but unlike Kuvalayananda and others, Ghosh and his students made no bones about their singular concern with the body. Although Ghosh claims to have also been a disciple of his spiritually inclined elder brother Yogananda, who taught and practised the principles of yoga self-realization in California, Bishnu Ghosh himself travelled to other parts of the world to promote postural yoga by demonstrating feats of physical strength—supporting the weight of a road-roller and elephant with his chest and bending iron bars with his teeth. In this respect he played the role of a side-show strongman, fitting a mould that was in large part shaped by Eugene Sandow who toured India in 1904.

Evidence for Ghosh's concern with the aesthetics of body building and muscle control is found in a volume entitled *Muscle Control and Barbell Exercises* (Sen Gupta and Ghosh 1930) co-written with Keshab Chandra Sen Gupta. The volume is remarkable for a number of reasons including photographs that provide valuable insight on the integration of yogic muscle control and body-building poses that are modelled on the statuary of classical Greece, as these poses were the stock-in-trade of early twentieth century physical culturists. As Ghosh points out, he received training from his guru, Mr R.N. Guha Thakurta of the All Bengal Physical Culture Association and Instructor of Physical Exercises at the University Law College, Calcutta. After transforming himself from a 68-pound weakling into a robust—if still rather small in stature—muscleman in Calcutta, he enrolled in the Bengal Engineering College at Sibpur.

> In all the college functions at Sibpur I used to entertain the gentlemen present with muscle control and many feats of strength, such as taking a roller (weighing about two tons) on my chest, lying under a bullock cart, allowing a motor car to run over me or a normal man to jump on my abdomen from a height of no less than 12 feet . . .
>
> I learnt muscle-controlling before all of this, when I was very young, from my beloved elder brother, Swami Yogananda Giri, B.A., the founder of the Yogoda System of physical culture. He is now in America and is helping the people there for the last twelve years. At the time when my borther was here I was very young and thin and would never practise it. But after Thakurta's system had improved my health, one day I happened to see Mr Chit Tun [a Burmese physical culturist] controlling his huge and shapely muscles. The audience shouted in wonder [for the art was then unknown in Bengal] and I knew that I could also perform the feat, *only that I required bigger muscles to be better appreciated.*
>
> I began to take regular exercise and started controlling my muscles again. *Soon I found that my muscles were becoming more and more shapely, and power of application of strength increased.* (Sen Gupta and Ghosh 1930: 52. Emphasis added)

Although the Yogoda Satsang Society of India, with central offices at the ashram in Dakshineswar, has a very clearly defined and well developed philosophy of meditation and divine consciousness, it is not very clear what constitutes 'Yogoda physical culture'. In his autobiography Yogananda makes reference to Yogoda as a 'unique system of physical development' he had discovered in 1916. This was integrated into the curriculum of the Brahmacharya Vidyalaya that was established on the grounds of the Kasimbazar Palace in Ranchi where Yogananda recruited his youngest brother, Bishnu Charan Ghosh, to direct the gymnasium and coordinate physical culture and sports.

Realizing that man's body is like an electric battery, I reasoned that it could be recharged with energy through the direct agency of the human will. As no action, slight or large, is possible without willing, man can avail himself of his prime mover, will, to renew his bodily tissues without burdensome apparatus or mechanical exercises. I therefore taught the Ranchi students my simple 'yogoda' techniques by which the life force, centred in man's medulla oblongata, can be consciously and instantly recharged from the unlimited supply of cosmic energy.

The boys responded wonderfully to this training, developing extraordinary ability to shift the life energy from one part of the body to the other, and to sit in perfect poise in difficult body postures. They performed feats of strength and endurance which many powerful adults could not equal. (Yogananda 1946: chapter 27)

It is not at all clear that Yogoda energizing techniques are based on the principles of either mediaeval hatha yoga or early twentieth century postural yoga. Rhythmic arm swinging, trunk twisting and walking in place are more akin to other forms of physical culture. Using one's hands to stimulate the *medulla oblongata* is something else altogether.

What seems clear, however, is that the two brothers ultimately chose divergent paths, but set out on their respective trajectories of self-development with reference to common principles in the philosophy of yoga. Even though it was Yogananda who set up shop very close to what became the Mecca of body-building in Venice Beach, the path taken by Bishnu Ghosh led to a point of direct intersection with the cult of the 'body beautiful' that emerged in counterpoint to the philosophy of self-discipline, masculinity and embodied spirituality in the articulation of sportive muscular Christianity.

Bikram Choudhury received his training in yoga asana and pranayama in the context of a unique gymnasium; but, like all gymnasia—and as the name itself suggests—The Yoga College was a place to engage in the practice of physical fitness and philosophy. As a gymnasium, The Yoga College has a complex history that combines elements of marketing, muscular Christianity, nationalism, and colonial masculinity as well as a range of different articulations of modern 'scientific' yoga, mediaeval tantrism, embodied alchemy, and permutations of 'traditional' practice that emerge from these articulations. It is not at all surprising, therefore, that the California-based owner of the Bikram Yoga trademark—who claims that he was invited to settle in the United States by President Richard Nixon, a patient he cured of a sciatica attack—embodies a truly post-modern pastiche of incongruous and manifestly inconsistent views that can only be made to make sense within the gambit of tantric logic.

In terms of this logic, gross materialism is not gross materialism, trademarks mean nothing and everything, and the organic spiritualism of Calcutta—invoked by Chaudhary in a CBS interview—is transplanted to the posh 'torture chambers' of Beverly Hills where instructors are made to 'suffer' through certification training—good for a limited period of three years—at $5000 a pop. Given his unambiguous concern with physical strength and its demonstration, and the convergence of an ideology of 'muscular Hinduism' manifest in mid-century Bengali nationalism with the globalization of sports in the early twentieth century, it is not surprising that Ghosh's disciple, Bikram Choudhury, became a champion of competitive yoga. According to literature provided by the world-wide Yoga College of India™, Bikram won the National India Yoga Championship in 1959 and held the title until he retired from competition three years later at the age of sixteen. (On this point of fact there is some ambiguity. According to other sources Choudhury won a national weightlifting championship in 1959, but after suffering an injury took up yoga and won the national yoga championship in 1969 when he was 23.)

Personalities aside, competitive yoga as an institutionalized sport is not very complex. It involves the performance of stipulated sequences of standardized asana postures that are judged on the basis of established criteria. The style of performance and the criteria for judgement reflect the specific manifestations of skill and proficiency that are involved in training and accomplishment. What competition produces, however, is a whole spectrum of meanings, attitudes, goals, valuations and configurations of 'talent' that effectively transforms the underlying structure of progressive self-realization and embodied self-perfection into a staged—and some would say contrived, superficial and distorted—enactment of that structure with reference to one-on-one, winner-take-all, best-of-the-best competition: a kind of last-yogi-standing that draws directly on, but displaces, the adamantine ideal of samadhi.

While the ripples of distortion produced by the conjoined disarticulation of *chittvritnirodh* and championship is in some ways unique, and characteristic of the post-modern age of global 'kaliyugification', in other ways it provides a clear and unfettered perspective on the relationship between sex and embodied perfection in the context of gymnastic self-discipline. Given the fact that a specific physiology of sex is central to asana and pranayama, a consideration of the more general problem—where kinetics, desire and fluid discharge come together—in relation to athleticism, can help to show that gymnastic asana in general, and Bikram Choudhury's super-heated antics in particular, might well be considered the perfect, modern manifestation of an ancient Greek problematic. In an interview for *Business 2.0* Bikram Choudhury has bombastically claimed that his yoga is the only yoga because he has 'balls like atom bombs, two of them, 100 megatons each. Nobody fucks with me.'

Hubris aside, another, more straightforward, if still somewhat tongue in cheek, way of putting this is that the instantiation of a world championship for postural yoga succeeds in producing a more complete physiological synthesis of self-discipline, care of the self and embodied perfection than was possible in the Olympian palaestra, where the issue of who got fucked and who did the fucking did not so directly factor into the triumphalism of championship *arete*. Whatever its limitations and contrived contortions of logic, world championship yoga succeeds in more completely making sex integral to the physical philosophy of sport than was possible in the ancient Olympics. If Bikram Choudhury succeeds in making yoga an Olympic sport, we will all have finally emerged from the darkness of the Platonic cave into the world of illusion-based reason.

To conclude on a slightly more serious note, postural yoga as a competitive gymnastic sport that is based on an aesthetic, evaluative judgement of what a person is able to do with his or her body fits easily into the framework of modern sports. As pointed out above, there is a clearly defined developmental history that explains this fit with regard to the profound influence of muscular Christianity on the articulation of athleticism in the colonial world (MacAloon 2007). Mark Singleton has made this point most forcefully with reference to the way in which asana are the product of colonial globalization wherein the form and function of physical training and gymnastics in Europe allowed for postural yoga—and Yogoda in Ranchi—to take shape as such (2010). Along the lines of this logic it is very important to point out that it makes as much sense to practise postural yoga as a sport as it does to run races, jump over bars, wrestle, box and swim on a synchronized team. But modern postural yoga fits into the rubric of contemporary sport for structural reasons as well; that is, for reasons that have to do with what the sensual body intimates in the slippery arena of signification and perception.

One of the most interesting features of modern sport and the performance of athletic competition is the way in which it transforms the athlete—or simply the athletic body—into an object of erotic desire. The preeminent historian of sport Allen Guttmann has made this point with reference to a spectrum of different ways in which individuals and groups either celebrate the erotic entailments of sportive athleticism, ignore them, deny them or engage in any number of different contortions of logic on the subject. In some respects the athletic body is objectified in relation to the subjective feeling of desire that is experienced by those who watch.

It is on this phenomenological level that I will conclude this chapter with reference to a simple, direct observation which puts two, very different perspectives on the embodiment of sex into a single gambit. Hatha yoga involves the internalization of the essence of sex in order to achieve immortality and embodied transcendent perfection. The performance of hatha yoga as a modern postural gymnastic sport has almost nothing whatsoever to do with this, but the structure of elision is almost identical: a championship performance of Bikram Choudhury's Hot Yoga routine is, in effect, an act that turns the history of yoga inside out, but with minimal contortions of logic and little of consequence with respect to changes in value, other than a significant transformation of consciousness.

'The Athlete Chandoo' from *Muscle Control and Barbell Exercise*: Bishnu Charan Ghosh
B.Sc. and Keshab Candhra Sen Gupta, B.A. Calcutta: Self Published 1930.

7

Conclusion
Signs of Sex and the Sex of Signs

Introduction: Sex and Structure

In the literature on sex and sexuality in South Asia the contrast between passionate, prescriptive admonitions to chastity on the one hand, and the celebration of things erotic on the other, is very well known. Certainly in the epics it is often the ascetic sage who embodies this opposition—contained, contrasted and secretly contrived in various ways—most dramatically.

> A sage performed great *tapas* lying in the water, and the gods feared his terrible powers. Agni sent five *apsara*s to the sage, who was overcome by lust and made them his wives. From then on he lived happily with them, having obtained youth through his *tapas*. (*Ramayana* III. 10. 12–17, in O'Flaherty 1973: 62)

Any number of myths recount how *rishi*s, engaged in dispassionate, earth-shaking *tapas*, are seduced by naked forest nymphs to the point of orgasm. And these orgasms often result in the autochthonous birth of powerful beings: Sharadvan sees the beautiful Janapadi—sent at the behest of a beleaguered Indra—and ejaculates onto a piece of cane that splits his seed into two, producing the twins Kripa and Kripi. The iconic ascetic Bharadvaja sees Ghritachi bathing. At the point of irrepressible ejaculation he manages to catch his seed in a clay pitcher, out of which is born Dronacharya, sage teacher-to-be of the Pandavas. While rubbing two fire-sticks together, Vyasa is 'overwhelmed by a violent storm of love' at the sight of Ghritachi. Unable to control the flow of his seed, but apparently able to keep control of himself, he ejaculates onto the lower of the two fire-sticks. After continued rubbing his son Shuka is born.

In a classic work on this subject, inspired by structuralism as a theory for understanding the logic of symbols, Wendy Doniger O'Flaherty has pointed out that Lord Shiva is the paradigmatic erotic ascetic. The power of his chaste self-abnegating tapas is the complementary opposite of his epic, ithyphallic eroticism (1973:10). Often it is the extent of the former in practice that ultimately produces a powerful expression of the latter. But it is just as often the other way around:

> After marrying Paravati, Siva made love to her for a thousand years, but then he lost all of his *tejas* and his virility was reduced. Seeing himself thus diminished, Siva resolved to perform *tapas*, and he undertook a great vow, wandering on earth, carrying a skull. (Vamana 34. 2–3 in O'Flaherty 1973: 296)

Thus, in effect, power derived through extreme chastity is reflected in specific instances of the extremely powerful, uncontrolled flow of sexual fluids. Many myths reflect the dynamic, powerful and complex relationship between chastity, sex, erections and desire, but versions of the Pine Forest myth are paradigmatic: Shiva seduces the wives and daughters of rishis, who are unaware of his power and true nature. As a result Shiva is cursed and castrated. Castration produces cosmic chaos, but also awareness of Shiva's true identity. Order is restored when the erect, castrated lingam, the very embodiment of opposition, penetrates the delusions of human consciousness as an object of worship—a symbol of structure itself.

While the structure of this opposition produces a dynamic paradox—rather than a logical contradiction—it is useful to focus on the iconographic physiology that reflects erotic asceticism in order to gain an important perspective on the analysis which follows, as it relates to this paradox.

> The ambiguity of ithyphallicism is possible because, although the erect phallus is of course a sign of priapism, in Indian culture it is a symbol of chastity as well. Siva is described as ithyphallic, particularly in the Pine Forest [where he seduces the wives of the sages], and this condition is often equated with a state of chastity: 'He is called *urdhvalinga* because the lowered *linga* sheds its seed, but not the raised *linga*.' The basic Sanskrit expression for the practice of chastity is the drawing up of the seed (*urdhvaretas*), but, by synecdoche, the seed is often confused with the *linga* itself, which is raised in chastity. (O'Flaherty 1973: 9–10)

Being 'that which cannot be controlled', an erection becomes a symbol of control itself, but only to the extent that its opposite is flagged or marked. Lord Shiva is not powerful because he is chaste; he is powerful because of the relationship between chastity and his unmitigated erotic passion. His erect phallus is a measure, and external sign, of sexual fluid that is drawn up and in. But not only this: ithyphallicism is integral to the production of semen as a fluid that has power in the body. However distracting the problem of desire may be, one must not lose sight of biomechanical dynamics, as these dynamics relate to the structure of symbols and signs. What I would like to draw attention to here is not simply the mythic structure of the paradox, but questions of anatomy, physiology and power in the structure of medical interventions that are rooted in this paradox.

A fundamental problem with sex is that it is all too easily reduced to the literalism of embodied experience at a singular moment in time. The intimacy of sex—as with sensuality in general—tends to produce a sense of two-dimensional pragmatism; instinctive responses along a trajectory of the sexual response cycle generate experience without signs, at least in the heat of the moment, and this experience extends outwards to take on profound meaning. Needless to say, the idea that sex is uninhibited by semiotic structures is an illusion; but it is an illusion that is most powerful and persuasive. Sex comes to mean a great deal, but within parameters that are tightly circumscribed by instinct and the fact that the signified of sex involves physical signs that point towards a single object, the erect lingam being iconic.

As intimated by the mythological preamble, lingams can be manipulated to mean various things. Most often their meaning is a function of outward projection. However, lingams point towards meanings that are embodied in different ways—involving secreted substances rather than emotions and desires—and a particular expression of masculinity involves sex as a sign of youthful strength and energy. *Gupt rog chikitsa* is a medical sub-specialty that deals with the paradoxical nature of sex in relation to masculinity, both as an outward projection of power, and an inward concern with youth, strength and the problem of time. Ripe with secreted significance, gupt rog chikitsa nevertheless takes shape in concrete, material things—herbs, pills, animals, oils—that stand in a direct relationship to the body. As such gupt rog chikitsa is inherently semiotic, and the semiotic structure, based on the logic of secrecy, reflects the ambiguity of ithyphallicism in real time.

As a time-tested theory of culture that involves the coupling of rules, perception and meaning, structuralism—however old and long in the tooth—is analytically seductive. Simple formulas of binary opposition—masculine/feminine, in/out, wet/dry, hard/soft—can be manipulated to reproduce whole worlds of suggestive cultural complexity. The nature of the seduction, at least in my memory of first reading *The Savage Mind* (1966), and now in the shadow of Levi-Strauss's death, is the endless anticipation of resolution; an analytical process that is equal parts evocation, procreation and fantasy; something new and unexpected merging perfectly with the structure of the subject at hand.

Having furtively characterized this vintage intellectual exercise rather erotically, I should back up and say that the seduction is not at all duplicitous, contrived or forced. If desire sets a trajectory bent on conquest, control, and domination—either intellectual, imperial or simply carnal—then by nature it is altogether something different: self-centred lust and violent projection, perhaps. Structural analyses most certainly can be crude. But the artful merger of analysis and subject is an ethnological romance. With luck it produces subtle poetic insight complete unto itself, encompassing the structural frame upon which it is built. On one level, therefore—and in the shadow of a great man who lived to be 100—this concluding chapter is a romantic homage to the savagery of the discontented mind and the structures of signification therein that are manifest as secrets about sex.

What I mean by 'secrets about sex' is signified by terminology; terminology that is used to denote a specific branch of medicine: gupt rog chikitsa—the treatment for secret diseases. Although gupt rog chiktsa has come to encompass a wide range of things including birth control, STD treatment and discourses of scientific celibacy, it is concerned, primarily, with sexual performance and the relationship between fitness, performance and masculinity. The essential core concern is with embodied power, as power is reflected in animals—elephants, lions, tigers, bulls and stallions: the erstwhile analogs of the virile king in the context of the physician Charaka's prescription of aphrodisiacs. Although gupt rog chikitsa is not by any means simply the modern articulation of Ayurveda's 'ancient' concern with *vajikarana* aphrodisiac therapy—whereby a king is transformed into a man with stallion-like size, strength and stamina—in an important sense the structural logic of inhibited 'secrecy' corresponds to the uninhibited expression of massive priapism reflected in the embodied lingam and the structural extension of the lingam into the form of the zoomorphized masculine body.

Critics of structuralism point to the limitations and distortions of decontextualized analyses and the articulation of 'voiceless' depersonalized constructs devoid of cultural meaning and lived experience. As indicated, structural analyses can be crude and formulaic. But this is only the case when they are reduced down to formulas and theorems. The virtue and power of structuralism, as an analytic sensibility, is that it is systematically *inconclusive* and thus properly reflects the nature of reality as mythological; purposefully and strategically it avoids the problematic attribution of agency to those involved in the production of meaning. Agency wedded to mythology produces a fragmentary world of deceptively definitive empiricism. As such, structuralism is diagnostic of the powerful myth that meaning is conclusive or transparent. This is particularly so when the nature of the mythic subject at hand is self-consciously defined as a secret, or as mysterious, and where the structures of signification involve the dynamics of secrecy.

Along parallel lines there is an interesting congruity between secrecy and the analytical seductiveness of structuralism. Secrecy stands, I think, as the not-quite-opposite of the arbitrariness of all signs, in the sense that it constantly begs the questions of randomness, while holding out hope that there is, on some plane, pure meaning; a world of uninhibited, unmediated perception: absolute truth. Both secrecy and structure are anchored, as it were, in the indeterminacy of oblique allusion to this possibility. Secrecy, almost by definition, exists in the domain of language. It is a part of speech although it can most certainly be inferred from and attributed to concrete or almost-concrete things—the philosopher's stone, the Sphinx, Aboriginal Churinga or a dark cave. It concerns tricks and deception as well as simply restricted information; uncertainty, as well as the truth about lies and lies about the truth, as lies and the truth involve real people and real things. As such, secrecy can derive from and devolve into concrete objects and experiences that are real but not very easy to grasp, either as such or in terms of what they mean. It is on this level that an affective analysis of manifest secrecy—in the form of gupt rog chikitsa—can engage with the disembodied, disoriented, voicelessness of structuralism.

The Lingam of Landour

In the north Indian tourist resort town of Mussoorie—affectionately known as 'queen of the hills'—there is an old clock-tower that dates back to the early twentieth century when the town was a hill station designed for the rest and relaxation of colonial administrators, officers, bureaucrats and their families. From the Doon Valley below, the night lights of the town appear as the layered strands of a pearl necklace resting against the dark mountain contours. The suggestive nickname of the town comes, in part, from the metaphorical entailments that ensue from this form of poetic anthropomorphism. But it also comes from the fact that in the nineteenth century the structured leisure of 'rest and relaxation' gave way to recreational pleasures of the flesh, to the extent that the town itself became gendered in the erotic imagination of late Victorian British India. As the story goes, the breakfast bell at the Grand Savoy was rung twice: once to ensure that everyone got back into the 'right' bed, and the second to call everyone, properly paired up, to the dining hall.

The old clock-tower, with its prominent four-faced clock, is an easily recognized landmark on the skyline. With each face arbitrarily reflecting a different fixed point in time—three o'clock in the south, five-to-five in the east—the erectile dysfunction rises up twenty metres above the rest of the town, marking the boundary between Mussoorie proper and the Landour bazaar. More than a few people have pointed out, without any particular Freudian insight, that it reflects a certain symbolic articulation of imperial conquest and colonial control. This reflection of power was with reference to literal function—the keeping of time, regulation, discipline and all that—as well as in terms of symbolic form. In terms of form, which is skewed in many ways, the broken clock-tower incarnates a degree of post-colonial irony.

Without any consciousness of being implicated in the magic realism of irony, but seeing in the clock-tower a definitive sign of masculinity, my young uncircumcised friends—who called me and my Christian and Muslim playmates *katue* (which means what it sounds like with reference to foreskin)—called it the lingam of '*Lund*'our; lund roughly meaning the same thing as lingam, although within the rubric of a structure that distinguishes subtle from gross, refined from course, civilized from savage. Communal affiliation, anatomy and aspersive bilingual puns aside, we also referred to it by the more direct double entendre of a cruder, penetrating, pendulous reference—*ghanta ghar*. Ghanta ghar does, in fact, just mean 'bell' tower, or 'home of the gong'—the clock and hourly chimes being denoted, at least on the level of literal meaning. By implication that which is denoted can be twisted and up-ended if said in a particular way to make the sound of the clapper sound like the clapper looks: the opposite of *urdhvalinga*. A gesture—using one's thumb and a quick, crotch-ward glance—providing pointed emphasis, makes ghanta mean the same thing as lund. Suggestive ambiguity is further encoded in the indeterminate and precisely unmarked question of where the term *ghar*—which means house—maps out on the sexed body. In other words, ghanta ghar invokes a range of sexual meanings by structuring the relationship between words, bodies and urban landscape. A slight, quick, knowing 'shift of the eyes south' references a range of slippages between the real and the imagined. A common practical joke among friends engages this slippage. It involves asking someone if they know their way around town. Regardless of the answer the victim of the joke is told that there is a map of the town right on his body, and that it is easy enough to see and to trace. Placing the tip of one's little finger on the crown of the victim's head, the joke proceeds by tracing out an imaginary map of locations and landmarks in 'Lund'our—nose to throat to chest to navel—ending with a vigorous goose in the ghanta ghar, bringing sign and signified emphatically together.

Meaning is thus complicated by the mysterious structure of words. Nothing is resolved by the apparent reality of the body. And this is the point with respect to the subject at hand. Sex as such, and sex in relation to words and things is increasingly complicated by actions designed to make sense. In a world of words—clock-towers, broken clocks, bells, clappers, foreskin—lingams define a mythology of post-colonial magic realism. Gupt rog chikitsa—a locus of concern about the illusiveness of lingams—is embrocated in this very tangible space.

One of the most striking memories I have of growing up in Mussoorie is of a sex clinic located at the base of the lingam of Landour.

At an angle in large English and Devnagari script it says 'Sex Specialist—World Famous Kaviraj Arjan Singh Vaidya and Sons'. On a placard beside the door is a picture of a man and a woman. The man, a look-alike of the freedom fighter Chandrashekhar Azad—left hand putting the final twist on an oiled and neatly pointed mustache—is standing to the side and behind the woman who is dressed in 'modern' western clothes.

As additional references on the door make clear, Kaviraj Arjan Singh Vaidya treats erectile dysfunction, premature ejaculation, impotence, wet dreams, and masturbation—'mistakes of childhood' as the euphemism has it—as well as V.D. and 'gas'. I figured that gas was just as embarrassing as sex, so the vertically arranged letters on one of the door jambs—GASVDSEX—made a certain amount of sense . . . although, not really.

What made more sense was the fact that Kaviraj Arjan Singh Vaidya advertised his expertise in the treatment of problems relating to the loss of strength and youthful energy—*takat jawani*. The cures that he provides for the 'secret diseases' or gupt rog are fundamentally treatments for this more generalized, pervasive somatic condition of masculinity-subject-to-time. From the base of the lingam he treats problems of masculinity that take shape in the language of sex.

Adjacent to a free homoeopathic dispensary and an antique shop that sells what now remain of the Empire's trappings, Arjan Singh's clinic is hardly ever open for business. In the 1960s and 1970s I only remember once or twice seeing a stern elderly Sikh gentlemen sitting in the narrow open doorway in front of a curtain and an array of boxes and bottles. I figured there was a secret, rear entrance, or that people made arrangements to meet with Dr Singh behind closed doors.

I also figured that Dr Singh's clinic was more or less unique, located where it was—in Mussoorie, that is, rather than at the base of the ghanta ghar—on account of the way in which the 'queen of the hills' has been billed as the 'Niagara Falls of North India': a preeminent place for middle-class newlyweds to come on their honeymoon. As an enterprising businessman, I reasoned, Dr Singh had identified a market niche at the point of intersection between masculinity, tourism and the consummation of matrimony: a circumscribed, self-consciously anxious 'consumer demographic' directly concerned with potency, performance and the twisted points of well-oiled mustaches.

But, somehow, between what seemed like an obvious, demographically articulated set of embodied problems—erectile dysfunction, premature ejaculation, and lack of stamina and strength—and the open, publicized information on Dr Singh's closed door, there was absolute ambiguity, uncertainty and mystery: an iconic black box. And, quite apart from the question of curing physiological conditions that have some relationship to cultural constructs like love, romance, and more basic feelings that tend in these directions, and many others, there are many questions: what is the tangible outcome of the cures to these interminable terminological problems? For instance, how do you measure 'enhanced erectile function'? How does one count, measure and tabulate numerous, strong, stamina-stimulated, orgasmically powerful and 'timely' ejaculations? Between what is deemed 'problematic' and what might be achieved there is a whole spectrum of imagined, fantastic possibility, which only resolves into deeper ambiguity. This is true even when—especially when—empirical answers are provided: Dr Singh's rigidly wiggling index finger signifying the recovery of an impotent sixty-year-old man. Between the physical member as such and the many discontents of embodied masculinity there is everything but certainty, including the fetishization of the desire for certainty—the pointed suggestion of a twisted mustache rather than its twisted point between thumb and forefinger.

As the designations '*Kaviraj*' and '*Vaidya*' would suggest, Dr Arjan Singh was, and his three sons continue to be, self-professed practitioners of Ayurvedic medicine. However, they claim authority on the basis of a long-standing family tradition of inherited expertise rather than the textual integrity of systematized, theoretical knowledge and conformity to the canonic structure of classical wisdom as codified by Charaka, Sushruta and Vagbhatta. What this means is that Kaviraj Arjan Singh's reputation as a healer derives from a combination of complex factors including the use of time-tested techniques and powerful testimonials of success, but also from the less direct mystique of maverick, one-of-a-kind invention, tempered by a sense of reputable, tried-and-true, father-to-son, family-name consistency.

As a vaidya with pedigree—which counts for a great deal in matters of sex—Kaviraj Arjan Singh draws, directly and indirectly, on the corpus of knowledge codified in the compounding of *vajikarana* aphrodisiacs (see Alter 2008). Quite apart from his skill, which by many accounts is considerable, his and his sons' authority derives from the way in which they are able to claim knowledge that is unique and secretly coded to lineage and word-of-mouth transmission, but is also linked, by a chain of complex signifiers, to a very real body of documented recipes and decoctions in the classical literature of Ayurveda as such.

The Structure of Sex in Relation to Time

It can be argued that Ayurvedic medicine as a whole, and most certainly theories of physiology and elemental metabolism that define an Ayurvedic understanding of the body, are structured with reference to semen as a sexual fluid, and vitality as a derivative of semen. According to the primary texts in the Ayurvedic corpus the body is supported or nourished by a process of *dhatu* transformation whereby *rasa* (chyle) is digested or 'cooked' so that it becomes *rakta* (blood); rakta is cooked so that it becomes *mamsa* (flesh); mamsa becomes *medas* (fat) by the same process, and so on from *asthi* (bone) to *majja* (marrow), from majja to *sukra* (semen), and from sukra to the elemental material essence of subtle energy known as ojas. The metabolic transformation of dhatu to dhatu is ongoing in the sense that food is consumed and transformed into rasa, thus regularly incorporating into the body raw material that will eventually manifest itself as ojas. The rate of transformation is understood to be about five days for each stage, or roughly a month from rasa to ojas. Similarly ojas is understood to be like a condensed distillate, being eight drops in volume and both located in the heart and 'pervading the whole body'.

Although there are a number of points of disagreement in the Ayurvedic literature about what exactly ojas is, and how it relates to other parts of the body and body functions, it is very clear that ojas is 'vital energy', and that vital energy is intimately linked to semen. It is the pure essence of 'cooked' semen in the same way that ghee is the essence of cooked butter.

A critical point in this regard is that in the transformation of sukra to ojas, sexuality is correspondingly transformed, or at least its significance is reconceptualized. Sex and the ability to have sex is less an end in itself and more a derivative of generalized vitality and robust health—it becomes a sign of youth in a body that is subject to the agency of time-bound transformation: a body that is constantly growing old and becoming less energetic.

The problem of aging is a paradigmatic problem in Ayurveda, and, in many ways, Ayurvedic therapy of the kind practised by Kaviraj Arjan Singh, must, in a general sense, be understood as an antidote to time, or specific complications that arise as a consequence of change as a function of time. With this in mind, the location of the medical shop-cum-clinic, at the base of the clock-tower, is not so much a case of coincidental irony as a manifestation of truth refracted in the concrete nature of magical realism.

What I mean is that the humours—*vata*, *pitta*, *kapha*—are by definition morbid and characterized by 'faults' precisely because the world is in flux, and flux is understood to be ontologically imperfect in relation to perfection as a condition that only exists outside of time. This is manifest even more clearly in the concept of guna which can perhaps best be translated as 'psychosomatic qualities that interweave like the strands of a rope'. All organic matter is constituted by the differential weave of three strands, sattva, rajas and tamas, which together derive from a perfect state of natural balance extant prior to creation. All living things are, by definition, out of balance as a function of time. Even the subtle, pure, bright radiance of sattva is best understood as an affected orientation towards perfect imbalance.

The problem of time is nowhere more clearly articulated than in the branch of Ayurveda known as *rasayana*. Rasayana is concerned with rejuvenation and may be understood as the penultimate solution to the paradigmatic problem. Rasayana is not just meant to prolong life; it is meant to extend life, and to extend it by restoring youthful vigour and vitality. In a sense it is therapy that turns back time. This is done quite literally. The restoration of normal humoural balance is understood to reflect an earlier stage of development. Although this is generally true, it is most graphically reflected in a description of rasayana therapy in the *Susruta Samhita*. Here a middle-aged patient undergoes *kuti-pravesika* treatment. He is isolated in a secluded room within a specially designed hut and restricted to a strict regimen.

After a series of purifying and lubricating procedures, along with sweating, he is given the elixir *soma* to drink. The effect of soma is significant. For the first seven days of treatment the patient vomits blood and worms, has diarrhoea with worms in it, and swells up. On the fourth day of treatment worms come out from all parts of his bloated body. On the seventh day he is reduced to skin and bones. On each of these days he is given milk that has been boiled and cooled, except that on day five and six he is given milk twice. On the seventh day his body is sprinkled with warm milk, and he is given a second dose of soma to drink. After this, his body begins to regenerate itself as his teeth, fingernails and hair fall out and his skin splits open and sloughs off. On the tenth day new skin appears; on the seventeenth, new teeth; on the twenty-fifth new fingernails appear, followed by new hair. By this point his new skin is radiant and lustrous.

It seems quite clear that rasayana involves structured rebirth. The aging body is killed off, and a new body emerges to take its place. But this new body is different in kind from the old body. It is immortal. It is a body that does not change.

> The visionary man who makes use of the king of plants, Soma, wears a new body for ten thousand years. Neither fire nor water, neither poison, blade nor projectile, are powerful enough to take his life. He gains the strength of a thousand well-bred, sixty-year-old, rutting elephants . . . He is as beautiful as the god of love, as attractive as a second moon (*Susruta Samhita*, 4:29 in Wujastyk 2003: 176)

As the shift in register from ageless immortality to martial invincibility to beauty-on-par-with-the-god-of-love would suggest, rasayana therapy anticipates sex and sexuality. The symbolism of elephants neatly, if rather awesomely, connects these themes. In the *Charakasamhita* the effect of rasayana therapy is almost always sensual, even though it is clearly not limited to sexual vitality. For example, one description of the effects is as follows: 'It alleviates hoarseness of voice, chest diseases, heart disease, *vatarakta*, thirst and disorders of urine and semen . . . If this rasayana [*chyavanaprasa*] is used by the indoor method [*kuti-pravesika*] even the old attain intellect, memory, lustre, freedom from diseases, longevity, strength of senses, sexual vigour, increased *agni* (digestion and metabolism), fairness of complexion and carmination of wind . . .' (*Chikitsasthanam* 1: 71–74). In the case of another rasayana decoction, Charaka claims that in addition to living for a hundred years without getting old, 'one attains sexual vigour in women and also is blessed with progeny.' (*Chikitsasthanam* 2: 4).

While there is no question but that rasayana anticipates sex as such, it also seems quite clear that it is linked to other concerns, and that long life—as cognate with immortality—is regarded as an important end in itself. On this level one can understand the logic of rasayana therapy in terms of broader philosophical concerns with time, change and flux in general and, in particular, the problem of rebirth as a symptom of the way in which reality is misperceived. To be immortal is to have escaped the snare of rebirth. To embody immortality is to embody consciousness of the Self as a transcendent, timeless principle. Certainly if one looks at alchemical medicine and at yoga—which are, like Ayurveda, inspired by *Samkhya* philosophy, in much the same way as the structure of biomedicine is Cartesian—there are very clear examples of how immortality is achieved by effectively stopping the flow and transformation of substances within the body.

Rasayana is, therefore, cognate with the ultimate goal of ascetic practice. Granted, the paradigmatic patient is most often a virile king, but the philosophical point of reference for his embodied power—with an emphasis here squarely on the body—is world renunciation. Speaking of *amalaka rasayana*, Charaka makes the following point:

> By this treatment, the sages regained youthfulness and attained disease-free life for many hundreds of years, and endowed with the strength of physique, intellect and senses practised penance with utmost devotion. (*Chikitsasthanam* 1: 75)

Although more sensual than erotic, one can clearly imagine the correlation between this medicalized image and the mythology of Shiva.

In any case, rasayana anticipates vajikarana, a branch of medicine directly concerned with aphrodisiacs. As the etymology of the term would suggest the goal is to 'make a horse out of a man', meaning that he will have the potency and power of a stallion. With the rather unfortunate stereotype of masculinity that this image brings to mind, it is important to point out that in vajikarana therapy size does, in fact, matter; but ithyphallic size is by no means the only thing or even the most important. In understanding sex and sexuality in the context of Ayurveda, it is of critical importance to appreciate the extent to which a concern for what might be called the physiological mechanics of kinaesthetic sex is linked to the metabolic production of semen in the body as a whole, quite apart from what the act of sex produces in terms of self-image.

Sexual potency has as much to do with the quantity and quality of semen that permeates the body—and is cooked into ojas—as it does with horse-like priapism. Clearly vajikarana 'maximizes pleasure during sexual congress' (*Chikitsasthanam* 2, in Rao 1987: 213). But, I would argue, it only does this within the context of a much more comprehensive transformation of the body: a person who lacks potency, lacks it as a consequence of old age and overindulgence; potency and virility decline when semen is depleted, dried up, diseased, or degenerated. Quite apart from the strength and stamina that horses are said to have, virility is directly correlated with comprehensive physical strength; for those who are strong and well balanced in terms of humoural criteria virility produces satisfaction (*vaidyaka-samgraha*). Although the *Charakasamhita* is concerned with therapeutic ithyphallicism, it is even more concerned with the production of semen, as healthy semen promotes strength and, most significantly, produces strong, healthy children.

Aphrodisiac compounds are significant insofar as they materialize the mystique of imagined possibility—with respect to size, stamina, and power, but also through radical ecological and herbal elaboration—while reproducing potency on the basis of what might be called *arcaneum ad infinitum*.

If one drinks milk after being satiated with sparrow meat one's penis will remain erect, retain semen and not become flaccid in the night. (*Chikitsasthanam* 2.1:46)

If one is satiated with cock's meat fried in crocodile semen, one maintains an erection all night long and never needs sleep. (*Chikitsasthanam* 2.1:48)

One should collect the semen of sparrows, swans, cocks, peacocks, tortoises and crocodiles, cow's ghee, lard and the fat of *kulinga* sparrows, and the powder of *sastika* rice and wheat. With these one may prepare various things to eat, such as *pupalika*, *saskuli*, *vartika*, *pupa* and *dhana*. By making use of these edibles one enjoys a woman with full satisfaction like a horse with a stiffened and semen-filled organ. (*Chikitsasthanam* 2.2:10–13)

Consider here the really exotic nature of crocodile semen, which signifies a scenario that is not in the least bit supernatural or based on the obscure logic of magic and myth-making. Since crocodile semen actually exists, to what extent, and on what level, is the relationship between signified and signifier dispassionately random, as it is in the case of cock meat and cocks? Much the same could be said with regard to the elemental nature, mythological significance and sheer volatility of mercury in *siddha* medicine and its various organic proxies in vajikarana. As a note on the question of passionate volatility, until one has watched a flock of sparrows getting down and dirty in the early spring, it is difficult to appreciate why this small creature—and its correspondingly small male member—signifies the same potential of endless, full satisfaction as that of the horse.

The point is that in the mix of vajikarana decoctions there are fabulous things that are tangibly real, and the exotic nature of their reality, or the possibility of their empirical reality—often sealed up in opaque bottles, or shrouded in a cloud of road-side dust kicked up by *kulinga* in rut—invokes a kind of power that combines magic with the potentiality of things you can touch, feel and smell. In this sense aphrodisiac compounds are seductive in the same way as sex, and the marketing of the former plays off of the mystique of the latter. The logic of aphrodisiacs is elisive, suggestive and analogic—it is the same logic reflected in the marketing genius of delineating, without calibration, regular, large and extra-large condoms.

The Seduction of Secrecy

To develop this point I will return to elements of Arjan Singh's practice, and, more generally, the unique way in which gupt rog chikitsa is advertised. But a specific example will provide an important perspective on the way in which secrecy allows for infinite elaboration, and how the sheer amplification of discreet information, on a number of different registers, produces and reproduces the infinite regress of secrecy by means of constantly imminent revelation that strains against the very medium of communication—images, words, and breathless sentence structure, too.

On the promenade leading up to the monumental façade of the Jumma Masjid in Old Delhi there are numerous hawkers of various items ranging from amulets to inexpensive zip drives. Each hawker's display occupies a designated space on the outer edge of heavily trafficked walkways on either side of a dried-up, narrow reflecting pool that extends east from the entry steps, prayer plaza and massive, marble-inlaid, central red sandstone archway between the minarets. At the far end of the reflecting pool, roughly in-between the *maidan* (field) in front of the entrance to Barkat Ali's akhara and the walled-off compound where wrestling tournaments are held on Sunday afternoons, is a wide, flagstone-covered space that is used for dignitary parking. On Fridays the Masjid grounds are crowded with people from all over southern Asia, and the promenade is bustling with activity. On other days there is not the same level of intensity, but the atmosphere is still carnivalesque. I always imagine the quick-money, buyer-beware culture of this place of prayer and pilgrimage as a kind of revenge of the Biblical money-changers: those iconic New Testament charlatans who were subject, several centuries earlier in Jerusalem, to the indignation of a righteous thrashing at the hands of Jesus, the Prince of Peace.

On any given day in the evenings one can find a rather nondescript middle-aged man carrying a large, brown briefcase standing in the middle of a crowd of boys and young men near the end of the reflecting pool in the parking lot for dignitaries. His teeth are stained with betel juice and his greying hair flecked with henna. He is in the business of selling pills for the enhancement of sexual performance and the treatment of 'embarrassing short-comings', real and imagined. The pills are home-made, rather nondescript and hardly more expensive than two cups of tea. However, the marketing technique is, as they say, priceless.

The man with the brown briefcase stands in the middle of an open space holding a binder notebook containing documents, letters and, most significantly, both black and white as well as colour photographs, some clear and sharp but obscure, others faded, blurred and unfocused. However unclear, they are unambiguous in terms of what they are supposed to reveal. In an easy, confident and reassuring tone he talks about problems that men might encounter with respect to sexual experiences and performance. He describes and elaborates on these problems in a very matter-of-fact tone, pointing out that if one suffers from wet dreams, there is a solution; that if one has difficulty getting and maintaining an erection, there is a solution, and one should not be concerned; if one's 'water falls too quickly' during intercourse, one should not be alarmed or dismayed, for there is a solution; if one's penis is too short or crooked, one need not be anxious or nervous, for there is a solution; if one is worried that excessive masturbation has resulted in weakness, watery semen and the signs of premature aging—sunken eyes, white hair and a sallow complexion—one should not be worried, for there is a solution. The monologue intensifies gradually over the course of ten or fifteen minutes, depending on the size of the crowd, with increasingly detailed references to the kinetic mechanics of sex—erection, thrusting penetration, orgasm.

As he talks, his eyes scan the crowd, but he does not meet any particular gaze; at times he looks out onto the maidan, or up to the minarets with studied, casual distraction. But his hands keep moving rapidly. With the notebook held open on his left hand and forearm, the fingers of his right hand are inserted between the laminated pages of photographs and official-looking—or, for all I know, official-in-fact—documents: letters, permits, testimonials. He flips these back and forth, just quickly enough to provide a brief glimpse of partial pages. The young men press close over his shoulder, those farther back on tiptoe, stretching their necks with hands on each other's backs trying to get a better view, arms around waists to keep balance. The constant, random flipping of pages draws one in. It is seduction.

I cannot accurately or completely describe the pictures in the notebook, for if I could the whole thing, the complex mix of mediated information that references information that is not complete, that produces imagination and wonder—and, at other times, in other places, fear, trembling and terror—would devolve into the completely transparent illusion of pornographic facticity and the confounding mimesis therein of desire and the kinetic mechanics of sex as an embodied act. Having looked more closely at what I imagine to be very comparable notebooks, I could fill in the gaps—extending my licence from ethnographer to pornographer—but the fact of the matter is that in this instance participant observation made the power of secrecy unambiguously clear in the open space between one kind of sign and another.

At a certain point in time, most likely having gauged the size of the crowd and the level of stimulation—an even mix of anxiety, assurance and anticipated euphoric affect—the nondescript man places the notebook back into the briefcase and removes a bag full of inexpensive, thin, matchbox-sized cardboard containers which he sells to men in the crowd for ten rupees each. You can buy as many as you like and ask no questions or you can buy as many as you like and ask for specific instructions, depending on the nature of your concerns.

Labelled as 'samples', they are billed as 'Empire Pills', invoking a prominent erection on the skyline of New York City rather than the long shadow of that upon which the sun never sets. Curiously, but in keeping with the argument presented throughout this book, they are indicated as 'blood purifiers' and 'the best herbal tablets for constipation and excess heat in the body'. Clearly meant to invoke the authority of scientific professionalization, place of manufacture and trademark are assigned to Bharat Pharmacy in Kanpur, a decidedly non-exotic, registered company under the management of Dr J.A. Sahaswani. Each box contains about ten pills with fairly clear instructions, subject modification and sentence structure notwithstanding: 'take one tablet before sleeping with water',which, I think, takes us back to the sage reference at the beginning of the chapter. Aside from this, the boxes of pills unto themselves mediate directly between key questions—how many? for what? and when?—and a host of variable answers.

The pills (*tikki*) are potent medicine. They function as a panacea, since specific symptoms resolve into a more general rubric of weakness wherein cause and effect—masturbation and *kamzori*; *svapan dosh* and weakness; old-age and erectile dysfunction—can be made to trade places like sign and signified in the transmutation of Sussureian to Lacanian structuralism: language into the order of the psyche.

Pills—and elsewhere potions and decoctions—are, in essence, elemental substances into which whole panoplies of concern resolve; they are also repositories of meaning: materialized points at which tangents of alternative and sometimes divergent significations intersect. In this sense a more literal translation of the term tikki conveys the appropriate connotation of that upon which information is inscribed and permanently preserved—a tablet. In relation to their elemental material form, and singular function, tablets stand in a particular relationship to the psychology of sex: they condense and reify unconscious secrecy much as an exorcism brings to light the dark, intransigent, unpredictable nature of maleficent spirits and malevolent demons.

The discussion will return to pills, potions and packaging, but the significance of these things must be understood with reference to other inscriptions, and to the direct indirectness of marketing gupt rog chikitsa.

Direct indirectness is not intended as a sophist turn of phrase; it is descriptively accurate in an empirically ethnographic sense, and stands to reason, albeit inconclusively.

Direct indirectness is not reflected in polite euphemisms—nightfall, dream error, hand embrace—or jocular mixed up references to kinship relations and sexed anatomy—*sala gandu bhen chod*—that presume a particular kind of kinetic sex. Direct indirectness is not in the play of signifier in relation to signified. It is about signs, and signs in relation to real and imagined restrictions on communication. It is, therefore, about the tension between referent and reality, but a purely discursive, textual reality, not the 'reality' of what secret knowledge is ostensibly about. The signs are about the radical contingency of communicating publicly about that which is, by definition, regarded as secret and private.

If you have travelled by rail or road in north India you will know what I am writing about. Billboards and advertisements are ubiquitous, come in many different shapes and sizes, and are presented on a range of different materials. Advertisements for clinics and doctors who specialize in the treatment of various diseases and conditions—diabetes, hypertension, malaria, asthma—appear in various forms, as do signs for private dispensaries and hospitals that specialize in specific diagnostic tests or offer new treatment technologies.

A distinctive type of advertising is characteristic of clinics and doctors who specialize in gupt rog chikitsa and associated conditions. The text of these advertisements are almost exclusively written in Devnagari or Arabic/Urdu script and usually read as follows—'Those with secret diseases should contact Dr X'; 'For the treatment of secret diseases, contact Dr Y' 'Clinic Z for the treatment of secret diseases'. Most often a basic location is indicated—near the clock-tower, Meerut; opposite the train station, Moradabad; on the main road, Kathauli; next to the clock-tower, Dehradun—and very frequently a telephone number is provided. Using inexpensive whitewash made from slaked lime, the signs are hand-painted with considerable care—not indiscriminately scrawled—often in grey, brown, or rust with a contrasting outline or shadow.

While these kinds of advertisement are not totally unique, they are very distinctive for several reasons beyond the obvious fact that as signs of a particular kind they make oblique reference to real problems of a very specific type.

The single most distinctive feature is that the signs are written in very, very large letters and consist exclusively of words and numbers on a massive scale—no illustrations, no sub-text elaboration, and absolutely no fine print. The scale of writing is made possible by the fact that the signs are painted on tall, one to five metre brick walls that extend for up to a hundred metres around mango and lychee orchards or peri-urban factory compounds. The signs are, in essence, painted on any large, flat surface that faces a road or rail line. Very few, if any, appear as 'commercial' billboard advertisements.

These signs, rather like the lingams of mythology, take shape in public view and enter into the economy at some point between what is formal and what is informal. And the fact that the signs are so enormous has always struck me as ironic to the point of farce. There is a degree of irony in all public secrecy, but viral 'graffiti' marketing one-upmanship to see who can make the most public statement about a subject that must be kept secret is, in essence, the queer, quirky, campy magic realism of Shiva in the pine forest: the lingam of 'Lundour'.

I will refrain from the obvious, tired jokes that might ensue about what does or does not matter with respect to size in relation to the subject at hand. But the sheer size of the painted words is noteworthy here for it is a distinctive, if not completely unique, feature of the advertisements. It says something significant about the structure of the message and the medium: semiotic realism—lingam as lingam.

Located in the relatively small town of Amroha between Delhi and Moradabad, Hashmi Dawakhana was established in the late 1920s by Hakim Hashmi, a practitioner of Unani medicine with specific expertise in the treatment of problems relating to sex, although it is not clear whether the more 'Ayurvedic' Sanskritic terminology of gupt rog was employed at the time. Recently, Hashmi Dawakhana has established a website to attract potential clients in the Middle East. While noteworthy, the fact of web access should not be confused with other forms of rapid, digital globalization. The vast majority of clients who make their way to Amroha follow a much older 'network' of petrol, diesel and coal-based transportation routes and information channels.

The clinic itself, which specializes in sex problems but also offers a range of other treatments, is tucked away along one of the many back allies of Amroha not far from the central bus depot. It is easy to locate only because it is very well known. Signs for Hashmi Dawakhana can be found from Dehra Dun and Haridwar towards the north and north-east, to Bareilly in the east, Delhi to the west and Agra to the south. In comparison to the signs along public transportation routes leading in to Amroha, the clinic signboard on Qazi Zada Street is very modest. The dawakhana office is on the ground floor of a three-storey building with a large waiting area appointed with couches and chairs. Brochures are available in racks in the waiting room, and newspapers and magazines are arranged on a central coffee table. The hakim, a middle-aged man dressed in starched white churidar pajama, sits behind opaque, curtained doors in a consulting office lined with books and photographs of himself with local and state dignitaries.

Having spent the night of a very hot mid-summer day in Moradabad I found my way to the clinic by taxi and was invited in to the hakim's consulting room where I intended to follow-up on an unanswered email sent from my office in Pittsburgh. I hoped to arrange an interview. As I entered and sat down, the hakim quickly gestured that I should quietly and calmly proffer my wrist for examination. Following a brief, awkward protest that was artfully deflected by various gestures of adamant refusal to speak—eyes closed, palms gently patting the air—I was directed to sit in a chair with my right arm extended, hand and wrist resting on a small pillow at the edge of the desk. With eyes closed, to concentrate and underscore the mystique of silence, the hakim felt my pulse for several minutes. Then he spoke in a very quiet, authoritative voice.

I was diagnosed with weakness, a lack of energy and a number of problems related to the physiology of arousal and the kinetics of sex. The prescription was an extended regimen of treatment that involved pills and follow-up visits at an initial cost of Rs 5,000 for the first dose of medicine.

Caught on the back foot by a kind of preemptive diagnosis that silenced my planned queries (although, why else would I have found my way to Qazi Zada Street in Amroha?), I indicated, quite honestly, that I could not afford the treatment and would not be able to schedule follow-up visits. After a brief discussion I agreed to purchase a bottle of Sikandar-e-Azam for Rs 500 rather than the more expensive, and more explicitly indicative, Hashmi Hardrock or Mughal-e-Penis. I kid you not: Mughal-e-Penis!

So what is noteworthy about the signs for gupt rog chikitsa, especially in terms of the specific history of objectionable advertising that incited the colonial and post-colonial state to act on behalf of decency (see Gupta 2002), is that there is nothing 'objectionable' about them. They are completely coded; completely transparent in the lack of transparency that is signified by three innocuous words—gupt, rog, chikitsa.

But the structure of advertising for gupt rog chikitsa also hinges on the seductive paradox of secrecy—the promise of revelation that is never fulfilled. In this sense all signs on the road lead to Mughal-e-Penis, or some facsimile of the same. The advertisements make no claim to anything in fact; and the ubiquitous inscriptions compensate, with the sheer size of words, for what ultimately cannot be communicated, as size itself becomes a visible sign of that which remains unspoken as well as unspeakable: it reflects the magnitude and scope of the public secret.

Ram Singh Ayurvedic Khandani Dawakhana in Dehradun specializes in gupt rog chikitsa, but the itinerant nature of this roadside, tent-based practice is at an opposite extreme from Hashmi Dawakhana.

Bijendra, a young man sitting in for his maternal uncle, claimed authority on the basis of lineage. As a practitioner of what he called 'dehati chikitsa'(country or 'folk' treatment), Bijendra repeatedly emphasized—as though playing a trump card to every question I put down—that dehati chikitsa is based on the expertise of traditional experience and is nothing at all like the 'English' medicine practised by Kaviraj Arjan Singh Vaidya or one 'Dr Anand' near the clock-tower in Dehradun.

Dehati chikitsa has an ambiguous status relative to textual and/or modern accredited Ayurveda, and Bijendra was not at all interested in the question of how his uncle's practice related, or did not relate, to the canonical writings of Charaka and Vagbhatta. To underscore the efficacy of the medicines that he sells he pointed out that processed and packaged drugs only have a temporary influence. What he sells—all made by hand from herbs picked in Himalayan forests—is permanently effective, the real thing!

From Bijendra I bought powdered herbs for Rs 1,100 and was instructed to consume about half a tablespoon mixed with 50 mg of glucose every morning, followed by a draught of raw milk. I was also prescribed an extended dosage of herbal pills to be consumed after each meal, again with milk. For Rs 500 I bought 10 gms of what I was told was musk oil infused with sixty herbs. Use of the oil involves strategic application fifteen minutes prior to acts of intimacy, avoiding the glans. While carefully measuring out each dosage and application, and showing me a book of anatomy, Bijendra explained that the oil would produce longer, harder erections. The powdered herbs would prevent premature ejaculation, and the pills would produce stamina and strength.

There you have it.

Given that gupt rog chikitsa is primarily concerned with problems of masculine potency and performance it is noteworthy that the *Charakasamhita* contains several chapters that are explicitly devoted to the detailed description of aphrodisiacs. While these have been touched on at various points in this book—and deserve a much more detailed and systematic analysis with respect to herbal botany, ecology and zoology—they require further comment here with respect to questions that relate to the ambiguity and secrecy of signification.

At first blush the recipes for aphrodisiacs in the chapters detailing vajikarana are noteworthy with respect to their transparency, and what might be regard as their rather two-dimensional empirical realism. Although obviously not intended to stand alone as such, one could follow the instructions of many of the annotated prescriptions since the weight and specific nature of each ingredient and notes on preparation are often provided in detail, at least in modern commentaries. Moreover, in a significant number of cases specific food items—ghee, milk, honey, meat soups, *shashtika* rice—either alone or in combination are said to have aphrodisiac qualities. In other words, Ayurvedic aphrodisiacs are not, in any sense, conceptualized as inherently super-natural, or based on procedures that combine exotic substances into magical formulas. As in the case of Bijendra's regimen of prescribed therapy, there is absolutely nothing 'gupt' about the structure of signification.

In keeping with the realist thrust of vajikarana, it is also important to note that Charaka and his various redactors seem to have been very pragmatic—and normatively literal rather than experimental—in their concern with sex, sexual health and the desire to promote potency and passion. This is reflected on two levels. First, the primary purpose of sexual intercourse is conceived of in the classical literature in terms of reproduction, and the function of aphrodisiacs is couched in terms of progeny and the production of numerous healthy male offspring. Not only this. The function of having male heirs is that they produce the material basis of wealth, fame, virtue and pleasure: pleasure, here, in the extended, rather than narrowly coital, sense of the term. Second, the Ayurvedic literature is not at all reductively medical in its delineation of pharmaceutical decoctions.

Unlike some modern practitioners of gupt rog chikitsa, Charaka makes it clear that mood, music, atmosphere and anticipation make a big difference. Although he can most certainly be faulted for a rather narrow, normative and gender-biased conceptualization of what stimulates desire, he does not overlook the obvious—good sex involves sensuality, and sensuality extends across the spectrum of senses, from touching the most intimate and sensitive parts of the body to 'the sound of drunken bees buzzing among the lotus blossoms', and the scent of jasmine in the evening air as mountains and rain clouds fade from dusky-blue to moonlit. Although written in verse form, Charaka's reference to the smell and touch of water-lilies, among other things, is not particularly poetic; but there is no question that romance and seduction is as important a part of the mix of medically enhanced eroticism.

But romance and sensuality aside—and quite apart from however complicated it might be to collect crocodile semen—vajikarana is not as straightforward and literal as it might seem. Vajikarana involves animals.

In ways that extend well beyond the scope of analysis here, the relationship between humans and non-human animals involves structures of reference, communication and reflexive discontent that blend mythology, magic and the empirical nature of reality. In this regard, the chapters on vajikarana in the *Charakasamhita* provide a kind of eco-pharmacological counterpoint to the zoological classification that is operative in the *Kama Sutra*—consuming the fat of a sparrow in one rubric and sparrow-like coital consummation in the other. The structure of reference involving animals and non-human animals is, by definition, mysterious. And this is what makes it directly relevant to the question of secrecy. Regardless of how exact and precise the comparison between one and the other, the comparison does not, and cannot resolve into equivalence.

Beyond this, whenever and wherever non-human animals are involved in the configuration of human sex, the metaphorical nature of the analogical correlation comes up against imagined possibilities that are not at all metaphorical: a shift from bestiary schema and the anatomy of beasts to bestiality.

In many respects everything hinges on language by virtue of the metaphorical entailments that are attendant on actual magical realism. What I mean is that vajikarana makes a man stallion-like with respect to sex, and stallion-like sex with a woman involves 'complete penetration with a penis gorged and stiffened with semen'. Other references to bulls, rutting elephants and sparrows—where seemingly endless stamina rather than size is what matters—are equally suggestive. Just imagine. Clearly the reference to animals, large or small, is neither generalized nor indiscriminate, and the entailments involve a precise delineation of physiological power, although not necessarily with reference to proportional size. Bulls, elephants and stallions are one thing, lions and tigers are emblematic of something else altogether. Hanuman's heroic celibacy notwithstanding, to invoke monkeys— who are all too human in any case—would be to confuse potency, wanton promiscuity, and almost certainly provoke nothing but lusty laughter.

What is going on here, by means of language rather than pictures, is a version of the sleight-of-hand manipulation of images put into play by the nondescript man between the Red Fort and the Jumma Masjid. Reference to bulls, elephants and stallions are the secret of sex turned inside out, not just a projection of overblown masculine fantasy, but an articulation of pervasive discontent concerning the paradoxical structure of secrecy and the uncertainty of inhibition With reference to the way in which sex almost always plays out, animals are the massively signified referents of the enormous words painted on gigantic walls that, like sparrows mating in the dust, seem to go on and on forever.

On the cover of this book we see an image of a man wrestling with a lion; with a sign of himself: intimations of victory lead not to resolution—the beast on its back—but to the structure of endless and limitless conquest. The infinite regress of culture-in-nature-in-culture-in-nature . . .

Having thought that I had purchased Sikandar-e-Azam from the hakim at Hashmi Dawakhana, I was surprised to find that the bottle was labelled Mughal-e-Azam: Alexander the Great having been sidelined by Dilip Kumar playing the role of the great emperor Jahangir in passionate embrace with the beautiful court dancer Anarkali. In any case, Mughal-e-Azam is of a type. There are many, many others. Here are how they are signified: 'Keep On', 'Body Line', 'Recharge Plus', and, directly in line with the theme of nominal greatness, 'Big Boss'. These fit into the rubric of other supplements that promise to reveal and transfer the secret of gupt rog chiktsa. The label Mughal-e-Azam invokes a world of romance and sensuality, but power is what is primarily at issue. Given the ubiquity of products that invoke the *Kama Sutra*, one might hope to find an iconic herbal supplement called 'Taj Mahal' that reflects Charaka's invocation of romance and heartache. But one is much more likely to find a tonic called 'Big Love'.

The maximum retail price for Mughal-e-Azam is listed as Rs 549 for a bottle of ten capsules manufactured by Hashmi Unani Pharmacy. Each bottle comes in a thin, gold-coloured, two-and-a-half inch square cardboard box with a bright red band at the top. The box is marked with a batch number, production date and a licensing code for the registered manufacture of Unani medicine.

Besides these facts—which confer legitimacy and legal status—the box provides two kinds of information about what is inside. On one side are the words, 'Enriched with Gold'. On the other side is a comprehensive list of ingredients. The list does not include 'gold' as such, but 10 mg of calcined gold leaf following an Ayurvedic process of *bhasmikarna*. The gold is included for 'stronger and sustained stamina and vitality', as this relates to a fairly straightforward syntagmatic chain of logic: the same logic of pure, rare, condensed value that was invoked by Bijendra the itinerant vaidya in Dehradun. Needless to say, gold is also a sign of wealth and power. So it is not at all surprising that one can find any number of products on the market that play off the standard of the name: '2 Much Gold', 'Energy 500 Gold', 'Vita-Ex Gold', 'Gold Night'.

But gold only 'fortifies' Mughal-e-Azam. Unto itself it is not a particularly noteworthy aphrodisiac, and, in fact, more often factors into Ayurvedic medicine analogically—as an inorganic sign of immortality—than as a substance unto itself such as ghee, pomegranate seeds, buffalo meat stew, black gram, goat's testicles, rooster meat fried in crocodile semen, and *shashtika* rice. Gold as *swarna bhasma* is, in effect, the equivalent of a transitive verb masquerading as a definitive noun. Fortified by gold, each capsule of Mughal-e-Azam contains 580 milligrams of ten different herbs, *bhasma*s and *kushta*s. In theory, it is the calibrated combination of these things—the only ones easily recognized being *swarna bhasma* and saffron—where the truth of the secret really lies.

From an intellectual standpoint it is reassuring that, despite the passage of time, the world is still structured in a way that inspired mediaeval alchemists intent on solving the problem of life and death—signified in the lingam—by developing exercises and breathing techniques to transmute semen into an elixir of immortality. Wherever we stand in relation to it, the ghanta ghar is a sign of the times.

In conclusion I will judge a book by the quirks of its cover.

The image that appears at the end of this chapter is of the artwork on the cover of a book written by Kaviraj Arjan Singh Vaidya, 'World Famous Sex Specialist' whose business card invites consultation 'for surely good treatment of all secret diseases'. Although the image might be even more apt for the cover of the Nepali Buddhist Padmashri's tenth-century *Nagarasarvasva*—'Entreaty of the Accomplishments of the Man-About-Town'— Singh's book invokes the *Koka Shastra*, a twelfth-century text composed by the poet Kokkoka (Comfort 1965), which is part of a distinctive body of mediaeval literature on sex and sexuality (Zysk 2002) that extended from the tenth century through to the present.

Singh is not at all unique or out of line in drawing on and rewriting the *Koka Shastra*. As Zysk points out, 'the Kama texts composed between the tenth and the nineteenth centuries were rarely inspired by independent thought. Rather, they borrowed extensively from one another, changing phrases or words to accommodate metre or individual taste, and adding new material when available' (2002: 6). No secrets or surprises in the *Ratirahasya* literature on the 'secrets of love'! But these texts serve as a reminder that the body and bodily experiences do not stand alone; sex is mediated through the medium of language.

Having been seduced by images such as that which appear on the cover of this book, Charaka's references to massively engorged elephant penises, a mysterious syntagmatic chain of one-dimensional advertisements anchored in Amroha, and flipped footpath pornography, it is easy to lose sight of that which is, in many ways, ethnographically grounded in the reality of a specific place and time: the social structure of romantic intimacy imagined, however normatively, by Dr Singh. While prescribing medicines to restore youthful strength, he treats secret diseases with the dissemination of marital advice. He does this from a clinic at the base of the lingam of Landour in the honeymoon resort town of Mussoorie, 'queen of the hills'. To quote the twelfth-century poet Kokkoka's invocation concerning the matter of real things and things that really matter in relation to the study of body types and the art of love:

A man may be young and pleasing to women, but if he is not soundly based in the study of body types, of habits, of preferences, of local customs, of instincts, of situations and of gestures, he invariably disgraces himself: of what use, indeed, is a coconut to a monkey. (Comfort 1965: 102)

All said, gupt rog chikitsa is diagnostic of sex and its discontents. As Dr Singh explained, and as the cover of his book intimates, the treatment of sexual problems involves communication and understanding more than anything else. Most of what he does involves straight talk with young couples about sex: language-based demystification. But a fundamental problem is that the desire for uninhibited intimacy and understanding—or absolute power—is always just beyond reach, provoking questions about what is wrong, what can and cannot be cured, and what is possible. A chronic, debilitating desire for everlasting youthful strength—and certain knowledge, mapped and traced on the body, that time is always running out—provokes the tyranny of open-ended fantasy: the possibility that someone, somewhere might have succeeded in extracting the secret essence of immortality from the morbid structure of sex.

Magic realism: Monkeys and coconuts; one lingam in relation to another.

The Art of Love: Gupt Rog Chikitsa

References Cited

'A Member of the Royal Asiatic Society of London.'
    1952   *Sex Life in India*. Calcutta: Medical Book Company.

Adams, Vincanne D. and Stacy Leigh Pigg (eds.)
    2005   *Sex in Development: Science, Sexuality and Morality in Global Perspective*. Durham, NC: Duke University Press.

Alloula, Malek
    1987   *The Colonial Harem*. Manchester and Minnesota: Manchester University Press.

Alter, Joseph S.
    1992a   *The Wrestler's Body: Identity and Ideology in North India*. Berkeley: University of California Press.
    1992b   'The Sannyasi and the Indian Wrestler: The Anatomy of a Relationship.' *American Ethnologist* 19:317–336.
    1993a   'The Body of One Color: Indian Wrestling, The Indian State and Utopian Somatics.' *Cultural Anthropology* 8:49–72.
    1993b   'Hanuman and the Moral Physique of the Banarsi Wrestler.' In *Living Banaras*, C.A. Humes and B. Hartel, eds. Pp. 127–44. Albany: State University of New York Press.
    1994   'Somatic Nationalism: Indian Wrestling and Militant Hinduism.' *Modern Asian Studies* 28, 3: 557–88.
    1996   'Gandhi's Body, Gandhi's Truth: Nonviolence and the Biomoral Imperative of Public Health.' *Journal of Asian Studies* 55:301–322.
    1997   'A Therapy to Live By: Public Health, The Self, and Nationalism in the Practice of a North Indian Yoga Society.' *Medical Anthropology* 17: 309–335.

2000a   'Subaltern Bodies and Nationalist Physiques: Gama the Great and the Heroics of Indian Wrestling.' *Body and Society* 6(2):45–72.

2000b   *Gandhi's Body: Sex, Diet and the Politics of Nationalism.* Philadelphia: University of Pennsylvania Press.

2002   'Nervous Masculinity: Consumption and the Production of Gender in Indian Wrestling. In Diane Mines and Sarah Lamb, eds. *Everyday Life in South Asia*. Pp. 132–145. Indianapolis: Indiana University Press.

2004   *Yoga in Modern India: The Body Between Philosophy and Science.* Princeton: Princeton University Press.

2006   'Yoga at the *Fin de Siècle*: Muscular Christianity with a 'Hindu' Twist.' *International Journal of the History of Sport* 23(5):759–776.

2007a   'Yoga and Physical Education: Swami Kuvalayananda's Nationalist Project.' *Asian Medicine: Tradition and Modernity* 3: 20–36.

2007b   'Yoga and Fetishism: Reflections on Marxist Social Theory.' *Journal of the Royal Anthropological Institute* (N.S.) 12: 763–783.

2008   'Ayurveda and Sexuality: Sex, Sex Therapy, and the 'Paradox of Virility.' In *Modern and Global Ayurveda: Pluralism and Paradigms*. Pp. 177–201. Dagmar Wujastyk and Frederick Smith, eds. Albany: SUNY Press.

Altmann, Denise
2001   *Global Sex.* Chicago: University of Chicago Press.

Anderson, Walter K. and Sharidhar D. Damle
1987   *The Brotherhood in Saffron: The Rashtriya Swayamsevak Sangh and Hindu Revivalism.* Boulder, Colo.: Westview Press.

Anderson, Benedict
1983   *Imagined Communities: Reflections on the Origin and Spread of Nationalism.* London and New York: Verso.

Anonymous
n.d.   *Brahmacharya Ki Prachand Shakti.* Barelli: Sanskriti Sansthan.

Antiyappan, Ira
2001   *Yoka and Ceks.* Chennai: Parati.

Ashby, Philip H.
1974   *Modern Trends in Hinduism.* New York: Columbia University Press.

Ashvalayana

1923 *Grhya Sutra*. Edited by Ganpati Shastri. Trivandrum: Government Press.

Atreya, Shanti Prakash

1974a 'Pahalwani me Dand Bethak ka Sthan.' *Bharatiya Kushti* 11 7–9: 21–26.

1974b 'Pahalwani me Dand Bethak Vyayam ka Sthan.' *Bharatiya Kushti* 11, 10–12; 19–27.

1984 'Ghee'. *Bharatiya Kushti* 21, 3: 21–36.

Ballhatchet, K. A.

1980 *Race, Sex and Class Under the Raj: Imperial Attitudes and Policies and Their Critics, 1793–1905*. New York: St. Martin's Press.

Barbach, L.G.

1975 *For Yourself: The Fulfillment of Female Sexuality*. New York: Doubleday.

Barrett, Ellen

2005 *Sexy Yoga: Forty Poses for Mind-Blowing Sex and Greater Intimacy*. Berkeley: Ulysses Press.

Bennett, Lynn

1984 *Dangerous Wives and Sacred Sisters*. New York: Columbia University Press.

Bhagavad Gita.

1945 Edited by Shripad Krishna Belvalkar. Poona: Bhandarkar Oriental Research Institute.

Bhagwandev, Yogacharya

1992 *Swasthya Aur Yogasana*. Delhi: Subodh Pocket Books.

Bhattacharya, Gargi

2002 *Sexuality and Society*. New York: Routledge.

Birken, Lawrence

1988 *Consuming Desire: Sexual Science and the Emergence of a Culture of Abundance, 1871–1914*. Ithaca, NY: Cornell University Press.

Brittan, Arthur

1989 *Masculinity and Power*. Oxford: Basil Blackwell.

Bose, Brinda and Subhabrata Bhattacharyya

2007 *The Phobic and the Erotic: the Politics of Sexualities in Contemporary India*. London: Seagull Books.

Brown, Peter Robert Lemont
    1988   *The Body and Society: Men, Women and Sexual Renunciation in Early Christianity.* New York: Columbia University Press.

Brown, Wendy
    1988   *Manhood and Politics: A Feminist Reading in Political Theory.* Totawa, N.J.: Rowman and Littlefield.

Cakravarti, Candra
    1963   *Sex Life in Ancient India: An Explanatory and Comparative Study.* Calcutta: Firmal K. L. Mukhopadhyay.

Calderone, M.
    1960   *Release from Sexual Tension.* New York: Random House.

Callaway, Helen
    1987   *Gender, Culture and Empire: European Women in Colonial Nigeria.* London: Macmillan Press.

Carka-Samhita
    1992   Translated and edited by Priavrat Sharma. Varanasi: Chaukhamba Orientalia.

Carstairs, G. Morris
    1957   *The Twice-Born.* London: Hogarth Press.

Chakravarti, Uma
    1990   'Whatever Happened to the Vedic *Dasi*? Orientalism, Nationalism and a Script for the Past.' In Kumkum Sangari and Sudesh Vaid, eds., *Recasting Women: Essays in Indian Colonial History*, pp. 27–87. New Brunswick: Rutgers University Press.

Chandra, Bipin
    1984   *Communalism in Modern India.* New Delhi: Vikas.

Chatterjee, Partha
    1986   *Nationalist Thought and the Colonial World.* London: Zed Books.
    1989   'Colonialism, Nationalism, and Colonized Women: The Contest in India.' *American Ethnologist* 16:622–633.
    1990   'The Nationalist Resolution of the Women's Question.' In Kumkum Sangari and Sudesh Vaid, eds., *Recasting Women: Essays in Indian Colonial History*, pp. 233–53. New Brunswick: Rutgers University Press.

Chetananda, Yogi
1977   *Sex and Yoga*. Delhi: Hind Pocket Books.
Chopra, Rakesh
1990   'Brahmacharya Ki Sadhana' (Celibacy). *Yog Manjari* 13:23–25.
Cohen, Lawrence
1995   'Holi in Banaras and the *Mahaland* of Modernity.' *GLQ* 2: 399–424.
Comfort, Alex
1965   'Introduction.' In *The Koka Shastra*. Edited and Translated by Alex Comfort. Pp. 43–79. New York: Stein and Day.
Cooper, Fredrick and Ann L. Stoler
1989   'Introduction—Tensions of Empire: Colonial Control and Visions of Rule.' *American Ethnologist* 16.4:609–21.
De Michelis, Elizabeth
2004   *A History of Modern Yoga: Patanjali and Western Esotericism*. London: Continuum.
Daniel, E. Valentine
1984   *Fluid Signs: Being a Person the Tamil Way*. Berkeley and Los Angeles: University of California Press.
Daniélou, Alain
2001   *The Hindu Temple: Deification of Eroticism*. Rochester VT: Inner Traditions.
1962   *L'Érotisme Divinisé*. Paris: Buchet-Chastel.
DeJean, Joan
1989   'Sex and Philology: Sappho and the Rise of German Nationalism.' *Representations* 27:148–171.
Demartino, M.F.
1974   *Sex and the Intelligent Woman*. New York: Springer Publishing Co.
Derné, Steve
2000   *Movies, Masculinity, and Modernity: An Ethnography of Men's Filmgoing in India*. Westport: Greenwood Press.
Dickie, Matthew W.
1993   'Callisthenics in the Greek and Roman Gymnasium.' *Nikephoros* 6: 105–151.
Dodson, B.
1933   *Liberating Masturbation*. New York: Betty Dodson.

Doniger, Wendy (O'Flaherty)

1973   *Asceticism and Eroticism in the Mythology of Siva.* London: Oxford University Press.

1980   *Women, Androgynes, and Other Mythical Beasts.* Chicago: University of Chicago Press.

Dumont, Louis

1986   *Essays on Individualism: Modern Ideology in Anthropological Perspective.* Chicago: University of Chicago Press.

Dwyer, Rachel

2000   *All You Want is Money, All You Need is Love: Sexuality and Romance in Modern India.* New York: Cassell.

Dyer, Alfred S.

1889   *Facts for Men on Moral Purity and Health; Being, Plain Words to Young Men upon an Avoided Subject; with, Safeguards against Immorality, and Facts That Men Ought to Know.* London: Dyer Brothers.

Edwards, James

1983   'Semen Anxiety in South Asian Cultures: Cultural and Transcultural Significance.' *Medical Anthropology* 7(3):51–67.

Eliade, Mircea

1990   *Yoga: Immortality and Freedom.* Princeton: Princeton University Press.

Elshtain, Jean Bethke

1981   *Public Man, Private Woman.* Princeton: Princeton University Press.

Embree, Ainslie T.

1990   *Utopias in Conflict: Religion and Nationalism in Modern India.* Berkeley: University of California Press.

Erikson, Erik H.

1969   *Gandhi's Truth.* New York: Norton.

Etienne, Mona and Eleanor Leacock

1980   *Women and Colonization.* New York: Praeger Press. Express Healthcare Management (www.expresshealthcare.in) June 30, 2004.

Filliozat, Jean

1991   'Continence and Sexuality in Buddhism and in the Disciplines of Yoga.' In *Religion, Philosophy, Yoga: A Selection of*

Articles by Jean Filliozat. Translated by Maurice Shukla. New Delhi: Motilal Banarsidass.

Feuerstein, Georg
  1998   *Tantra: The Path of Ecstasy*. Boston: Shambhala Publications.

Foster, Lawrence
  1984   *Religion and Sexuality: The Shakers, the Mormons and the Oneida Community*. Urbana: University of Illinois Press.

Foucault, Michel
  1980   *Power/Knowledge: Selected Interviews and Other Writings, 1972–1977*. C. Gordon, ed. New York: Pantheon Books.
  1984   Nietzsche, Genealogy, History. In *The Foucault Reader*. P. Rabinow, ed. Pp. 76–100. New York: Pantheon Books.
  1988   *The Care of the Self: The History of Sexuality, Vol. 3*. New York: Vintage Books.
  1990a   *The History of Sexuality: An Introduction, Vol. 1*. New York: Vintage Books.
  1990b   *The Use of Pleasure: The History of Sexuality, Vol. 2*. New York: Vintage Books.

Fox, Richard
  1989   *Gandhian Utopia: Experiments with Culture*. Boston: Beacon Press.

Freud, Sigmund
  1965 (1933)   *New Introductory Lectures on Psychoanalysis*. New York: W. W. Norton and Company.

Gallagher, Catherine and Thomas Walter Laqueur
  1987   *The Making of the Modern Body: Sexuality and Society in the Nineteenth Century*. Berkeley and Los Angeles: University of California Press.

Gandhi, Mohandas K.
  1929   *An Autobiography: The Story of My Experiments with Truth*. Boston: Beacon Press.
  1948   *Key to Health*. Ahmedabad: Navajivan Publishing House.
  1949   *Diet and Diet Reform*. Ahmedabad: Navajivan Trust.
  1954   *Nature Cure*. B. Kumarappa, ed. Ahmedabad: Navajivan Trust.
  1958   *Self-Restraint and Self-Indulgence*. Ahmedabad: Navajivan Trust.
  1964a   *The Law of Continence*. A.T. Hingorani, ed. Bombay: Bharatiya Vidya Bhavan.

1964b   *Through Self-Control.* A. T. Hingorani, ed. Bombay: Bharatiya Vidya Bhavan.

1965a   *The Nature Cure.* A. T. Hingorani, ed. Bombay: Pearl Publications.

1965b   *The Health Guide.* A. T. Hingorani, ed. Bombay: Pearl Publications.

Gandhi, Ramchandra

1982   'Brahmacharya.' In *Way of Life: King, Householder, Renouncer. Essays in Honor of Louis Dumont.* T. N. Madan, ed., Pp. 205–222. New Delhi: Vikas Publishing House.

Gangadhar, D. A.

1984   *Mahatma Gandhi's Philosophy of Brahmacharya.* Bangalore: Christian Institute for the Study of Religion and Society.

Garrison, Omar

1964   *Tantra: The Yoga of Sex.* New York: Julian Press.

Gellner, Ernest

1983   *Nations and Nationalism.* Oxford: Basil Blackwell.

Gherandasamhita

[1914–1915] 2007   Translated and edited by Rai Bahadur Srisa Chandra Vasu. Delhi: Munshiram Manoharlal Publishers.

Gillis, John R.

1974   *Youth and History: Tradition and Change in European Age Relations, 1770–Present.* New York: Academic Press.

Gilmore, David D.

1990   *Manhood in the Making: Cultural Concepts of Masculinity.* New Haven, CT: Yale University Press.

Gotham, Chamanlal

n.d.   *Brahmacharya Ki Prachand Shakti.* Barelli: Sanskriti Sansthan.

Gupta, Charu

2002   *Sexuality, Obscenity, Community: Women, Muslims, and the Hindu Public in Colonial India.* New York: Palgrave.

Guttmann, Allen

1996   *The Erotic in Sports.* New York: Columbia University Press.

Haich, Elisabeth

1972   *Sexual Energy and Yoga.* London: Allen and Unwin.

Hare, E.H.
    1962   'Masturbatory Insanity: The History of an Idea.' *The Journal of Mental Science* 108:2–25.

Hathayogapradipika
    1997   Translated by Pancham Sinh. New Delhi: Munshiram Manoharlal.

Hiralal
    1983   *Brahmacharya Vivaha Ke Pahle Aur Vivaha Ke Bad*. Unnau (Magrawara): Prakritik Chikitsalaya.

Hobsbawm, Eric J.
    1990   *Nations and Nationalism Since 1780: Program, Myth, Reality*. Cambridge: Cambridge University Press.

Howe, Joseph W.
    1974 (1887)   *Excessive Venery, Masturbation, and Continence*. New York: Arno Press.

Hyam, Ronald
    1990   *Empire and Sexuality: The British Experience*. Manchester: Manchester University Press.

Iyengar, B.K.S.
    1993   *Light on Yoga*. New York: Schoken Books.

Jacquemart, Pierre and Saïda Elkéfi
    1992   *Yoga, Sexualité et Stress*. Paris: Maloine.

John, M. E. and J. Nair
    1998   *A Question of Silence: The Sexual Economies of Modern India*. Delhi: Kali for Women.

Kakar, Sudhir
    1981   *The Inner World: A Psycho-Analytic Study of Childhood and Society in India*. New Delhi: Oxford University Press.
    1982   *Shamans, Mystics and Doctors: A Psychological Inquiry into India and Its Healing Traditions*. New Delhi: Oxford University Press.
    1990   *Intimate Relations: Exploring Indian Sexuality*. Chicago: University of Chicago Press.
    1996   *The Colors of Violence: Cultural Identities, Religion and Conflict*. Chicago: University of Chicago Press.

Kakar, Sudhir and John Ross
    1987   *Tales of Love, Sex, and Danger*. London: Unwin and Hyman.

Kama Sutra
    1993   Translated by Sir Richard Burton. New Delhi: Penguin
            Books.
Kapur, Teg Bahadur
    1977   *Yoga for Healthy Sex Life.* Delhi: Shksha Bharati.
Keuls, Eva C.
    1993   *The Reign of the Phallus: Sexual Politics in Ancient Athens.*
            Berkeley: University of California Press.
Khandelwal, Meena
    2004   *Women in Ochre Robes: Gendering Hindu Renunciation.*
            Albany: SUNY Press.
Khandelwal, Meena, Sondra L. Hausner and Ann Grodzin Gold
    2006   *Women's Renunciation in South Asia: Nuns, Yoginis, Saints
            and Singers.* New York: Palgrave Macmillan.
Khare, R.S.
    1976   *Culture and Reality: Essays on the Hindu System of
            Managing Food.* Simla: Institute of Advanced Study.
Khare, R.S. and M.S.A. Rao
    1986   *Food, Society and Culture: Aspects in South Asian Food
            Systems.* Durham, NC: Carolina Academic Press.
Koka Shastra.
    1965   Edited and Translated by Alex Comfort. New York: Stein
            and Day.
    n.d.   Edited and Translated by Kaviraj Arjan Singh Vaidya.

'Krish' Shri Vishnudata
    n.d.   *Brahmacharya Sadhan.* Delhi: Dehati Pustak Bhandar.
Kumar, Surindar
    n.d.   *Yogic Cure for Urinary and Seminal Diseases and Hernia.*
            New Delhi: Books for All.
Kurtz, Stanley
    1992   *All the Mothers are One.* New York: Columbia University
            Press.
Lal, Kanwar
    1967   *The Cult of Desire: An Interpretation of the Erotic Sculpture
            of India.* New Hyde Park, NY: University Books.
Lalvani, Vimla
    1997   *Yoga for Sex.* London: Hamlyn.

Langford, Jean
    2002   *Fluent Bodies: Ayurvedic Remedies for Postcolonial Imbalances*. Durham, NC: Duke University Press.

Laqueur, Thomas Walter
    1986   'Orgasm, Generation and the Politics of Reproductive Biology.' *Representations* 14:1–41.

Lea, Henry Charles
    1884   'A Historical Sketch of Sacerdotal Celibacy in the Christian Church.' Boston: Houghton Mifflin and Co.

Leslie, Charles
    1992   'Interpretations of Illness: Syncretism in Modern Āyurveda.' In *Paths to Asian Medical Knowledge*. Edited by Charles Leslie and Allan Young, pp. 177–208. Berkeley: University of California Press.

Levi-Strauss, Claude
    1966   *The Savage Mind*. Chicago: University of Chicago Press.

Loraux, Nicole
    1990   'Herakles: The Super-Male and the Feminine.' In David Halpern, John W. Winkler and Froma I. Zeitlin, eds., *Before Sexuality: The Construction of Erotic Experience in the Ancient Greek World*. Princeton: Princeton University Press.

Lynch, Owen M.
    1990   *Divine Passions: The Social Construction of Emotion in India*. Berkeley and Los Angeles: University of California Press.

MacAloon, John J.
    2007   *Muscular Christianity and the Colonial and Post-Colonial World*. New York: Routledge.

MacDonald, Robert H.
    1967   'The Frightful Consequences of Onanism: Notes on the History of a Delusion.' *Journal of the History of Ideas* 28:723–731.

MacMunn, Sir George
    1933   *The Martial Races of India*. London: Sampson, Low and Company.

Maheshwari, Prabhudiyal
    1992   'Yuva Shakti Rashtra Pranshakti Hai.' *Yog Manjari* 11:15–16.

Mahindra, Ramcharan
    1985   *Sau Varsh Tak Swasth Rahen*. Barelli: Sanskriti Sansthan.

Mani, Lata
    1987   'Contentious Traditions: The Debate on Sati in Colonial
            India.' *Cultural Critique* 7:119–156.
Manava Dharmashastra
    2005   Translated and Edited by Patrick Olivelle. Oxford: Oxford
            University Press.
Marglin, Frederique Apffel
    1985   *Wives of the God-King: The Rituals of the Devadasis of
            Puri.* Delhi: Oxford University Press.
Marriott, McKim
    1976   'Hindu Transactions: Diversity without Dualism.' In
            Transaction and Meaning. Bruce Kapferer, ed. Pp. 109–142.
            Philadelphia: University of Pennsylvania Press.
    1977   'Towards an Ethnosociology of South Asian Caste Systems.'
            In *The New Wind: Changing Identities in South Asia.*
            Kenneth David, ed. Pp. 227–238. The Hague: Mouton.
    1990   *India through Hindu Categories.* New Delhi: Sage Publications.
    1991   'On Constructing an Indian Ethnosociology.' *Contributions
            to Indian Sociology* (n.s.) 25:295–308.
    1992   'Alternative Social Sciences.' In *General Education in the
            Social Sciences: Centennial Reflections.* J. MacAloon, ed.
            Pp. 262–278. Chicago: University of Chicago press.
Martin, Emily
    1987   *The Women in the Body: A Cultural Analysis of Reproduction.*
            Boston: Beacon Press.
    1989   'The Cultural Construction of Gendered Bodies: Biology and
            Metaphors of Production and Destruction.' *Ethnos* 54.3–4:
            143–60.
    1990   'Toward an Anthropology of Immunology: The Body
            as Nation State.' *Medical Anthropology Quarterly* 4.4:
            410–26.
    1991   'The Egg and the Sperm: How Science Has Constructed a
            Romance Based on Stereotypical Male-Female Roles.' *Signs*
            16:485–501.
Martin, Thomas
    1996   *Ancient Greece: From Prehistoric to Hellenistic Times.* New
            Haven: Yale University Press.

Massyngberde, Ford J.
    1967   *A Trilogy of Wisdom and Celibacy*. Notre Dame, IN: University of Notre Dame Press.
Masters, R.E.L.
    1967   *Sexual Self-Stimulation*. Los Angeles: Sherbourn.
Mather, Cotton
    1723   *The Pure Nazarite*. Boston: John Phillips.
Mazzarella, William
    2001   'Citizens Have Sex, Consumers Make Love.' In Brian Moern, ed., *Asian Media Productions*. Honolulu: University of Hawai'i Press.
    2003   *Shoveling Smoke: Advertising and Globalization in Contemporary India*. Durham, NC: Duke University Press.
Mead, George Herbert
    1977   *On Social Psychology*. A. Strauss, ed. Chicago: University of Chicago Press.
Meyer, Johann Jakob
    1930   *Sexual Life in Ancient India, 2 vols*. New York: Routledge.
Moore, Marcia and Mark Douglas
    1970   *Diet, Sex and Yoga*. York, ME: Arcanum Publications.
Mosse, George
    1985   *Nationalism and Sexuality*. Madison: University of Wisconsin Press.
Mujumdar, D.C.
    1950   *Encyclopaedia of Indian Physical Culture*. Baroda: Good Companions.
Muller, F. Max
    1879 (1965)   *The Sacred Laws of the Arayas*. Delhi: Motilal Banarsidass
Nanda, Serena
    1990   *Neither Man nor Woman: The Hijras of India*. Belmont, CA: Wadsworth Publishing.
Nandy, Ashis
    1980   *At the Edge of Psychology: Essays in Politics and Culture*. Delhi: Oxford University Press.
    1983   *The Intimate Enemy: Loss and Recovery of Self Under Colonialism*. Delhi: Oxford University Press.

Narayananda, Swami
 1950   *The Way of Peace, Power and Long Life*. Rishikesh, India: N.K. Prasad.
 1965   *The Mysteries of Man, Mind, and Mind-Functions*. Rishikesh, India: Universal Yoga Trust.
 1976   *Brahmacharya: Its Necessity and Practice for Boys and Girls. 2nd. ed*. Rishikesh, India: Universal Yoga Trust.

Navarya, Prem Chand
 1988   'Yog Dwara Kam-Shakti Ka Rupantaran.' *Yog Manjari* 11:15–16.

Newman, R.P.
 1975   'Masturbation, Madness and the Modern Concepts of Childhood and Adolescence.' *Journal of Social History* 8:1–27.

Nichter, J.S.
 1981   'Negotiation of the Illness Experience: Ayurvedic Therapy and the Psychosocial Dimensions of Illness.' *Culture, Medicine, and Psychiatry* 5:5–24.

Noelle, Jacquie
 2003   *Better Sex through Yoga*: DVD: Starlight Home Entertainment.

Obeyesekere, Gananath
 1976   'The Impact of Ayurvedic Ideas on the Culture and the Individual in Sri Lanka.' In *Asian Medical Systems, a Comparative Study*. C. Leslie, ed. Pp. 201–226. Berkeley and Los Angeles: University of California Press.
 1981   *Medusa's Hair: An Essay on Personal Symbols and Religious Experience*. Chicago and London: University of Chicago Press.

O'Flaherty, Wendy Doniger—See Doniger, Wendy

O'Hanlon, Rosalind
 1991   'Issues of Widowhood: Gender and Resistance in Colonial Western India.' In Douglas Haynes and Gyan Prakash, eds., *Contesting Power: Resistance and Everyday Social Relations in South Asia*, pp. 62–108. Berkeley and Los Angeles: University of California Press.

Oldenberg, Veena Talwar
 1991   'Lifestyles of Resistance: The Case of the Courtesans of Lucknow.' *In Contesting Power: Resistance in Everyday Social*

Relations in South Asia. Douglas Haynes and Gyan Prakash, eds. Pp. 23–61. Berkeley: University of California Press.

Olivelle, Patrick
2005   *Manu's Code of Law: A Critical Edition and Translation of the Manava-Dharmasastra*. Oxford: Oxford University Press.

Osella, C. and F. Osella
2007   *Men and Masculinities in South India*. London: Anthem Press.

Patwardhan, Anand
1995   DVD: *Father, Son and Holy War (Pita, Putra aur Dharmayuddha)*.

Peiss, Kathy, Christina Simmons, and Robert A. Padgug
1989   *Passion and Power: Sexuality in History*. Philadelphia: Temple University Press.

Pinch, William R.
2006   *Warrior Ascetics and Indian Empires*. Cambridge: Cambridge University Press.

Powell, Jim
1985   *Energy and Eros: Teachings on the Art of Love*. New York: Morrow.

Prasad, S.N.
1983   *Kalyānamalla's Ananga Ranga: An Indian Erotic*. Varanasi: Chaukhamba Orientalia.

Raghavan, V.
1979   *Festivals, Sports and Pastimes of India*. Ahmedabad: B.J. Institute of Learning Research.

Raheja, Gloria Goodwin
1988   *The Poison in the Gift: Ritual, Prestation and the Dominant Caste in a North Indian Village*. Chicago: University of Chicago Press.

Raheja, Gloria Goodwin, and Ann Gold
1994   *Listen to the Heron's Words: Reimagining Gender and Kinship in North India*. Berkeley: University of California Press.

Rai, Indrisan
1984   *Prachin Bharat me Malla Vidhya*. Ph.D. dissertation, Banaras Hindu University, Varanasi.

Ramayana of Valmiki
1990   Translated by Robert Goldman. Princeton: Princeton University Press.

Rao, S.K. Ramachandra
    1987   Encyclopaedia of Indian Medicine. Bombay: Popular
            Prakashan
Reddy, Gayatri
    2005   *With Respect to Sex. Negotiating Hijra Identity in South
            India.* Chicago: University of Chicago Press.
Rele, Vasant Gangaram
    1927   *The Mysterious Kundalini: The Physical Basis of 'Kundalini
            (Hatha) Yoga' According to Our Present Knowledge of Western
            Anatomy and Physiology.* Bombay: D.B. Taraporevala.
Roland, Alan
    1988   *In Search of Self in India and Japan.* Princeton, NJ: Princeton
            University Press.
Rosselli, John
    1980   'The Self-Image of Effeteness: Physical Education and in
            Nineteenth-Century Bengal.' *Past and Present* 86: 12 1–48.
Rudolph, Susanne, and Lloyd Rudolph
    1967   *The Modernity of Tradition.* Chicago: University of Chicago
            Press.
Russett, Cynthia Eagle
    1989   *Sexual Science: The Victorian Construction of Womanhood.*
            Cambridge, MA: Harvard University Press.
Said, Edward
    1978   *Orientalism.* New York: Vintage.
Salam, Abdus
    1895   *Physical Education in India.* Calcutta: W. Newman and
            Co.
Sangari, Kumkum, and Sudesh Vaid
    1990   *Recasting Women: Essays in Indian Colonial History.* New
            Brunswick, NJ: Rutgers University Press.
Saraswati, Swami Yogananda
    1982   *Brahmacharya Raksha Hi Jiwan Hai.* Alwar: Ramji Lal
            Sharma.
Scanlon, Thomas F.
    2002   *Eros and Greek Athletics.* Oxford: Oxford University Press.
Sen Gupta, Keshub Ch. and Bishnu Charan Ghosh
    1930   *Barbell Exercise and Muscle Control.* Calcutta: Published by
            the Authors.

Sharma, Pandit Shiv and Kailash Nath Sharma
  1991 [1973] *Yoga and Sex*. New Delhi: B. I. Publications Private Limited.
Shastri, Jagatkumar
  1970   *Brahmacharya Pradip*. Delhi: Madhur Prakashan.
Shastri, Kaviraj Jagannath
  n.d.[a] *Brahmacharya Sadhan*. Delhi: Dehati Pustak Bhandar.
  n.d.[b] *Brahmacharya ka Anubhav*. Delhi: Dehati Pustak
           Bhandar.
  n.d.[c] *Bhojan aur Swastiya*. Delhi: Dehati Pustak Bhandar.
Siddhantalankar, Satyavrata
  1983   *From Old Age to Youth through Yoga (with Homoeopathic
           and Other Treatments)*. New Delhi: Chandravati Lakhanpal
           Trust Society.
Singleton, Mark
  2010   *Yoga Body: The Origins of Modern Postured Practice*. Oxford
           and New York: Oxford University Press.
Sivasamhita
  1996   Translated by Rai Bahadur Srisa Chandra Vasu. New Delhi:
           Munshiram Manoharlal.
Sivananda, Swami
  1974   *Mind: Its Mysteries and Control*. Sivanandanagar: Divine
           Life Society.
  1984   *Brahmacharya Hi Jiwan Hai*. Allahabad: Adhunik Prakashan
           Graha.
Smith, Anthony D.
  1971   *Theories of Nationalism*. New York: Harper and Row.
Sood, Yogacharya R.L.
  1985   'Yoga for Younger Generation.' *Yog Manjari* 7:17–19.
Spratt, Philip
  1966   *Hindu Culture and Personality*. Bombay: Manaktalas.
Srivastava, Sanjay
  2004   *Sexual Sites, Seminal Attitudes: Sexualities, Masculinities
           and Culture in South Asia*. New Delhi: Sage.
  2007   *Passionate Modernity: Sexuality, Class and Consumption in
           India*. London: Routledge.
Stevenson, Sinclair
  1991   (1920) *The Rites of the Twice-Born*. Delhi: Munshiram
           Manoharlal.

Stoler, Ann L.

    1989   'Making Empire Respectable: The Politics of Race and Sexual Morality in 20th-century Colonial Cultures.' *American Ethnologist* 16.4:634–60.

Strauss, Sarah

    2005   *Positioning Yoga*. New York: Berg.

Strobel, Margaret.

    1987   'Gender and Race in the 19th and 20th Century British Empire.' In R. Bridenthal et al., eds. *Becoming Visible: Women in European History*, pp. 375–96. Boston: Houghton and Mifflin.

Sur, Atul Krishna

    1973   *Sex and Marriage in India; an Ethnohistorical Survey*. Bombay: Allied Publishers.

Sushruta Samhita

    2006   Edited and Translated by Kaviraj Kunjalal Bhishagratna. New Delhi: Cosmo Publications.

Tharu, Susie

    1990   'Tracing Savitri's Pedigree: Victorian Racism and the Image of Women in Indo-Anglian Literature.' In Kumkum Sangari and Sudesh Vaid, eds., *Recasting Women: Essays in Indian Colonial History*, pp. 254–68. Brunswick, NJ: Rutgers University Press.

Thomas, Paul

    1960   *Kama Kalpa; or, The Hindu Ritual of Love. A survey of the customs, festivals, rituals and beliefs concerning marriage, morals, women, the art and science of love and sex symbolism in religion in India from remote antiquity to the present day. Based on ancient Sanskrit classics, Kama Sutra, Ananga Ranga, Ratirahasya, and modern works*. Bombay: D.B. Taraporevala.

Tissot, S.

    1781   *On Onania: or, a Treatise upon the Disorders Produced by Masturbation*. London: D. Bell, R. Gray, and W. Thompson.

Trawick, Margaret

    1990   *Notes on Love in a Tamil Family*. Berkeley: University of California Press.

Urban, Hugh B.
  2003   *Tantra: Sex, Secrecy, Politics and Power in the Study of Religion.* Berkeley: University of California Press.
Vanita, Ruth
  2002   'Dosti and Tamanna: Male-Male Love, Difference, and Normativity in Hindi Cinema.' In Diane P. Mines and Sarah Lamb, eds., *Everyday Life in South Asia.* Bloomington: Indiana University Press.
  2007   *Queering India: Same-Sex Love and Eroticism in Indian Culture and Society.* New York: Routledge.
Vashisht, Ramesh Chandar
  1992   'Yuvon Ka Ekmatra Shaktistrot—Brahmacharya.' *Yog Manjari* 15:25–26.
Verma, Ravi K., Pertti J. Pelto, Stephen L. Schensul and Archana Joshi
  2004   *Sexuality in the Time of AIDS: Contemporary Perspectives from Communities in India.* New Delhi: Sage Publications.
Volin, Michael and Nancy Creagh Phelan
  1967   *Sex and Yoga.* New York: Harper and Row.
Wadley, Susan
  1975   *Shakti: Power in the Conceptual Structure of Karimpur Religion.* Chicago: University of Chicago Studies in Anthropology, No. 2.
Walters, Margaret
  1978   *The Nude Male.* New York: Paddington Press.
Weeks, Jeffrey
  1985   *Sex, Politics, and Society: The Regulation of Sexuality Since 1800.* New York: Longman.
  1989   *Sexuality and Its Discontents: Meanings, Myths and Modern Sexualities.* Boston: Routledge and K. Paul.
White, David Gordon
  1996.   *The Alchemical Body: Siddha Traditions in Medieval India.* Chicago: University of Chicago Press.
  2003   *Kiss of the Yogini: 'Tantric Sex' in Its South Asian Context.* Chicago: University of Chicago Press.
Wujastyk, Dominik
  2003   *The Roots of Ayurveda: Selections from Sanskrit Medical Writings.* New York: Penguin.

Yoga Sutra of Patanjali
1961   Translated with commentary by I.K. Taimni. Wheaton, IL: Theosophical Publishing House.
Yogananda, Paramahansa
1946   *Autobiography of a Yogi*. New York: Philosophical Library.
Yogeshwaranand
1985   *First Steps to Higher Yoga*. Delhi: Yoga Niketan Trust.
Zimmermann, Francis
1998   *The Jungle and the Aroma of Meats*. Berkeley and Los Angeles: University of California Press.
Zysk, Kenneth G.
2002   *Conjugal Love in India: Ratisastra and Ratiramana. Text, Translation, Notes*. Leiden: Brill.

Index

adultery, 56, 83

advertising, consumption and commodification, 7, 200–01, 203

aesthetic stimulation, 166

aggression, 10, 51, 96

alchemical tradition, 14, 15, 154, 173

Alexander, 89, 208

All Bengal Physical Culture Association, 171

All India Ayurvedic Congress, 134

Anand, Dr, 204

Anand, Mool Raj, 64

Ananda Ashram, Pondicherry, 133, 168

Anderson, Benedict, 22

androgynous onanism. *See* masturbation

anthropomorphism, 185

aphrodisiac compounds, 194, 195, 205

arcaneum ad infinitum, 194

Aretaeus, 11

Aristotle, 11, 156, 157, 158, 160

Arjun, 122

arousal, 11, 74, 75, 203

coitus, orgasm, and ejaculation, 156, 160

artha (advantage), 25, 67

asana and *pranayama*, 14, 62, 126, 130–34, 137–38, 147, 164, 170, 173, 175

ashtanga practice, 128

goraksasana, 139, 141

halasana, 141

kukkutasana, 145, 164–65

mayurasana, 165

padmasana, 141, 164

shavasana, 141

siddhasana, 79, 145, 162, 164, 168

stambhanasana, 139

virasana, 141. *See also* yoga

ashrama cycle, four-fold, 25

Ashvalayana Grhya-Sutra, 25

athletes, adolescent and adult trainers, sexual relationship, 166–67

athleticism and sex, 141, 143–44, 147, 149–54, 176. *See also* wrestling, yoga

233